RAMADAN:
MOTIVATING BELIEVERS
TO ACTION

AN INTERFAITH PERSPECTIVE

EDITED BY

LALEH BAKHTIAR

FOREWORD BY
SEYYED HOSSEIN NASR

Book Designer
Liaquat Ali

Library of Congress Cataloging in Publication Data
Bakhtiar, Laleh
    Ramadan: Motivating Believers to Action:
    An Interfaith Perspective

    Includes bibliographical references.
    1. Islam, Practices. 2. Psychology, Religious.
    I. Bakhtiar, Laleh. II. Title.
BL 53.U45   200'.1975.16302
ISBN: 0-934905-25-8

Published by:
The Institute for Traditional Psychoethics and Guidance

Distributed by:
KAZI Publications, Inc
3023 W. Belmont Avenue
Chicago IL 60618
Tel: 312-267-7001; FAX: 312-267-7002

CONTENTS

FOREWORD: WHY DO MUSLIMS FAST?

Seyyed Hossein Nasr

Certain truths are by nature evident and need not be discussed in normal circumstances. But, in a day and age when the most evident truths are shrouded by the clouds of doubts and questioned, one is forced to discuss even the most obvious of them. One such truth is the necessity for an ascetic element in human life. Without an element of self-denial and asceticism no religion and therefore no human culture is possible. One must withdraw occasionally from the full life of the senses even in order to be able to enjoy the fruit of sensual perception. As the Taoist saying affirms, it is the empty space of the wheel which makes the wheel. It is only a certain degree of restraint from the material objects of the senses that makes even the life of the senses balanced, not to speak of making possible an opening in the human soul for the spiritual life.

One such practice of restraint is fasting, promulgated in Islam as obligatory for the month of Ramadan and recommended for other periods of the year. As the Holy Quran asserts, it is a practice which existed in older religions and in Islam it was only revived and institutionalized in the form of the *sawm* of Ramadan. Fasting during this month possesses, of course, many social and external benefits and features which have been discussed often and in fact even somewhat overemphasized in certain quarters, where the chief virtue of fasting is reduced to charity towards the poor. This element of charity is, of course, there but like all true charity it becomes spiritually significant only when it is directed towards God. And in fasting it is the obeying of the Divine Will which has as its fruit charity towards the poor and the needy and an actual participation in their hunger and thirst.

But the most difficult aspect of the fast is the edge of the sword of abstention directed toward the carnal soul, the *al-nafs al-ammarah* of the Holy Quran. In fasting, the rebellious tendencies of the carnal soul are gradually dampened and pacified through a systematic submission of these tendencies to the Divine Will, for at every moment of hunger the soul of the Muslim is reminded that it is in order to obey a Divine Command that the passions of the carnal soul go unheeded. That is also why the fast does not include only food but also abstention from every form of lust and carnal passion.

As a result of this systematic restraint, the human soul becomes aware that it is independent of its immediate natural environment and conscious that it is in this world but not of it. A person who fasts with complete faith becomes aware very rapidly that he is a pilgrim in this world and that he is created as a creature destined for a goal beyond this material existence. The world about him loses somewhat its materiality and gains an aspect of 'vacuity' and transparency which in the case of the contemplative Muslim leads directly to a contemplation of God in His creation.

The ephemeral and 'empty' nature of things is, moreover, compensated by the appearance of those very things as Divine gifts. Food and drink which are taken for granted throughout the year reveal themselves during the period of fasting more than ever as gifts of heaven (*ni'mah*) and gain a spiritual significance of a sacramental nature.

To fast is also to wear the armor of purity against the passions of the world. It is to incorporate even 'physically' in one's body the purity of death which is of course coupled with spiritual birth. In fasting, man is reminded that he has chosen the side of God over the world of passions. That is why the Holy

Prophet loved fasting so much. It was a basic element of that 'Muhammadan spiritual poverty' (*faqr*), about which he said, '*al-faqr fakhri*' (spiritual poverty is my glory).

This death of the passions cleanses the human soul and empties it of the putrid water of its negative psychic residues. The individual and through him the Islamic community is renovated through this rite and reminded of its moral and spiritual obligations and goals. That is why the arrival of the blessed month is greeted with joy. For in it the doors of heaven are opened further for the faithful and the Divine Compassion descends upon those who seek it. To have completed the fast of Ramadan is to have undergone a rejuvenation and rebirth which prepares each Muslim to face another year with determination to live and act according to the Divine Will. The fast also bestows a spiritual perfume upon the human soul whose fragrance can be perceived long after the period of abstinence has come to an end. It provides for the soul a source of energy upon which it feeds throughout the year. The holy month has therefore been called 'the blessed', *mubarak*, one in which the grace or *barakah* of God flows upon the Islamic community and rejuvenates its deepest sources of life and action.

INTRODUCTION

Laleh Bakhtiar

Motivating believers to action is based on seven key qualities which when consciously developed lead to positive action. Positive action in religious terms means doing what the Source wants them to do with their lives by submitting to God's Will.

These seven qualities, in turn, form a threefold process of how to learn to do exactly this—what nature has programmed the individual human being to do through conscious choice.

KNOWLEDGE, PROCESS, ACTION

The threefold method works through knowledge, process, action. Knowledge refers to knowledge of the outer world as well as of the inner workings of nature. Such knowledge in the traditional view leads to knowledge of the Source. This is confirmed by the well-known Tradition, "One who knows self, knows one's Lord."

This knowledge is then inwardly processed, placed within the alchemical oven, so to speak, for transformation. The result of the transformation, the proof of having transformed is through a third stage called action. Action towards the Source, towards self and towards others is proof of the extent or quality of transformation.

Knowledge incorporates two of the seven major qualities of a believer who is both responsible and committed—responsible for self and committed to the Source and fellow human beings. These two qualities are purpose or goal and belief. Process involves three of the seven characteristics, namely, strategy, moral values and energy. Having strategies makes it possible to realize one's goals and beliefs when they are based on moral values and receive the necessary energy to carry out these strategies. Action, proof of the strategies having worked, result in human bonding and mastering communication.

The essays in this collection are divided into these seven characteristics to show how a practice like prescribed fasting during the month of Ramadan can reinforce the motivations of a believer towards action.

In this sense, believers are of two types: those who practice prescribed fasting during the month of Ramadan and those who want to understand them, to observe what they do during this month and how and if it helps them become better human beings.

GOAL-SETTERS

As goal-setters, believers have a consuming purpose that drives them to grow and to transform. The purpose in this case is to practice the prescribed fast for one month out of every year throughout their adult lifetime. Through this spiritual practice, as their goal, believers are invigorated and fueled by having meaning in their life. It mobilizes them to try to be all that they can be in the human sense which is ultimately the spiritual sense. They envision self through the model of the perfect human being—Muhammad ibn Abd Allah (ص)—and surround themselves with people—relatives, friends, acquaintances—who share similar goals.

Syed Anwer Ali explains the goal, purpose, spiritual passion behind the prescribed fast. "The Goal of Prescribed Fasting," reflects on the goal of piety (*taqwa*), being God-fearing, guarding against wrongdoing. "The Mysteries of Prescribed Fasting" by Muhammad al-Ghazzali has been a classic for almost 800 years. There are few writers who have exceeded his depth of understanding of the spiritual practice of prescribed fasting as well as other types of spiritual practice. A person who succeeded to what should today be considered a Secretary of the government left it all to become a Sufi because he realized that his breadth of knowledge was not being processed to lead to better action towards others. He left his position and turned to writing and mysticism. In this article, al-Ghazzali outlines the outer and inner duties of a person who has set the goal of fasting, the duties described being based on the *sunnah* or sayings and actions of the Messenger Muhammad (ﷺ) as related by his Companions.

For the Sufi, the goal of piety is understood at the deepest level. This is called spiritual poverty and prescribed fasting is one of the best methods to attain it. Javad Nurbakhsh, the master of the Ni'matullahi order, has collected sayings of Sufis over the centuries on fasting and spiritual poverty.

BELIEVERS

After goal-setting, the second important aspect of outer and inner knowledge is belief. Belief encompasses a wide range of subcategories. For the religious believer, belief about what they are and what they can be determines who they will be. As they believe in a higher power to be the best possible understanding of the universe given the miraculous events of the past which cannot be scientifically explained in a conclusive manner, their belief supports their goal. The goal of piety and its quality of spiritual poverty expands the possibility of self attaining human perfection.

Abul Ala Mawdudi's "Commentary: Quranic Verses Prescribing Fasting" are based on knowledge of the Traditions recorded from the Messenger's Companions. This is the traditional method of commentary and explains the historic as well as the philosophic basis of the verses. Muhammad Zakariyya Kandhlawi goes deeper into the Traditions and relating to prescribed fasting in "The Virtues of Ramadan," commenting on them from his wide base of traditional learning.

The Traditions have been compiled on various topics and one of the most important areas have been that of traditional medicine. Several of such compilations exist and one of the best among them is that of Imam Jawziyya. Muhammad al-Akili not only translated this but embedded the translation with modern equivalents. His article on prescribed fasting according to the Traditions on traditional medicine as compiled by Imam Jawziyya helps believers by reinforcing their knowledge of prescribed fasting. It was a practice initiated in its particular form of performance during the month of Ramadan by the Quran—revelation—and reinforced by the Messenger's actual practice of it (*sunnah*). Therefore, for a believer whose two main sources for knowledge are the Quran and the *sunnah*, this essay further confirms the belief that they can actually attain the goal by practicing the prescribed fast. Muhammad al-Akili further points out that prescribed fasting, on the one hand, and prayers and supplication, on the other, go hand in hand for spiritual transformation to occur.

STRATEGISTS

Moving, then, towards process, the goal-setting believer looks for strategies. With their resource being the self consisting of body, soul, spirit and center in what is called the heart—they want to learn what they need to do to organize this resource. How can they have their goal and belief achieve the greatest potential? What is the most effective way to use the resource of self and its subparts? The most effective strategy has always been modeling the behavior of others who have the same goal and the same belief. For the believer, this model is that of the Messenger Muhammad (ﷺ) who was the perfect human being.

Strategies he used included performing the prescribed fast as well as prescribed prayer, supplication and continuous recitation of the revelation. In "Strategies for Prescribed Fasting," Pervez Hanif points these out. As he indicates, the month of fasting is not just performing the prescribed fast, although this sets the stage for other strategies and spiritual practices which the remaining articles each relate to in one way or another.

For the believer, revelation brought both a Law and a Way. Both serve as strategies of how to approach life in the manner in which the model approached life. As the model did not always do things in exactly the same way, five schools of interpretation developed of the *sunnah* formulated in the Traditions. These five schools are the Hanafi, Hanbali, Shafi'i, Maliki and Jafari schools of law so called after the name of the person who founded them. They were all completed within 150 years after the death of the Messenger. In 1963, the head of al-Azhar university in Cairo, Shaykh Shaltut, issued an edict that all of these five schools are recognized schools of law and that any believer will be considered to have followed the *sunnah* if they follow any aspects of any of these five schools.

Whatever strategy is chosen—that of one particular school of law or cutting across the views, for the believer, it becomes an important part of goal-setting and belief to follow the strategy of prescribed fasting as recorded in the Divine Law. Herein lies the importance of the article by Muhammad Mughaniyyah and the reason for its inclusion in this compilation of essays.

As indicated by the Traditions on medicine, fasting will not have a psychological-spiritual effect unless it be accompanied by prescribed prayer and supplication. The remaining three articles emphasize their importance as a strategy for a believer to be able to process prescribed fasting. It is only when the process resulting from fasting and supplication are internalized that transformation in terms of actions will have a positive effect on the person who is performing the prescribed fast as well as those around him/her. Otherwise, as a Tradition points out, they will only receive hunger and thirst for their efforts.

While one example of Quranic commentary was included as reinforcement of the belief system, another by Muhammad Husayn Tabataba'i, "Quranic Commentary on '*I answer the prayer...*' (2:186)," also a contemporary religious scholar, reinforces the strategy of supplication. Supplication is a daily strategy of believers but it is of particular importance during the month of the prescribed fast and his commentary on a verse which falls between two verses prescribing fasting as a religious duty is most informative. It shows the importance of supplication while at the same time is proof of the wealth of traditional commentary where one verse out of the 6600± can receive so much attention and yet still not exhaust the possibilities of what it could mean.

The strategy of Quranic recitation is yet another form of spiritual discipline encouraged during the month of prescribed fasting. The Quran is traditionally divided into thirty parts so that the believer reads one part each night during this month. It is also an integral part of the special night prayer as pointed out by Muhammad Husayn Tabataba'i, in his essay.

One of the verses of the Quran says, "Remember Me and I will remember you," making this form of supplication a very rich traditional strategy to attain spiritual energy. Munir Abu Salman points out the different prayers recorded in the Quran by prophets like Abraham, Ishmael, Moses, Jesus and Muhammad, peace be upon them all, as well as those of great women like Asiyah, the foster mother of Moses, wife of Pharaoh, the Queen of Sheba and Hannah, the mother of Mary and grandmother of Jesus, used in the remembrance of God.

MORAL HEALERS

Strategies and the process of self transform only if they are accompanied by positive values and if they receive the necessary energies to be accomplished. Values are the fundamental moral and practical judgments a person makes about what is most important to them. They are specific beliefs about what is right and wrong. In the traditional view, the human being has the innate possibility to know right from wrong. The Quran speaks to this innate ability as a verse describes it as "a guidance and criterion." A person who performs the prescribed fast, while not believing that it is right, will develop inner conflict and this will undermine the attaining of the goal. Therefore, recitation of the Quran as well as remembrance is reinforced during this month to further elucidate the values which lead to human perfection.

Psychologically goals are effected by beliefs—the more a person believes he or she can accomplish a certain goal, the more energy that person invests in doing it. Beliefs, in turn, need strategies. Strategies are effected by values. If they do not agree, the person begins to undermine self success because of the internal conflict between what the person internally values and a strategy that person may use to achieve success in the goal set for self. For the believer, positive values when consciously internalized, lead to moral healing. Moral healing is another term for the greater struggle where reason and the passions battle within for the attention of the heart. Prescribed fasting enhances the possibility of reason succeeding and morally healing by lessening the energies of the passions as pointed out in the article by Laleh Bakhtiar.

While believers spend eleven months of the year oriented towards this world, emphasis in this one month a year is towards the spiritual. The dangers of too much attachment to this world are pointed out by Muhammad al-Ghazzali. Although he wrote some 800 years ago, his words are as relevant today as if they had been written now. Attachment to this world to an extent which goes beyond moderation holds the believer back from serving God and His creatures because excessive attachment to the world increases the passions (lust and anger) and reduces the possibility of the eternal preservation of self.

With a de-emphasis on this world, at least one month a year, prescribed fasting takes on the quality of what might be called "spiritual fasting" as described in an article by Muhyiddin Abdul Qadir Gilani, one of the great Sufi masters. Having morally healed to a certain extent by accepting the command to perform the prescribed fast and actually fasting, the believer is led towards a desire to extend the fasting beyond what is prescribed, to work overtime in a sense. As the Shaykh points out, all of the senses of hearing, seeing and touching should also fast along with that of tasting and smelling.

ENERGIZERS

The final aspect of process which is considered in this collection is that of being an energizer. Nothing happens without a source of energy. The more energy a person has, the more vibrancy he or she has. While it is usually thought that if a person eats better food, that person will have more energy, and this is true to some extent, there is also a qualitative energy which comes from spiritual practices which cannot be measured in the usual sense. Its presence can only be known through the resulting actions.

"The Therapeutics of Prescribed Fasting" are discussed by a practicing physician, Shahid Athar. Practical suggestions are given along with the medical benefits of fasting. The article "Medical Benefits of Fasting," by Dr. Ebrahim Kazim, show the medical implications to the body of prescribed fasting. Dreams are yet another source of energy although less considered as so simply because we do not clearly understand their effects. What is known is that they arise from our unconscious state and the traditional interpretations of dreams about fasting as recorded by Ibn Sirin and translated by Muhammad al-Akili prove most interesting reading. Ramadan recipes by Shabnam Zaman brings the reader back to the world of food and how various cultures follow different patterns in the pre-dawn meal and the daily ending of the fast. Living in a world that puts such emphasis on material consumption, recalling how a believer can do so much with so little is food for thought.

HUMAN BONDING

Finally, the last two parts, Human Bonding and Mastering Communication are aspects of action—proof of the extent of transformation through attaining the goal and having performed the prescribed fast. The power to bond with others is an extraordinary human power. It comes in the true sense when bonding develops from the heart and not from either the intellect or the passions. It comes from a deep love for one's fellow human being and arises when a person tries to meet the needs of others before his or her own needs, much like a mother with her new born child.

Here a reader might ask if the strategies have worked reinforcing the goals and beliefs. The first article in this section, "Ramadan and Interfaith Bonding," by Shahid Athar is a good example of the transformed spirit at work putting forth energies to bond with others. He cites examples of interfaith meetings in the Indianapolis area which have had a positive effect on the community.

M. A. Choudhery looks at fasting from the historic perspective showing how the concept of fasting has existed among many peoples in the past. She then compares and contrasts the various reasons behind the religious practice of fasting, the motive behind the prescribed fast being the ability to grow closer to God and not because of sorrow for a calamity or atonement for wrongdoing. Through this historical development, prescribed fasting has now become a means of positive bonding with God.

MASTER COMMUNICATORS

Believers should conceivably be master communicators on all three levels—with self, with others and with the Source. How they communicate determines the quality of their lives. Through spiritual disciplines like prescribed fasting, believers are given an opportunity, a challenge. If they are able to communicate that challenge to themselves successfully, they will find the ability to change. This is not to accept prescribed fasting as only a religious duty but rather as a divine challenge, as a chance for growth instead of an experience which limits self. In this way they will become master communicators because their very life will communicate their vision, goal and beliefs to others to help them change for the better, as well.

Traditional methods to master communication with the Source as well as with other people are multiple during the month of the prescribed fast. Tariq Butt summarizes them in his article "Utilizing Ramadan to Communicate." An article on each traditional method of fostering communication follows his essay including "The Special Night Prayer (*tarawih*) of

Ramadan" by Muhammad Aslam, "Retreat to a Mosque (*i'tikaf*) by Muhammad Zakariyya Kandhlawi, "The Night of Power" by Seyyid Qutb, "The Poor-due of Ramadan" by Navid Hanif and "The Festival: Suggestions for School Celebrations by Ismat Bano Siddiqi.

Ramadan is considered by believers to be a blessed month because in it previous scriptures were said to have been revealed as well as the Quran. As the Islamic calendar is based on the moon, the month is celebrated ten days before the preceding year except in leap years when it comes eleven days sooner. It is a month when believers renew their covenant with the Creator through prescribed fasting and prayers as well as the special night prayer of Ramadan said in congregation. There is also a retreat to the mosque during the last ten days of the month where the believer remains in the mosque fasting during the day, performing the prescribed prayers and supplicating throughout the day and night. The retreat is traditionally said to anticipate the Night of Power, the night which is better than 1000 months. Finally, at the end of the month, each believer pays the poor-due which is then given to the poor and needy. The month ends with a Festival where the entire community gathers to share in celebration with each other.

Prescribed fasting, then, motivates believers to action. The action may be manifested as either an enthusiastic audience to the spiritual disciplines of other faiths or as a practitioner of this faith in particular. For the practitioner, the first stage is to make the prescribed fast a goal and then to believe that he or she can do it. Strategies like prescribed prayers, supplications, recitation of the Quran, remembrance of God help make the goal a reality. Believers who are clear on their values and what is most important to them in their life allow their reason to rule over their passions. Believers seek out the necessary material and spiritual energies to be able to work toward their goal, bonding with others of the same and different faiths, looking for commonalties and differences. They then practice as master communicators at all three levels through the same means God communicates to them.

PART ONE:
GOAL-SETTERS

1

SETTING THE GOAL OF THE PRESCRIBED FAST

Syed Anwer Ali

The third pillar of Islam is the prescribed fast, that is, fasting during the entire ninth month of the Islamic lunar year, known as the month of Ramadan. Fasting, as a matter of fact, has been one of the forms of worship in almost all the nations of the world right from the days of Adam. It is prevalent even today, in one or the another form among Christians, Jews and followers of other religious traditions as well as among non-believers. As regards the prophets of God and their true followers, they all used to keep fast in obedience to the Divine Command.

The Quran makes fasting obligatory for the believers and says, *"Oh you who believe, fasting is prescribed for you, as it was prescribed for those before you, so that you may guard against wrongdoing* (that is, attain piety)" (2:183). Fasting is for the complete month of Ramadan. The Quran says, *"Whoever of you is present in that month, he shall fast therein"* (2:185).

The Editor

THE MEANING OF FASTING

Fasting means complete abstinence from eating, drinking, smoking and indulgence in sex throughout the day, that is, from dawn until sunset. According to the Traditions of the Messenger, one must take some sort of food before dawn in order to sustain the rigors of hunger and thirst ahead in the day. This is technically known as the pre-dawn meal (*suhur, sahar*). The Quran says, *"Eat and drink until the whiteness of the day becomes distinct from the blackness of the night at dawn, then complete the fast until nightfall"* (2:187). The fast ends at sunset just after the evening prayer. This is technically known as post-sunset ending of the fast. Then, throughout the night, that is, until dawn of the next day, one can eat, drink, and smoke as well as have sexual intercourse with one's spouse.

If one eats, drinks, smokes or mates with one's spouse by mistake while fasting, but immediately after realizing the mistake, withdraws from such a lapse and remains in fast until the post-sunset ending of the fast time, then he or she has to only repeat the fast of this day, which is considered to be a broken fast, after the month of Ramadan. But if he or she eats, drinks, smokes or mates with his or her spouse intentionally and knowingly or after realizing the mistake does not abstain from it forthwith and keeps the fast during the rest of the fasting time until sunset, as a penalty, he or she has to keep fast continuously for sixty days after the month of Ramadan. In case of any gap falling in the period of sixty days, fasting shall again have to be resumed for a continuous period of sixty days. If, however, one is unable to keep fast for sixty days due to old age or sickness or other reasons permitted by the Quran, he or she is allowed to free a slave or feed sixty persons at a time with food which he or she usually eats.

EXCEPTIONS

Those who are sick or on journey during the month of Ramadan are allowed not to fast, but they must compensate the loss of fasting days with an equal number of days' fasting afterwards when the illness or journey ends. If on a journey, the comfort or ability of a man or woman to fast are immaterial. The Companions of the Messenger used to keep or end the fast while on journeys and nobody objected.[1] During war, also, the Messenger asked the believers not to keep the fast so that their physical ability against the enemy would not be diminished. There is also an exception for those who are unable to fast. This covers the case of a woman who is nursing, one with child, or an elderly man or woman who cannot bear fasting,[2] as well as a sick person whose sickness is prolonged or a person whose journey extends over a whole year. This exception was first available to all the believers as provided by 2:84 of the Quran, but subsequently this general exception was taken away and fasting was made obligatory by verse 2:185 and only the sick and those on a journey were allowed to postpone fasting until the end of sickness or journey as the case may be. As regards persons for whom fasting was extremely difficult, the exception, however, remained intact. However, they have to compensate for the loss of fasting, and in place of each day's fast, they have to feed a poor person twice a day with wholesome meals.[3]

DURATION

Fasting, as already stated, is for the whole of the day from dawn until sunset for a complete month. There are, however, countries in which the days are sometimes very long and it is beyond the power of the ordinary human being to abstain from food from appearance of the dawn until sunset, or even to have a division of twelve months of a year, although, no doubt, such a case is of rare exception. Companions of the Messenger are reported to have asked him about their prayers in a day which extended to a year or a month and he answered that they should measure the day according to the measure of their days.[4] From this it follows that in the countries where the day is too long, the time of fasting may be measured in accordance with the length of an ordinary day, or, where practicable, fasting may also be postponed to a shorter day of about normal length.

PURPOSE

The Quran says that fasting has been ordained *"so that you may guard against wrongdoing"* (that is, attain piety) (2:183). The goal is for the human being to learn to shun wrongdoing. Fasting in Islam, as such, does not simply mean abstaining from food but, in addition to or along with this, abstaining from every kind of wrongdoing.[5]

PIETY

The purpose of fasting is to gain piety which means to fear God alone. The Quran repeatedly asks the believers to fear God alone. It says, *"O people, be pious towards He Who created you from a single being"* (4:1); and, *"Be pious. Surely He is severe in requiting wrongdoing"* (5:2); and, *"Whosoever fears God alone and acts aright shall have no fear, nor shall he grieve"* (7:35); and *"O you who believe, be pious and speak straight words"* (33:70); and, *"Be pious, surely God is All-hearing and All-knowing"* (49:1); and, *"Be pious so that Mercy may be given unto you"* (49:10); and *"O you who believe, be pious and believe in His Messenger. He will give you two portions of His Mercy, and give you a light in which you shall walk, and forgive you"* (57:28); and, *"Be pious surely God is aware of what you do"* (59:18); and *"Be pious oh people of understanding"* (65:10). The prophets Noah (26:163), Hud (26:126), Saleh (26:144), Lot (26:163), and Shuyib (26:179)[6] all called their people to piety. Their people turned away from them and were ultimately destroyed.

Piety, in fact, is the most effective and the strongest possible check against wrongdoing. He/she will instinctively shun all conceivable moral lapses affecting his/her person or society at large, be it theft or robbery, rape or adultery, and the like. He/she will neither abuse nor fight, neither commit murder nor deprive anybody of his/her property, will not give or take bribes or draw upon unlawful gains, will refrain from causing nuisances, disturbing the peace, becoming unjust or imprudent, will not trespass the bounds of justice or deny anybody's lawful right. This is because he/she fears that he/she will have no excuse before God on the Day when he/she will have to ultimately stand before Him to account for his/her deeds.

He/she knows that the punishment of hellfire is grievous and bitter (54:46). It is an terrible place (64:10). It is a flaming fire plucking out the extremities (70:15-16). It neither leaves nor spares (74:28). Thus piety is the foundation of morality which is essential for the maintenance of absolute peace and tranquillity. Piety is fostered by prescribed fasting. It ensures the ultimate well-being of society at large.

HUMANITY

The prescribed fast also make people realize the hardships which others endure for lack of sustenance for their life. Only those who themselves undergo the hardship of hunger and thirst can understand the miseries of those who, inspite of labor, are not able even to meet their basic needs. This naturally induces people to help others in need and to abstain from hoarding wealth—which ultimately proves to be of no avail to them. This really creates a sense of humanity in people in its true sense and teaches them not to be unmindful of the oppressed class of human society. It also helps them to understand the true spirit and the real purpose of the Quran which repeatedly asks the believers to pay the poor-due and to spend for the help of the poor and needy persons of society.

UNIFORMITY

The prescribed fast establishes a unique and singular type of uniformity between all the believers throughout the world in the timings of when to eat and when to drink and to abstain from doing so at certain times. All the believers around the world take their meals and keep the fast from dawn until the setting of the sun and then end the fast all at one and the same time without any exception. It appears as if the entire world of believers on earth is but one family wherein all are on the dining table at one and the same time and all abstain from eating, drinking, smoking and even mating with their mates during one and the same period of time.

SINCERITY

The prescribed fast is also the real test of the sincerity of devotion and obedience to God. When believers keep the fast and abstain from eating, drinking and other things prohibited by God during fasting, only God knows whether they are actually doing so or not. It all depends upon the truthfulness of the person himself or herself whether what is shown externally is actually true or false. If a person were to outwardly behave as if he/she were not eating, drinking or smoking, but, in fact, secretly does all this, nobody will check this out or disbelieve the person. Only God bears witness to all the pretensions and deceptions. Fasting is in fact something like an undeclared bond between the human being and God alone and it is for this reason that God says that fasting is for Me and I am its reward.[7]

REMEDY AGAINST EVIL

The prescribed fast strengthens the heart against wrongdoing. When one can abstain from all that is otherwise lawful and permissible, merely because God orders one to abstain from it during a particular time, there is no doubt that he/she can quite easily and readily abstain from wrongdoing and what is forbidden by God. Thus to abstain from some thing lawful on account of the Command of God is really to prove that one can most certainly abstain from all that is really unlawful and forbidden by God and this closes the doors of wrongdoing once for all for that person.

STRUGGLE IN THE WAY OF GOD

The prescribed fast prepares a person for the greater struggle in the way of God (*jihad al-akbar*) along with the discipline and spirit of obedience which prescribed prayer teaches. The willingness to bear the hardships of hunger and thirst and restraining from lust and desires for wrongdoing which prescribed fasting creates, are ultimately the basis for the greater struggle in the way of God. The purpose is to establish peace, tranquillity and social justice in human society wherein everybody should have equal rights and liberties without the least disturbance to others.

In short, the prescribed fast really teaches a person to obey the Commands of God with all sincerity, whether it be at the suffering of hunger and thirst or control of sexual urges. In fact it is a means of training to prepare a person to pass his/her entire life in a manner which satisfies God. A person should live and die for God's satisfaction and this is the real purpose of sending guidance in the form of the revealed religion through the prophets of God.

ACHIEVEMENTS OF THE PURPOSE

The real purpose underlying the prescribed fast, however, can only be achieved when one inculcates in oneself the fear of God or piety, when one does what God wishes one to do and abstains from what God orders one not to do. If this is not done, then mere abstaining from eating and drinking is of no avail. The Messenger Muhammad (ﷺ) says that when one does not give up telling lies and acting upon falsehood, God does not need his/her abstaining from eating and drinking. He also says that there are many persons who fast but they do not get any thing except hunger and thirst.[8] On the contrary, the wrongdoings of one who keeps the prescribed fast with its real spirit are forgiven. According to another Tradition of the Messenger, one who keeps the prescribed fast with faith and fear of accountability will have all of his/her wrongdoing forgiven. The prescribed fast is, in fact, a shield against the attacks of satanic temptations or egocentric desires.[9]

THE NIGHT OF POWER
AND RETREAT TO THE MOSQUE

The Night of Power is one of the last ten nights of Ramadan. It has been described in the Quran as better than 1000 months. The Quran, a guidance and a criterion, (2:185), was revealed on this Night. This Night, according to the Traditions of the Messenger, falls on either the 21st, 23rd, 25th, 27th or 29th nights of the month of Ramadan. To keep awake and spend the auspicious moments of this Night in prayer and remembrance of God is of great spiritual importance.

The spirit of devotion which the prescribed fast creates in the human being ultimately makes him/her submit completely and exclusively to the Will of God. As a result of it, he/she voluntarily gives up all affairs of his/her life, takes leave of his/her house, family, business, wealth, property, profit and loss, and comes with his/her bedding to stay in a corner of the mosque for the last ten days of the month of Ramadan. There, the only engagement for him/her is to remember God in all postures even when he/she is not engaged in prescribed prayers.

This is technically known as retreat to the mosque (*i'tikaf*). This begins after the afternoon prescribed prayer on the 20th of Ramadan and ends on seeing the new moon of the next month of Shawwal. It is a binding Tradition—which means that if any one or more persons of any locality undertakes it, every one of that locality also shares the blessings, and if none from a locality volunteers himself/herself for it, all persons of that locality will be treated as having defied the important command and thus pay for their lethargy and unresponsive behavior, inviting God's displeasure. For retreat in the mosque, intention and purity in all respects are required. According to the Traditions of the Messenger all wrongdoings of one who sits in retreat are forgiven and virtues are added to his/her credit.9

MYSTIC POINT OF VIEW

1. 2:183: This verse sanctions spiritual exercises for the mystics.

2. 2:186: The words, *"I am indeed close to them,"* *fa inni qarib,* indicate achievement of nearness to God which is the ultimate goal of mystic life.

3. 2:187: The words, *"on the night of the fasts is the approach,"* *lailat as-siyamir rafasu,* require mystics to be moderate in their spiritual exercises.10

2

ON THE MYSTERIES
OF PRESCRIBED FASTING

Muhammad al-Ghazzali

Muhammad al-Ghazzali (d. 1111 CE), known in the West as Algazel, is considered to be one of the greatest thinkers not only in Muslim philosophy, but in human thought, as well. His work influenced Jewish thinkers like Maimonides (d. 1204 CE) who wrote in Arabic and derived his knowledge of Greek philosophy from Arabic translation. Christian thinkers did not remain without influence from al-Ghazzali, as well. The Dominican Raymund Martin was thoroughly acquainted with al-Ghazzali's major works as was his contemporary, Thomas Acquinas (d. 1274 CE). Al-Ghazzali is considered to be the best known writer on moral subjects. As both a theologian and Sufi, he was able to bridge the Law and the Way as a great synthesizer of intellectual thought which preceded him. His work, "On the Mysteries of Fasting," has been a classic in the Islamic world from the time that it was written.

The Editor

INTRODUCTION

Praise be to God who has shown great favor unto His servants by delivering them from the satanic temptations that the ego imprints in their hearts and minds. God has successfully opposed the hopes of these satanic forces and frustrated its designs by making the prescribed fast a shield for His servants. He has opened the gates of paradise unto His servants and taught them that negative forces find the way to their hearts through inappropriate lust and anger. He has made known unto them that only through subduing inappropriate lust and anger can the soul at rest assert its superiority.

In accordance with the words of Muhammad (ﷺ), "The prescribed fast comprises half of patience,"[1] and "patience forms half of belief,"[2] the prescribed fast equals one-fourth of belief. Furthermore, it is distinguished from the other pillars of Islam by its special and peculiar position in relation to God, since He said through the mouth of His Messenger, "Every good deed will be rewarded from ten to seven hundred fold except prescribed fasting which is endured for My sake and which I shall reward."[3] God also said, "Verily, the patient shall be repaid: their reward shall not be by measure" (39:13.)

Prescribed fasting comprises one-half of patience while its reward transcends reckoning and calculation. To have an idea of its excellence you have only to remember the words of Muhammad (ﷺ) when he said, "By Him who holds my life in His hand, the soul breath of the person's mouth who is performing the prescribed fast is more fragrant before God and more pleasing to Him than the perfume of musk."[4] "I shall reward the person who performs the prescribed fast and forgoes food and drink and suppresses the appetite for My sake."[5] Muhammad (ﷺ) also said, "Verily paradise has, [among other things], a gate which is called *al-rayyan* and through which no one shall enter except those who have observed the prescribed fast."[6] And again, "Two joys are prepared for him who observes the prescribed fast, the joy of ending the prescribed fast and that of meeting his/her Lord."[7] On another occasion he said,

"Everything has a gateway and the gateway to worship is prescribed fasting."[8] And again he said, "The sleep of the person performing the prescribed fast is worship."[9]

The Messenger once said, "When the month of Ramadan arrives, the gates of paradise are flung open while those of hellfire are closed. At the same time all the satans are put in chains and a herald cries out, 'Oh you who seek good come forward and you who desire wrongdoing desist'."[10]

Commenting on the words of God, *"Eat and drink with healthy relish, for what you did before in the days that have gone by,"* (69:24).Waki[11] said that *"the days that have gone by"* were the days of prescribed fasting, since during those days [men and women] abstained from food and drink.[12]

On another occasion Muhammad (ﷺ) himself included the prescribed fasting in the list of things which lift the human being to the rank of the angels when he said, "Verily God will make His angels vie with the ascetic young people saying, 'Oh young people who have suppressed your carnal lust for My sake and who have consecrated the prime of your life unto Me, you are in My sight as one of My angels'."[13]

And again Muhammad (ﷺ) said that God would address His angels concerning fasting and say, "O My angels I behold My servant. He/she has suppressed his/her carnal lust, abstaining from pleasures and giving up his/her food and drink—he has done all that for My sake."[14]

Concerning the words of God, *"No soul knows what joy is reserved for them in return for their works,"* (32:17) it has been said that *"their works"* refer to the prescribed fast, since God said, *"Verily the patient shall be repaid. Their reward shall not be by measures"* (39:13).

Thus will the reward of the person performing the prescribed fast be generous and even profuse. It will be beyond imagination or estimate. It is fair that it be so, because the prescribed fast belongs to God and, by virtue of this relationship, it has been rendered noble, although all the acts of worship belong to God, just as the House (*al-bayt*)[15] has been made noble by its special relationship to God, although the whole earth is His also.

Prescribed fast belongs to God in two respects: First, because it is a form of abstaining from pleasures which are otherwise lawful. It is concealed from human sight because of its very nature whereas all the other acts of worship are apparent and exposed to it. It stands alone as the only act of worship which is not seen by anyone except God. It is an inward act of worship performed through sheer endurance and patience.

Second, prescribed fasting belongs to God because it is a means of defeating the enemy of God, the human ego, which works through inappropriate lust and anger. This lust and anger are strengthened by eating and drinking. For this reason Muhammad (ﷺ) said, "Verily the untamed ego affects the son of Adam by pervading his/her blood. Let him/her therefore make this difficult for the untamed ego by means of hunger."16 For the same reason he told Ayisha, "Persist in knocking the door of Paradise." When she asked, "With what shall I knock on the door of Paradise?" he replied. "With hunger."17

Whereas the prescribed fast is primarily a method of subduing temptations of the ego, blocking its path, and placing obstacles in its way, it deserves a special place in relation to God, since subduing the enemy of God is to help Him, and His help is not forthcoming unless people first help Him. Thus He said, *"If you help God, He will help you, and will strengthen you"* (47:8). The servant of God should take the initiative. God will crown him/her with success by further guiding him/her to His ways. For this reason God said, *"And whoso make efforts for Us in Our ways will We guide them."*(29:69) God also said, *"Verily God changes not what a people have until they change it for themselves."*(13:12).

Change increases temptation and strengthens the desires of lust and anger, which are the grazing grounds of the satanic forces and their pasturing land. As long as the ground is fertile, these forces will continue to frequent them. As long as they frequent them, the majesty of God will not be revealed to the servant. His glory will remain concealed from a person. The Messenger said, "Had it not been for the fact that these forces hover around the hearts of the children of Adam, the latter would have readily lifted their hearts unto the Kingdom of Heaven."[18]

In this respect the prescribed fast becomes the gateway to worship and a protection against hellfire.[19] Since its excellence has become so very important, it is necessary to describe its outward and inward conditions by enumerating its principles and regulations as well as its inward rules. We shall discuss this under three sections.

SECTION 1
ON THE OUTWARD DUTIES OF PRESCRIBED FASTING

THE OUTWARD DUTIES

The outward duties relative to prescribed fasting are six. The first duty is to watch for the beginning of the month of Ramadan and announce it upon the observation of the new moon (al-hilal). But if the clouds should make the observation of the new moon impossible, then the length of Shaban (the month which precedes Ramadan) should be extended to thirty days. By observation we mean actual sighting of the new moon. It is established by the word of one truthful and trustworthy witness, while that of the new moon of Shawwal (the month following Ramadan) is not established except by the word of two witnesses. This is merely a means of precaution for the preservation of the purity of worship. Anyone who hears a trustworthy witness assert that he has seen the new moon and believes him, the prescribed fast thereupon becomes incumbent upon him, even though a religious judge should fail to announce the arrival of the new month. In the matter of worship, therefore, let each person do whatever he/she deems best.

Whenever the new moon is seen in one town, but is not seen in another and the distance between the two is less than two days' journey, prescribed fasting becomes incumbent upon both towns alike. But if the distance were more than two days' journey, each town would have its own arrangement, and what would be incumbent upon the one would not extend to the other.

The second outward duty is intention (*niyyah*). Every night before the dawn of the following day, the person should specifically and deliberately entertain the intention of prescribed fasting. If he/she should entertain the intention to perform the prescribed fast in the month of Ramadan, but fail to renew his/her intention every night, his/her fast would not be valid. This is what we mean when we said every night. If he/she should entertain the intention during the daytime, his/her fast would not be valid. This is true of the fast of the month of Ramadan and of the prescribed fasts, but voluntary fasts are excepted. This is what we mean when we said that the intention of fasting should be entertained during the night before the following day of prescribed fasting.

If one should entertain the intention to fast either the month of Ramadan or the obligatory fasts but fail to be specific, his/her fast would not be valid. The prescribed fast is ordained by God and its observance should be the result of specific intention.

If during the doubtful night (*laylah al-shakk*), one should entertain the intention to fast the following day, if it should belong to Ramadan, then the prescribed fast would not be valid, unless the intention is supported by the word of a trustworthy witness. The possibility that the trustworthy witness might be mistaken or even lying should not affect the determination of the person who has planned to begin the prescribed fast the following day. Similarly any attendant circumstances such as doubt concerning the last night of Ramadan would not prevent the person from entertaining the intention to begin the prescribed fast the following day. Nor would the intention to begin the prescribed fast be affected if its entertainment depended upon mere conjecture, as in the case of a person imprisoned in a dark dungeon who thinks that the month of Ramadan had arrived whatever doubt he/she might have would not prevent him/her from entertaining the intention to begin the prescribed fast.

Again, if a person should be uncertain of the night of doubt, the verbal expression of his/her intention to begin the prescribed fast the following day would not be possible because the seat of intention is the heart, wherein it is inconceivable to entertain doubt in conjunction with certainty. Thus, if in the middle of Ramadan one should say that he/she would begin the prescribed fast the following day if that day belonged to the month of Ramadan, no harm could be done because it is mere repetition of words, while in the seat of intention there would be no room for doubt or hesitation, rather it is positively certain that the following day is of Ramadan. One who formulates his/her intention during the night and decides to fast the following day and then eats while it is yet night will not invalidate his/her intention. If a woman in a state of menstruation should entertain the intention of prescribed fasting on the following day and her period come to an end before dawn, her fast would be valid.

The third duty is that, as long as he/she remembers that he/she is fasting, the individual should abstain from intentionally allowing any material substance such as food, drink, snuff and enema, to enter his/her body. All these render the prescribed fast invalid. It is not, however, invalidated by phlebotomy and cupping nor by forcing the probe into the ear or the orifice of the penis unless the probe reaches the bladder. Whatever enters the body unintentionally, such as dust, flies or water during the rinsing of the mouth will not invalidate the prescribed fast. Water which enters the body during the rinsing of the mouth, however, will invalidate the prescribed fast if the individual goes to excess in rinsing his/her mouth, because he/she would then be deliberately negligent. This is what we meant when we said "intentionally." We said "as long as he/she remembers that he/she is fasting" in order to exempt from this ruling the one who has forgotten that he/she was fasting and whose eating will not invalidate his/her prescribed fast. But if the person should intentionally eat either at the beginning or at the end of the day and later find that his/her eating has encroached upon the actual period of daylight, it would be his/her duty to make amends. But if he/she should, to the best of his/her ability, continue to believe that he/she had not eaten outside the prescribed time, he/she would not have to make amends. Yet he/she should not eat either in the early morning or in early evening except after careful and thorough examination of the time.

The fourth duty is abstinence from sexual intercourse. The definition of sexual intercourse is the disappearance of the glans of the penis in the vulva. If the person, forgetting that he/she is fasting, should have sexual intercourse, he/she would not, because of it, break the fast. If, during the night, he/she should either have sexual intercourse or experience an erotic dream and wake up in the morning in a state of prescribed impurity, his/her prescribed fast would not thereof be broken. If the dawn breaks while he/she is copulating with his/her spouse and stops immediately, his/her fast remains intact; but if he/she continues until reaching orgasm, his/her fast will be invalidated and atonement (*kaffarah*) becomes incumbent upon him/her.

The fifth duty is abstinence from deliberate seminal emission either through sexual contact or through no sexual contact because deliberate seminal emission breaks the fast. The person, however, will not break his/her fast if he/she kisses his/her spouse or lies with him/her unless in so doing he/she emits seminal fluid. Nevertheless both are disapproved except where the person is advanced in age and in full control of his/her impulses, in which case there will be no harm in kissing, although abstinence therefrom is better and more desirable. It he/she fears that as a result of kissing and toying he/she may emit seminal fluid, and yet kisses with the result that seminal fluid is emitted, he/she breaks the prescribed fast because he/she was deliberately negligent.

The sixth duty is abstinence from vomiting because it renders the prescribed fast invalid. But if one cannot help it, his/her prescribed fast remains intact and valid. And if a person swallows phlegm or mucus from his throat or chest he/she will not invalidate the fast. This has been made permissible because of the prevalence of the affliction. But if he/she swallows either after it had gotten to his/her mouth, he/her will break his/her fast.

The duties attending the breaking the prescribed fast are four, namely, making up, atonement, expiation and abstinence from food and drink for the rest of the day in imitation of those who are performing the prescribed fast.

Making amends is obligatory upon every responsible Muslim who has neglected to observe the prescribed fast with or without any excuse. Thus the menstruating woman is under obligation to make amends for every prescribed fasting which she fails to observe; while the unbeliever, the minor, and the insane are under no such obligation. Making amends for days omitted in Ramadan need not be consecutively performed but may be performed either at different intervals or all at once.

The atonement is not obligatory except after sexual intercourse. Seminal emission, food and drink require no atonement. The atonement consists of freeing one slave. If this is not possible, the fasting of two consecutive months will suffice. However, if this also be beyond the person's ability, he/she should feed sixty poor people, giving each a bushel of wheat or barley or dates.

As to abstinence from food and drink for the rest of the day, it is obligatory upon anyone who broke the fast without a valid excuse or failed to carry out all its requirements. The menstruating woman is under no obligation to perform the prescribed fast for the rest of the day if she has already become pure. Similarly the traveler, who at the end of two days' journey, arrives not in a state of prescribed fasting, is under no obligation to perform the prescribed fast for the rest of the day.

It is also obligatory to abstain from food and drink on doubtful days when only one trustworthy witness has declared that he has seen the new moon. Furthermore, when one travels, unless it is unbearable, it is better to perform the prescribed fast than not to do so. No one should end his/her prescribed fast on the day when he/she embarks on a journey if he/she has already begun that day by prescribed fasting, nor on the day when he/she comes in from a journey, if he/she has already begun that day by prescribed fasting.

As to expiation, it is obligatory upon pregnant and nursing women if they should not fast for the sake of their children. Besides making amends for days thus omitted, they should give in expiation a bushel of wheat to the poor for each day they did not fast. The elderly person who does not fast because of infirmity should give a bushel of wheat for every day thus omitted.

THE PRACTICES CONNECTED WITH THE PRESCRIBED FAST

The practices connected with the prescribed fast are six. They are delaying the time of the pre-dawn meal, speeding the ending of the prescribed fast by eating dates or drinking water before performing the prescribed prayer, putting away the toothpick after sunset, generous giving during the month of Ramadan especially because of its special excellencies,[23] reading or reciting a 30th part of the Quran every day, and retreating into the mosque, especially during the last ten days of the month of Ramadan. It was the custom of Muhammad (ص), upon the arrival of the last ten days of the month of Ramadan, to roll up his mattress, fasten his mantle around his waist, and, making his family do the same, continue in his worship until the end of the ten-day period. The Night of Power (*laylah al-qadr*) falls during these ten days.[20] More probably the Night of Power falls on an odd night. Most likely among these is the 21st, 23rd, 25th or 27th. During this ten-day retreat, continuous observance is preferred.

If a person vows or states his/her intention to observe these days of retreat continuously, the continuity of his/her observance is broken if he/she leaves the mosque without justifiable necessity, such as leaving in order to call on some sick person, or to attend a funeral, or to visit a friend. But if he/she interrupts the retreat in order to answer a call of nature, the continuity of the observance will not be broken. The person may, during the period of retreat, perform ablutions at his/her own home, but he/she may not attend to any other work on the way from and back to the mosque.

Muhammad (ص) used to leave the mosque only in order to answer the call of nature. On his way from and back to the mosque, he did not inquire about the sick except as he passed by without stopping.[21] The continuity of the observance of the retreat will be broken through sexual intercourse, but not through kissing. While in the mosque the person may use perfumes and contract marriage. Continuity is not broken through eating, sleeping, and washing of the hands in a basin because they are all unavoidable and necessary. Nor is it broken by the emergence of a part of the body from the mosque, for the Messenger used to put his head out to be massaged by Ayisha who was in an adjacent chamber.[22] Whenever the person leaves the retreat in order to answer a call of nature, he/she should restate his/her intention upon returning to resume the retreat, unless he/she had stated his/her intention for the ten day period in advance. Despite this, however, the renewal of the intention is better.

SECTION 2
ON THE MYSTERIES OF PRESCRIBED FASTING AND ITS INWARD CONDITIONS

Prescribed fasting is of three successive grades, namely, the prescribed fasting of the general public, the prescribed fasting of the select few, and the prescribed fasting of the elite among the select few. The prescribed fasting of the general public involves refraining from satisfying the appetite of the stomach and the sexual appetite, as has already been discussed. The prescribed fasting of the select few is to keep the ears, eyes, tongue, hands and feet as well as the other senses free from wrongdoing.

The prescribed fasting of the elite among the select few is orienting the prescribed fast to a fast of the heart. A fast of the heart is to abstain from mean thoughts and worldly worries. It is complete unconcern with anything but God. Such a fast is broken by thinking about anything other than God and the Last Day, as well as by concerning the self with things of this world, except in so far as it promotes religion which belongs to the Hereafter. Thus those whose hearts are sanctified have said, "Those who spend their day worrying over what they will have to eat to end their prescribed fast sins." This is because they have little confidence in the bounty of God and little faith that the livelihood promised unto them will be received. In this rank stand the prophets and saints. We shall not dwell on the verbal description of the kind of fasting but shall define it through its active operation. It is to seek God with all of one's strength and to turn away from all other things besides Him. In short it is to embody the words of God when He said, "'*Say God,' then leave them in their pastime of vain discourse and triflings*" (6:91).

The prescribed fasting of the select few, which is the prescribed fasting of the virtuous people, is to keep the senses free from wrongdoing. It is accomplished through six things: To refrain from looking at anything blameworthy and disapproved or anything which occupies the person and diverts him/her from remembering God. The Messenger said, "The coveting glance is one of the poisoned arrows of satan. He who because of piety abstains therefrom will receive from Him a belief the sweetness of which will fill his heart."[27] In another Tradition, he said, "Five things break the prescribed fast: the telling of lies, backbiting, tale-bearing, perjury, and the casting of coveting and lustful eyes."[28]

The second is to keep the tongue free from raving, lying, backbiting, tale-bearing, obscenity, abusive speech, wrangling, and hypocrisy and to impose silence upon it. Furthermore the tongue should be employed in the remembrance and glorification of God and engaged in reading and reciting of the Quran. This is the fasting of the tongue. A Sufi once said, "Backbiting renders prescribed fasting of no effect."[29] Another[30] once said, "Two traits render prescribed fasting of no effect: backbiting and lying."

The Messenger said, "Verily, fasting is like unto a shield, therefore whenever one of you performs the prescribed fasts let him not speak unseemly or act foolishly. If anyone disputes with him or swears at him, let him say, 'I am performing the prescribed fast, verily I am fasting'."[31] In another Tradition we read about two women who lived during the lifetime of Muhammad (ﷺ). As they were fasting one day the pangs of hunger and the darts of thirst proved too much for them to endure, and they almost collapsed. Consequently they sent Muhammad (ﷺ) asking him permission to break their fast. In reply he sent them a cup saying, "Vomit into this cup what you have eaten." To the amazement of all present the one filled half the cup with pure blood and tender flesh and the other filled up the second half of the cup with the same thing. Thereupon Muhammad (ص) said, "These two women have tasted from that which God has made lawful unto them and have broken their prescribed fast by doing that which He has made unlawful unto them. They sat down and engaged in backbiting. The flesh and blood which they vomited is the flesh and blood of those people whom they have betrayed."27

The third is to close the ears to every reprehensible thing because everything which is unlawful to utter is also unlawful to hear. For this reason God regarded the listener and the "sharks" of unlawful trade alike when He said, *"Listeners to falsehood are sharks of unlawful trade"* (5:46). And again, *"Had not the masters and the divines forbidden their uttering wickedness and devouring unlawful trade, bad indeed would have been their deeds"* (5:68). Silence therefore, in the face of backbiting is unlawful. Said God, *"You are, then, like unto them"* (4:139). Muhammad (ص) also said, "The backbiter and he/she who listens unto him/her are partners in wrongdoing."28

The fourth is constraining the rest of the senses from wrongdoing, restraining the hand from reaching evil, and curbing the foot from pursuing wickedness, as well as avoiding questionable foods at the daily end of the prescribed fast. Otherwise, if the prescribed fast is going to be abstinence from lawful things and partaking, on the daily ending of it, of unlawful things, it will have no significance at all. Such a person is like one who builds a building but destroys the capital. For lawful food is harmful not because of its quality, but because of its quantity. Prescribed fasting is designed to induce moderation. Similarly the person who, for fear of the bad effect of an excessive does of medication, resorts to taking a dose of poison, is indeed foolish. The unlawful is poison detrimental to religion while the lawful is like a medication, a little of which is beneficial, but the excess of which is harmful. The purpose of fasting is to induce moderation therein. Muhammad (ص) said, "Many a man gets nothing out of his fast except hunger and thirst."29 In explanation of this, it has been said that the Messenger is referring to the person who ends the prescribed fast with unlawful things. Others said that he meant the person who abstains from lawful food and ends his/her prescribed fast on the flesh of people through backbiting, which is unlawful. Still others said that the Messenger meant the person who does not keep his/her senses free from wrongdoing.

The fifth is that when ending the prescribed fast, a person should not overeat of even lawful food, thereby stuffing his/her belly full. For there is no vessel more abominable unto God than a belly stuffed with lawful food. How could any one expect to overcome the enemy of God and subdue his/her own inappropriate desires through prescribed fasting if, when ending the prescribed fast, compensates himself/herself for what had missed during the day and even helps himself/herself to more food and drink of diverse kinds. It has thus become the custom to store up all the food for the month of Ramadan, wherein more food and drink are devoured than in several months. Yet it is well known that the purpose of prescribed fasting is hunger and the suppression of lust so that the self might be able to attain piety. If the stomach were not given any food from the early morning until the evening so that its appetite became aroused and its desire increased and then it were fed with delicacies and stuffed to satiety therewith, its pleasure would be enhanced and vitality doubled, consequently giving rise to passions otherwise dormant. The spirit as well as the secret of prescribed fasting is to weaken the flesh which is the human ego's tool for turning the self back to wrongdoing. The weakening of the flesh is never achieved unless a person reduces his/her food to the amount of food which he/she would have eaten in the evening if he/she were not fasting.

But if, on ending the fast, believers should eat an amount of food equivalent to what they would have eaten during both the daytime and the evening, they would reap no benefit from their prescribed fast. As a matter of fact among the proprieties of prescribed fasting is that the person should not sleep much during the daytime, but rather stay up so that they might feel the pangs of hunger and the flames of thirst and become conscious of the weakness of the flesh, with the result that their heart would be cleansed and purified. They should maintain their body in such a state of weakness during the Night of Power so that they might find their night worship (*tahajjud*) easier to perform and their night portions (sing. *wird*) easier to read.

It is hoped, then, that satanic temptations will not hover around their heart and that they will be able to lift their eyes unto the kingdom of heaven. In this connection the Night of Power represents the night on which a glimpse of the invisible world is revealed to the human being. It is also the night which is alluded to by the words of God when He said, *"Verily We have sent it down on the Night of Power"* (97:1). Those who bury their head deep into a nose-bag full of food cannot hope to see the invisible world. Even if they keep their stomach empty, they will not be able to remove the veil and see the invisible world unless they also empty their mind from everything except God. This is the whole matter, the basis of which is to cut down the amount of food one eats.

The sixth is that their heart should remain in a state of suspense between fear and hope, after the daily ending of the prescribed fast, because they do not know whether or not their prescribed fast will be accepted. Will they be among the friends of God or among the rejected by God? They should remain in such a state of suspense after every act of worship.

It has been related that Hasan al-Basri (a well-known early Sufi) once passed by a group of men who were rollicking with laughter. He said to them, "Verily God has made the month of Ramadan a race-course where men compete in His worship. Some have won their race and been crowned with success while others lagged behind and lost. We are surprised and astonished at the man who wastes his time in indolence and laughter on the day when the earnest finish victorious and the idle meet with failure and disaster. By God, if the veil were to be removed, you will find the good man occupied with his good works and the wrongdoer with his wrongdoings." In other words the joy of those whose prescribed fast has been accepted will occupy them and keep them from indolence, while the agony and regrets of the person whose prescribed fast has been rejected will take all joy from their heart and make laughter impossible.

It was related that Hasan al-Basri was once told, "You are an old man. Prescribed fasting would make you weak." To which he replied, "This prescribed fast is my preparation for a long journey. Verily to endure the yoke of God's service is easier than to endure the yoke of His torture." Such words depict the inward meaning of fasting.

If you then ask, "How can the jurisprudents approve the prescribed fasting of those who confine themselves to restraining the appetite of their stomach and their sexual urges, but neglect these inward aspects of the prescribed fast, how, then, can they say that their prescribed fast is valid?" Then know that the jurisprudents of the outward law support its formal requirements by means of proof far weaker than that of angels. Angels stand in close proximity to God and whoever follows in their footsteps and emulates their example is drawn, like them, near to God. This proximity, however, is not one of location, but one of qualities and attributes.

If, among the people of insight and the physicians of the heart, this be the secret of prescribed fasting, what good-will is there in delaying a meal and combining two at sunset while indulging in the satisfaction of all the other physical desires and lusts throughout the day? And if there were good in such behavior what would the words of Muhammad (ﷺ) mean when he said, "Many a person gets nothing out of the prescribed fast except hunger and thirst?"[30] For this reason Abu al-Darda (a Companion of the Messenger) once said, "How good is the sleep of the wise and how excellent is their eating. Behold how they put to shame the wakefulness of the foolish and their fasting. Verily the weight of an atom of the worship of the faithful and pious is better than the weight of mountains of the worship of those who are misguided and those in error." Consequently one of the learned said, "Many a person performing the prescribed fasting is not truly fasting. and many a person not abstaining from food and drink is truly fasting."

Those who are truly fasting while not abstaining from food and drink are those who keep themselves free from wrongdoing. Those are not truly fasting are those who, while they are hungry and thirsty, allow themselves every freedom to commit wrong. But those who truly understand prescribed fasting and its secret knows that they who abstain from food, drink and sexual intercourse, but commit all manner of wrongdoing are like those who, in performing the ablution, run their hand over one of their limbs three times for the prescribed ablution, thereby outwardly fulfilling the Law as far as the limb is concerned, but neglecting the truly important thing which is attaining the state of prescribed purity. Consequently because of their ignorance, their prayer is rejected.

On the other hand, those who break the prescribed fast through eating, but observe it by keeping themselves free from wrongdoing are like the those who, in performing the ablution, wash each of the limbs of their body once only. Their prayers are, by the will of God, accepted because they have fulfilled the principal thing in the ablution although they have failed to fulfill the details. But those who do both are like those who, in performing the ablution, wash each member of their body three times, thereby fulfilling both the principal purpose of ablution as well as its elaborate details, which constitutes perfection. Muhammad (ص) once said, "Verily prescribed fasting is a trust. Let each, therefore, take good care of His trust."[31]

Again when he recited, "*Verily God enjoins you to give back your trusts to their owners,*"(4:61) he raised his hands and touching his ears and eyes said, "The gift of hearing and the gift of seeing are each a trust from God." Similarly the gift of speech is a trust, for if it were not so Muhammad (ص) would not have said, "If anyone disputes with another and swears at him, let the latter say, 'I am performing the prescribed fast, verily I am fasting'."[32] Or, in other words, "I have been given my tongue in order to keep and hold, not in order to give it free rein in retort and reply to you."

It is clear, then, that every act of worship is possessed of an outward and an inner form, an external husk and internal pith. The husks are of different grades and each grade has different layers. It is for you to choose whether to be content with the husk or join the company of the wise and the learned.

3

SUFIS ON PRESCRIBED FASTING AND SPIRITUAL POVERTY

Javad Nurbakhsh

Mystics have continued over the centuries to emphasize the importance of fasting as a spiritual discipline, the goal of which is to fast from everything but experiencing the Presence of God. In the following sayings collected by Javad Nurbakhsh, it will be observed how the goal of the prescribed fast is processed by the mystic resulting in a quality known as spiritual poverty.

Spiritual poverty is a major characteristic of a person who has a Muhammadan character (*al-khulq al-muhammadi*). "Adorned by the virtues of sincerity, generosity and humility or truthfulness, nobility and simplicity, the Messenger was also touched by the perfume of kindness and the effusion of happiness...."[1] Prescribed fasting is one of the disciplines that leads the mystic towards these character traits in modeling the Messenger Muhammad (ص).

Muhammadan character as summarized in the character trait of spiritual poverty is also a trait called *hilm* or the moral reasonableness of a religiously cultured monotheist. Spiritual poverty or moral reasonableness are described for modeling purposes in the character of the Messenger in the following way:

> He does not become unnecessarily angry, is calm and collected, has patience and is kind to others. It means that he is in a state of joy and felicity and not given to constant agitation and protest. Muslims do not fail to remember that the Messenger always smiled and had a sense of happiness and joy emanate from his face which did not of course exclude 'holy anger' when he faced those who opposed the Truth,but what is remarkable is that there existed within his soul both vigor and gentleness, both the severity and purity of the desert and the gentle breeze and perfume of a rose garden. He transformed the world and carried out the most remarkable tasks under unbelievable hardships, but always with the kindness and generosity which characterizes the friends of God. In him the highest perfections were assembled. He was in reality that perfect human being before whom the angels were ordered to prostrate themselves. That is why God and His angels praise and bless him and those who are faithful are commanded to also praise and bless him and to model their lives after him.[2]

The Editor

A Sufi said, "Fasting means becoming absent from consciousness of the creation through beholding God."[3] Prescribed fasting in this sense means the fasting of the inner consciousness, not the external fast. When one restrains the outer being from lust and personal desires, one is merely performing prescribed fasting according to the Divine Law. When one restrains the inner being from the passions of the ego and attraction to the world, on the other hand, one is fasting according to the dictates of Reality.

Shibli asked one of his disciples if he could maintain a permanent prescribed fast. "What is that?" the disciple inquired. Shibli explained that it is to make one's entire life a single day in which one keeps the prescribed fast which is broken solely by the beholding of the Presence of God.[4]

Abu Sa'id Abi'l-Khayr said, "The world is a day in which we are fasting."[5] This means that we should expect nothing from the world and not be bound by it. Muzaffar Kermanshahi said, "Fasting is of three types: fasting of the spirit which involves the curbing of expectations; fasting of the intellect which involves the curbing of the passions; and fasting of the animal soul which is to refrain from eating, drinking and sexual desire."[6]

Prescribed fasting is also described by Shah Ni'matu'llah-i Wali[7] to be of three kinds: The first is prescribed fasting of the common people which is to abstain from drink, sex and food from the first to the last light of day with an expressed intention to do so. The second is the prescribed fasting of the elect which entails continuous fasting from all wrongdoing and error on the part of all the faculties and parts of the body. The third is the prescribed fasting of the elect of the elect who are the intimates of the circle of the Compassionate and retainers of the court of the Most Praised. This group observes an outer and inner fast, every day, from that which is other than the love of God and they wear the subtle vesture of honor which embodies the message, "Fasting is Mine and I am the reward for it."[8]

In yet another Sufi view,

> Know that, in the view of the verifiers, fasting has three degrees. The common people fast by refraining from food, drink and sexual intercourse from morning to the sunset prescribed prayer. The elect fast by preserving the seven bodily members from wrongdoings and acts of disobedience. They prevent the tongue from lying, obscenity and backbiting; the eye from looking with caprice and appetite; the ear from listening to nonsense, obscenity, idle talk, and their like; and the hand, foot and other members from acts made unlawful and forbidden by the Divine Law. The revelation gives news of this meaning when it says, *'The hearing, the sight, the heart—all these shall be questioned'* (17:36). The Messenger Muhammad (ص) said, 'Five things break the fast of the person faster—lying, backbiting, slander, ungodly oaths,

and looking with lust.' The elect of the elect perform
the prescribed fast by also examining their thoughts
and preventing their innermost consciousness from
paying attention to anything other than God. These
are the people of poverty and their capital and provisions for wayfaring on the path to God are nothing-
ness.

> God's Being inclines
> > only toward not-being—
> In this path, take not-being
> > as your provision.

*"God has brought from the faithful their selves and
their possessions in order that they should have the
Garden,"* (9:111). I have sold myself at the auction of
'I don't care,' and bought You! As long as an atom of
them remains, they will not have bestowed the
degree of beauty upon the perfection of prescribed
fasting.

> A man of perfection
> > walked the path of annihilation
> and departed from existence
> > like dust.
> A thread of his being
> > went along with him—
> > in spiritual poverty's eye,
> > that thread was an infidel's belt.[9]

Spiritual poverty, then, arises from, among other spiritual
practices, the practice of prescribed fasting. It is characterized
by destitution, impoverishment and neediness as contrasted to
'wealth' which connotes 'independence' and 'self-sufficiency'.
Spiritual poverty is in reality a devotee's attribute whereas
wealth is an attribute of the Lord. In this sense, the Quran
declares, *"Oh humanity! You are poor in relation to God and
God is the Rich, the Glorious"* (35:15).

The term spiritual poverty has various meanings. First of
all, sometimes it implies straightened circumstances and material need. In this case the word *faqir* or poor one means only a
beggar in contradistinction to *miskin*, one who is lowly and destitute. A distinction is often made between the two insofar as a
faqir is considered to be a dervish who has the ability to support

himself/herself and family for a few days whereas the *miskin* is someone afflicted by extreme need and impoverishment.

Secondly, sometimes spiritual poverty implies an individual's spiritual impoverishment and need for God. In this case, the term *faqir* has different shades of meaning. It may be synonymous with the ascetic who renounces the world to attain a reward in the Hereafter or it may be synonymous with the Sufi who renounces both this world and the next to attain the Truth. Here the term *faqir* is identical in meaning with the perfect human being and the Sufi who has attained total mystical reabsorbment in the Truth.

The main verses in the Quran which refer to spiritual poverty which is synonymous with the term Sufi are: "*And God is Rich and you are poor*" (47:38); "*So Moses watered their flocks for them.. Then he turned aside into the shade and said, 'My Lord, I am needy (faqir) of whatever good you send down for me'*" (28:24) as well as the verse mentioned above (35:15).

Various Traditions of the Messenger (ﺹ) also refer to spiritual poverty: "Spiritual poverty is my pride and I glory in it."[10] This has been annotated with the following verse:

This is clear proof enough for me
    of poverty's real wealth:
That it was the pride of the Messenger,
    master of the pilgrims of spiritual poverty[11]

"Spiritual poverty is to be shame-facedness in this world and the next."[12] The esoteric interpretation of this Tradition is that the human being is 'possible being' while God is Necessary Being. Without Necessary Being the human being has no existence. That is to say, his/her existence in its contingence is in need of Necessary Being. Thus the existential poverty of his/her possible being culminates in shame-facedness and disgrace in this world and the next.

A third Tradition is, "Spiritual poverty approaches the point of infamy."[13]

In the words of the mystic poet Attar:
In the land of infamy
The mystic pitches his tent,
Dressed in the vestment of spiritual poverty
Approaches a point and secluded from the rabble

By a shamefaced visage here and hereafter.

"Spiritual poverty is glory to its possessor."[14] is another Tradition.

In a commentary upon the Quran, Ansari says, "Know that there are two kinds of spiritual poverty. One against which the Messenger of God cautioned when he said, 'In You I seek asylum from poverty'. Concerning the other he commented, 'Poverty is my pride'. The former approaches impiety, the latter, Reality. The poverty resembling impiety pertains to the heart; it deprives the heart of all knowledge, wisdom, virtue, patience, contentment, humble submission and trust in God until from all these higher states it is impoverished. But that poverty of the Spirit which the Messenger deemed an honor is that which divests a person of worldliness and approximates him/her to true piety or real faith."[15]

Ruwaim says, "There is majesty in spiritual poverty which requires that it remain hidden, inviolate and jealously protected. Whoever divulges it and flaunts it before people ceases to belong to this company and has no eminence in spiritual poverty." [16] When asked of the reality of spiritual poverty, he replied, "To select things justly and when needy, to choose the lesser over the more."[17]

Hamdun Qassar says, "The natural state of the *faqir* is humility. If he/she becomes proud of his/her spiritual poverty, he/she surpasses all the wealthy in pride."[18] Shaqiq Balkhi says, "Spiritual poverty is accompanied by three things: a heart that is carefree, a conscience at ease and a soul in peace, at rest."[19] Abu Hafs Haddad says, "Spiritual poverty is not complete until one likes giving more than receiving."[20] And, "The best way for a devotee to draw near to God is by constant spiritual poverty in every state, careful adherence to the Tradition of the Messenger in every action and pursuit of a lawful livelihood."[21]

Finally, Abu'l Fadhl Hasan says, "Reality consists in two things: First, integrity of one's spiritual poverty before God which is among the principles of devotion. Second, the meticulous following of the example of the Messenger which means the denial of all ease and advantage to oneself."[22]

PART TWO: BELIEVERS

4

COMMENTARY: QURANIC VERSES PRESCRIBING FASTING

Abul Ala Mawdudi

The following is a traditional commentary on the Quran written by a contemporary Muslim religious scholar. The scholar first repeats the verse of the Quran and then comments.

The Editor

(2:183) *Believers! Fasting is enjoined upon you as it was enjoined upon those before you that you become God-fearing..*[1]

1 Like most other injunctions of Islam, those relating to prescribed fasting were revealed gradually. In the beginning, the Messenger (ص) had instructed the Muslims to fast three days in every month, although this was not obligatory. When the injunction in the present verse was later revealed in 2 AH, a degree of relaxation was introduced. It was stipulated that those who did not fast despite their capacity to endure it were obliged to feed one poor person as an expiation for each day of obligatory fasting missed (see verse 184). Another injunction was revealed later (see verse 185) and here the relaxation in

respect of able-bodied persons was revoked. However, for the sick, the traveler, the pregnant, the breast-feeding women and the aged who could not endure fasting, the relaxation was retained.

(2:184) *Prescribed fasting is for a fixed number of days and if one of you be sick, or if one of you be on a journey, you will perform the prescribed fast the same number of other days later on. For those who are capable of performing the prescribed fasting (but still do not fast) there is a redemption: feeding a needy person for each day missed. Whoever voluntarily does more good than is required will find it is better for him.[2]and that you should perform the prescribed fast is better of you, if you only knew[3]* (2:184).

2 This act of extra merit could either be feeding more than the one person required or both fasting and feeding the poor.

3 Here ends the early injunction with regard to fasting which was revealed in 2 AH prior to the Battle of Badr. The verses that follow were revealed about one year later and are linked with the preceding verses since they deal with the same subject.

(2:185) *During the month of Ramadan the Quran was sent down as a guidance to the people with clear signs of the true guidance and as the criterion (between right and wrong). So those of you who live to see that month should fast it and whoever is sick or on a journey should fast the same number of other days instead. God wants ease and not hardship for you so that you may complete the number of days required,* [4] *magnify God for what He has guided you to, and give thanks to Him.*[5]

4 Whether a person should or should not perform the prescribed fast while on a journey is left to individual discretion. We find that among the Companions who accompanied the Messenger on journeys some performed the prescribed fast whereas others did not; none objected to the conduct of another. The Messenger himself did not always perform the prescribed fast when traveling. On one journey a person was so overwhelmed by hunger that he collapsed; the Messenger disapproved when he learned that the man had been performing the prescribed fast. The Messenger used to prevent people from per-

forming the prescribed fast during wars so that they would not lack energy for the fight. It has been reported by Umar that two military expeditions took place in the month of Ramadan. The first was the Battle of Badr and the second the conquest of Makkah. On both occasions, the Companions abstained from prescribed fasting, and, according to Ibn Umar, on the occasion of the conquest of Makkah, the Messenger proclaimed that people should not perform the prescribed fast since it was a day of fighting. In other Traditions, the Messenger is reported to have said that people should not fast when they had drawn close to the enemy, since abstention from fasting would lead to greater strength. The duration of a journey for which it becomes permissible for a person to abstain from performing the prescribed fast is not absolutely clear from any statement of the Messenger. In addition, the practice of the Companions was not uniform. It would seem that any journey which is commonly regarded as such, and which is attended by the circumstances generally associated with traveling, should be deemed sufficient justification for not fasting. Jurists agree that one does not have to fast on the day of commencing a journey; one may eat either at the point of departure or after the actual journey has commenced. Either course is sanctioned by the practice of the Companions. Jurists, however, are not agreed as to whether or not the residents of a city under attack may abstain from prescribed fasting even though they are not actually traveling. Ibn Taimiyyah favors the permissibility of abstention from prescribed fasting and supports his view with very forceful arguments.

5 This indicates that prescribed fasting need not be confined exclusively to Ramadan. For those who fail to perform the prescribed fast during that month owing to some legitimate reason, God has kept the door of compensation open during other months of the year so that they need not be deprived of the opportunity to express their gratitude to Him for His great bounty in revealing the Quran.

It should be noted here that fasting in Ramadan has not only been declared an act of worship and devotion and a means to nourish piety, but has also been characterized as an act of gratefulness to God for His great bounty of true guidance in the form of the Quran. In fact, the best way of expressing gratitude for someone's bounty or benevolence is to prepare oneself, to the best of one's ability, to achieve the purpose for which that bounty has been bestowed. The Quran has been revealed so that we may know the way that leads to God's satisfaction, follow that way ourselves and direct the world along it. Prescribed fasting is an excellent means by which to prepare ourselves for shouldering this task. Hence, prescribed fasting during this month of the revelation of the Quran is more than an act of worship and more than an excellent course of moral training. It is also an appropriate form for the expression of our thankfulness to God for the bounty of the Quran.

(2:186) *(Oh Muhammad!) When My servants ask you about Me, tell them I indeed am quite near; I hear and answer the call of the caller whenever he calls Me. Let them listen to My call and believe in Me;*[6] *perhaps they will then be guided aright.*[7]

6 Even though people can neither see God nor subject Him to any other form of sense perception, this should not make them feel that God is remote from them. On the contrary, He is so close to each and every person that whenever any person so wishes, he can communicate with his Lord. So much so that God hears and responds even to the prayers which remain within the innermost recesses of the heart. People exhaust themselves by approaching false and powerless beings whom they foolishly fancy to be their deities, but who have neither the power to hear nor to grant their prayers. But God, the omnipotent Lord and the absolute Master of this vast universe, Who wields all power and authority, is so close to human beings that they can always approach Him without the intercession of any intermediaries and can put to Him their prayers and requests.

7 This announcement of God's closeness to human beings may open his eyes to the Truth, may turn him to the right way wherein lies his success and well-being.

(2:187) *It has been made lawful for you to go into your wives during the night of the prescribed fast. They are your garment and you are theirs.*[8] *God knows you betrayed yourselves and He mercifully relented and pardoned you. So you may now associ-*

ate intimately with your wives and benefit from the enjoyment
God has made lawful for you;[9] and eat and drink[10] at night
until you can discern the white streak of dawn against the black-
ness of the night,[11] then (give up all that and) complete your fast-
ing until night sets in.[12] But do not associate intimately with
your wives during the period when you are on retreat in the
mosques.[13] These are the bounds set by God; do not, then, even
draw near them.[14] Thus does God make His signs clear to
humanity that they may stay away from wrongdoing.

8 Just as nothing intervenes between a person's body and
his clothes, so nothing can intervene between a man and his
wife; it is a relationship of inalienable intimacy.

9 Although there was no categorical ordinance in the early
days prohibiting sexual intercourse between husband and wife
during the nights of Ramadan, people generally assumed that
this was not permissible. Despite the feeling that their action
was either not permitted or was at least disapproved of, they
did at times approach their spouses. Such a betrayal of conscience can encourage a sinful disposition. God, therefore, first
reproaches them with their lack of integrity, for this is what
was objectionable. As for the act itself, God makes it clear that
it is quite permissible. Henceforth they might engage in sexual
intercourse as a perfectly lawful act unencumbered by feelings
of guilt.

10 In this connection, too, there was a misapprehension at
first. Some thought that eating and drinking were absolutely
prohibited after the performance of the night prescribed prayer.
Others thought that one could eat and drink so long as one had
not fallen asleep, but that if one had, it was not permissible to
eat on reawakening. These were people's own fancies and often
caused great inconvenience. This verse seeks to remove all such
misconceptions. It clearly lays down the duration of the fast:
from dawn until sunset. Between sunset and dawn it is permissible to eat, to drink, and to indulge in the legitimate gratification of sexual desires. At the same time, the Messenger introduced the pre-fasting meal recommending a good meal just
before dawn.

11 In fixing the time of obligatory rites, Islam has been

mindful that these timings should be so clear and simple that people, at all stages of development, should be able to follow them. This is why Islam bases its timing on conspicuous natural phenomena and not on the clock. Some people object that this principle of timing is untenable in areas close to the poles where night and day each last for about six months. This objection is based on a very superficial knowledge of geography. In point of fact, neither day nor night lasts for six months in those areas—not in the sense in which people living near the equator conceive of night and day. The signs of morning and evening appear at the poles with unfailing regularity and it is on this basis that people time their sleeping and waking, their professional work, their play and recreation. Even in the days before watches were common, the people of countries like Finland, Norway and Greenland used to fix the hours of the day and night by means of various signs that appeared on the horizon. Just as those signs helped them to determine their schedules in other matters, so they should enable them to time their various prescribed prayers, the pre-dawn meal and the post-sunset daily ending of the fast.

5 Complete your prescribed fasting until night sets in means that the time of prescribed fasting ends with nightfall, that is, sunset marks the ending of the fast. The precise time of the end of the pre-dawn meal is when a lean strip of aurora appears at the eastern end of the horizon and begins to grow. The time to end one's prescribed fast starts when the darkness of night seems to have begun to appear over the eastern horizon. Some people in our own time have adopted an attitude of extreme caution with regard to the time of both the end and start of prescribed fasting. The Law has not fixed these schedules with rigid precision. If a person wakes up just at the crack of dawn, it is proper for him to eat and drink hastily. According to a Tradition, the Messenger said, "If anyone of you hears the call for the morning prescribed prayer while he is eating, he should not stop immediately, but should finish eating to the extent of his bare need."

Similarly, one need not wait for the light of day to disappear fully before breaking the prescribed fast. The Messenger, for instance, used to ask Bilal to bring him something to drink as soon as the sun had set. Bilal expressed his astonishment, pointing out that the light of day could still be observed. To this the Messenger replied that the time of fasting came to an end when the darkness of night began to rise from the east.

13 On retreat in the mosque refers to the religious practice of spending the last ten days of Ramadan in the mosque, consecrating this time to the remembrance of God. In this state, known as *i'tikaf*, one may go out of the mosque only for the absolutely necessary requirements of life, but one must stay away from gratifying one's sexual desires.

14 The directive here is neither to exceed nor draw near the limits set by God. This means that it is dangerous for a person to skirt the boundaries of disobedience; prudence demands that one should keep some distance from these lest one's steps inadvertently lead one to cross them. The same principle has been enunciated in a Tradition in which the Messenger said, "Every sovereign has an enclosed pasture and the enclosed pasture of God consists of His prohibitions. So whosoever keeps grazing around that pasture is likely to fall into it." It is a pity that many people who are not conversant with the spirit of the Divine Law insist on using these boundaries to the limits. Many religious scholars exert themselves in finding out arguments to justify this attitude and a point is thus reached where only a hair's breadth separate obedience from disobedience. Consequently many people fall prey to disobedience, even to downright error and wrong-doing. For once a person arrives at this point, he is seldom capable of discerning between right and wrong and maintaining the absolute self-control needed to keep within the lawful limits.

5

THE VIRTUES OF RAMADAN SEEN THROUGH THE TRADITIONS

Muhammad Zakariyya Kandhlawi

The Traditions (pl. *ahadith,* sing. *hadith*) refer to the sayings, customs and actions of the Messenger as related by his Companions. Various compilations of the Traditions have been done based on the reliability of the transmitter. A science developed called the Science of Transmitters in which certain rules were developed for choosing a particular Tradition as reliable or not. The Traditions in the following essay are all considered to be reliable because they are found in the collection known as *Sahih al-Bukhari.*

The Editor

TRADITION

On the last day of Shaban, Muhammad (ﺹ) addressed us and said,

> Oh people, there comes upon you now a great month, a most blessed month, in which lies a night

greater in worth than one thousand months. It is a month in which God has made compulsory that the prescribed fasting should be observed by day; and He has made the Special Prayer (*tarawih*) by night a Tradition. Whosoever tries drawing nearer to God by performing any virtuous deed in this month, for him/her shall be such reward as if he/she had performed a prescribed act of worship in any other time of the year. And whoever performs a prescribed act of worship for God, for him/her shall be the reward of seventy prescribed acts of worship in any other time of the year. This is indeed the month of patience, and the reward for true patience is paradise. It is the month of sympathy with one's fellow human beings; it is the month wherein a true believer's provisions is increased. Whosoever feeds a person performing the prescribed fast in order to end the fast at sunset, for him/her there shall be forgiveness of his/her sins and emancipation from the hellfire, and for him/her shall be the same reward as for him/her whom he/she fed, without that person's reward being diminished in the least.'

Thereupon we said, 'Oh Messenger of God, not all of us possess the means whereby we can provide enough for a prescribed fasting person to break the prescribed fast.' The Messenger replied, 'God grants this same reward to one who gives a person who is performing the prescribed fast a single date or a drink of water or a sip of milk to end the prescribed fast. This is a month, the first part of which brings God's Mercy, the middle of which brings God's forgiveness and the last part of which brings emancipation from hellfire. Whosoever lessens the burden of God's servants in this month, God will forgive that person and free him/her from hell-fire.'

He also said, 'And in this month, four things you should endeavor to perform in great number, two of which shall be to please your Lord, while the other two shall be those without which you cannot make do. Those which shall be to please your Lord, are that you should in great quantity recite the testimony bearing witness to the oneness of God, "*la ilaha illa Lah,*" (there is no god but God) and beg God's forgiveness for your wrongdoings. And as for those two without which you cannot make do you should beg God for entry into paradise and seek refuge with God from hellfire.'

And whoever gave water to drink to a person who had performed the prescribed fast, God shall grant him/her a drink from my fountain such a drink where after he/she shall never again feel thirsty until he/she enters paradise.'

COMMENTARY

Abraham (ع) received his scriptures on the first or third of this month, and David (ع) received the Psalms on the twelfth or eighteenth of this month. Moses (ع) received the Pentateuch on the sixth; Jesus (ع) received the New Testament on the twelfth or thirteenth. From this we note the close connection between the Divine Scriptures and the month of Ramadan. For this reason, as much recitation of the Quran should be done as possible during this month; such was the habit of our saints.

Gabriel used to recite the whole Quran to Muhammad (ص) in the month of Ramadan. In some Traditions, it is stated that Muhammad used to recite and Gabriel used to listen. By combining these Traditions, the religious scholars have said that it is recommended to recite the Quran in such a manner that while one person recites, the others listen. Thereafter another person recites while the others listen. So recite the Quran as much as possible; whatever time remains thereafter should also not be wasted. Muhammad (ص) has drawn our attention to four other things and advised that we should practice them as much as possible. These are the recitation of the Quran, seeking God's forgiveness for our wrongdoings, begging for admittance to paradise and seeking refuge from hellfire.

Therefore any spare time should be spent on these things. What is so difficult about keeping the tongue busy with the recitation of "there is no god but God" while engaged in our daily tasks?

In the same Tradition, Muhammad (ص) has said a few more

things, "Ramadan is the month of patience." Hence, even if great difficulty is experienced in prescribed fasting, one should bear it cheerfully with patience; one should not complain, as people are likely to do during the hot summer days. Similarly, if the pre-dawn meal is missed, one should not complain. Should we feel fatigued at the time of the Special Prayer (*tarawih*), this too should be borne with patience. Do not consider it a great imposition or trial otherwise these performances may lose credit with God. When we turn our back on worldly comforts, forsake our eating and drinking for the sake of livelihood, then in comparison with God's pleasure what are these little difficulties?

Further, the Traditions states that this is the month of sympathy, especially with the poor and destitute. Sympathy should be of a practical nature; when ten things are placed before us for post-sunset meal, at least three or four of them should be set aside for the poor and needy, even if we cannot treat them equally well as ourselves. In showing sympathy for the poor, as in all other matters, the Companions were living examples, and in this respect, it is our duty to follow or at least try to follow them.

There are hundreds and thousands of incidents that leave us astonished. Look at the following example: Abu Jahm relates that during the battle of Yarmouk he went in search of his cousin, taking with him a leather bottle full of water so as to give him a drink and wash his wounds if he were alive and wounded. He found him lying among the wounded. He says, "When I asked him whether he wanted some water, he indicated 'Yes.' At that moment, someone near him moaned. My cousin pointed to that, indicating that I should first quench the thirst of the neighbor. I went to him and found that he, too, needed water, but, just as I was about to give it to him, a third person groaned near him. The second one pointed to this third one, meaning that I should give the third one a drink first. I went to the third man, but before he could drink he passed away, whereupon I returned to the second one, only to find that he, too, had passed away. When I returned to my cousin, he, too, had become a martyr." This is the spirit of sacrifice that our forefathers possessed. May God be pleased with them and grant us the ability to follow in their footsteps.

Umar ibn al-Khattab (a Companion of Muhammad (ص) and the second rightly-guided caliph) has reported a statement of Muhammad (ص), who said that there are at all times five hundred chosen persons who enjoy God's favor, as well as forty saints. When any one of them dies, another takes his place. The Companions asked about their peculiar virtuous deeds. Muhammad (ص) said, "They forgive the oppressor, show kindness to the evil-doer and, out of their love for the common man, share their provisions with the needy."

In another Tradition, it is stated that whosoever feeds the hungry, clothes the naked, and grants refuge to the traveler, surely God shall save him from the terrors of the Day of Judgment. Yahya Garmaki used to give Imam Sufyan Thawri one thousand dirhams every month, whereupon Imam Sufyan used to prostrate himself before God, praying, "Oh God, Yahya has provided sufficiently for my worldly needs; You, through Your Great Mercy, see to his necessities in the Hereafter." After the death of Yahya, some people saw him in their dreams and on inquiring what had happened to him in the Hereafter, he replied, "Through the prayers of Sufyan, I have been forgiven by God."

Further, Muhammad (ص) has mentioned the virtue of feeding a person performing the prescribed fast at the time of the post-sunset ending of the fast. In one Tradition it is reported that the angels invoke blessings during the nights of Ramadan upon a person who feeds a person who is performing the prescribed fast to end the fast out of his/her legitimate (*halal*) earnings and, on the Night of Power (*laylat al-qadr*), Gabriel shakes hands with him/her. The sign of this is that one's heart becomes soft, while tears flow freely from one's eyes. Hamad bin Salamah, a very famous recorder of Traditions, used to feed fifty people every day in Ramadan at the post-sunset ending of the prescribed fast.

TRADITION

Another Companion reports that Muhammad (ص) said:

One day when Ramadan had drawn near, "The month of Ramadan, the month of blessings has come to you, wherein God turns towards you and sends down to you His special Mercy, forgives your faults, accepts prayers, appreciates your competition for the greatest good and boasts to the angels about you. So show to God your righteousness; for verily, the most pitiable and unfortunate one is he who is deprived of God's Mercy in this month.

COMMENTARY

In this Tradition, we read about the spirit of competition among the believers, each one trying to do more good deeds than the other. In our own home, I am greatly pleased on seeing how even the women compete with each other, the one trying to recite more of the Quran than the others, so that, in spite of domestic responsibilities, fifteen to twenty parts of the Quran are read by each one daily. I mention this only out of a sense of gratitude to God, mentioning His favor, and not to boast of it. May God accept their deeds and ours, and increase us all in good deeds.

TRADITION

The Messenger Muhammad (ﷺ) said:

Verily God and His angels send mercy upon those who eat the pre-dawn meal.

COMMENTARY

How great is God's favor upon us that even the partaking of food before dawn for prescribed fasting is so greatly rewarded. There are many Traditions in which the virtues of the pre-dawn meal are expounded and the rewards mentioned. A commentator on Bukhari (one of the most reliable collection of Traditions) has quoted the virtues of the pre-dawn meal from seventeen different Companions and all the religious scholars are agreed on its being recommended. Many people are deprived of this great reward because of their own laziness. Some even go so far as to finish the special prayer (*tarawih*), eat what they suppose to be pre-dawn meal and go to bed. What great blessings do they lose! The pre-dawn meal actually refers to partaking of food shortly before dawn. Some authorities say that the time for pre-dawn meal commences after half the night has passed. Then it must also be remembered that to eat at the latest possible time is better and greater in reward than eating earlier, subject to the condition that no doubt remains as to whether the pre-dawn meal had been eaten before the time of dawn. The Traditions are full of virtues about the pre-dawn meal.

Muhammad (ﷺ) said, "The difference between our prescribed fasting and that of the People of the Book (Jews and Christians) lies in our partaking of food at the pre-dawn meal which they do not." He has said, "Eat the pre-dawn meal because in it lie great blessings." And again, "In three things, are there great blessings: in companionship, in eating baked bread stuffed with ground meat (*tharid*) and in the pre-dawn meal." In this Tradition, the use of the word companionship is general, where from we deduce that it includes the prescribed prayers in congregation as well as the Friday congregational prayer and all those righteous deeds done in company, as thus God's help comes to them. Baked bread stuffed with ground meat is a tasty preparation The third thing mentioned in this Tradition is the pre-dawn meal. When Muhammad (ﷺ) used to invite any of the Companions to eat the pre-dawn meal with him, he used to say, "Come and partake of blessed food with me." One Tradition says, "Eat the pre-dawn meal and strengthen yourself for the fast. And sleep in the afternoon so as to gain assistance in waking up in the latter portion of the night for worship."

One of the Companions said, "I once visited Muhammad (ﷺ) at a time when he was busy in partaking of the pre-dawn meal. Muhammad (ﷺ) then said, "This is a thing full of blessings, which God has granted you. Do not give it up." Muhammad (ﷺ), in urging us repeatedly to partake of the pre-dawn meal, has said, "Even though there be no food, then one date should be eaten or a drink of water taken."

Thus, when there are definitely great advantages and

reward in the pre-dawn meal, Muslims should endeavor to observe this practice as much as possible. However, in all things moderation is important. Going beyond the bounds of moderation is harmful: neither should so little be eaten that one feels weak throughout the period of prescribed fasting, nor should so much be eaten that it causes discomfort. Repeatedly, we have been prohibited from filling the stomach excessively.

In his commentary on *Sahih Bukhari*, a religious scholar has mentioned various reasons for the blessedness of the pre-dawn meal: It is based in a Tradition and by doing it, one follows the Tradition; through the pre-dawn meal, we differentiate ourselves from the ways of People of the Book, which we are at all times called upon to do; it provides strength for worship; it promotes greater sincerity in worship; and it aids in elimination of bad temper, which normally comes about as result of hunger.

TRADITION

Another Tradition reports that Muhammad (ص) said:

> Many of those who fast obtain nothing through such prescribed fasting except hunger, and many a one performs the prescribed prayer by night but obtains nothing by it, except the discomfort of staying awake.

COMMENTARY

With regard to this Tradition, the religious scholars have mentioned three different interpretations: First, this Tradition may refer to those who fast during the day and, then, for post-sunset ending of the fast, eat food that is not legitimate (*halal*); all the reward for prescribed fasting is lost because of the greater wrongdoing of eating unlawful (*haram*) food, and nothing is gained except remaining hungry. Secondly, it may mean those who fast duly but, during prescribed fasting, engage themselves in backbiting and slandering others. Thirdly, the person referred to may be one who, while prescribed fasting, did not stay away from evil and wrongdoing. In this Tradition, all such possibilities are included. Similar is the case of the person performing the prescribed prayer all night voluntarily; because of backbiting or any other sinful act (e.g. missing the dawn prescribed prayer or keeping awake for show), his/her night of devotion goes unrewarded.

TRADITION

It is reported in another Tradition:

> I have heard Muhammad (ﷺ) saying, 'Prescribed fasting is a protective shield for believers, as long as they do not tear up that protection.'

COMMENTARY

"Protective shield" here means just as a person protects the self with a shield, similarly prescribed fasting protects one from one's well-known enemy—one's untamed ego. In other Traditions we are told that prescribed fasting saves one from God's punishment and hellfire in the Hereafter. Once somebody inquired from Muhammad (ﷺ), "What invalidates the prescribed fast?" He replied, 'Telling lies and backbiting."

This Tradition, when read in conjunction with so many others, actually tells us to avoid such actions which cause prescribed fasting to be wasted. In our times, we are fond of whiling away the time with unnecessary conversations. Some religious scholars are of the opinion that lies, backbiting, slander, etc., actually undo the fast just like eating and drinking, but the great majority of religious scholars believe that the fast is not totally undone, but loses its blessings. The religious scholars of Islam have mentioned six things, about which care should be taken in prescribed fasting:

First, one should keep the eyes away from any place where one should not look. Some go so far as to prohibit looking at one's own wife with desire, let alone another woman. Similarly, looking at any evil action or where evil is committed should be avoided. Muhammad (ﷺ) said, "The glance is like an arrow from inappropriate lust. Whosoever, out of fear for God, prevents the self from looking at evil, God shall grant that person such light of faith, the taste and ecstasy of which one will feel in the heart." The Sufis interpret the above saying to mean that those sights which should be avoided include all such places and things that distract the mind from the remembrance of God.

Secondly, one should guard the tongue against lies, unnecessary conversation, backbiting, arguments, swearing, etc. In *Bukhari*, we read that prescribed fasting is a shield for the prescribed fasting person. For this reason, those who fast should avoid all useless talk, joking, argument, etc. Should anyone pick an argument, then respond with, "I am performing the prescribed fast." In other words, one should not start an argument and if someone else starts it, then too, one should avoid taking it up. When the person who starts an argument is not an understanding person, then at least one should remind oneself that, "I am performing the prescribed fast."

Backbiting during prescribed fasting makes this spiritual discipline much more difficult. Similar is the case with other acts of wrongdoing. Experience shows that for the faithful, God-fearing persons, prescribed fasting is no hardship, whereas the wrongdoing find it too hard to bear. One should therefore stay away from sins and especially from major wrongdoings, like backbiting and slander, which are often indulged in to while away the time. God says in the Quran that backbiting is tantamount to the actual eating of the flesh of one's dead brother. We find this also narrated in various Traditions.

Once Muhammad (ص), on seeing some people, asked them to pick their teeth. They said that they had not tasted any meat that day. He said, "So and so's flesh is sticking to your teeth." It transpired that they had been backbiting. May God keep us safe from this evil, because we are very neglectful of this warning. All are guilty of this. This includes the average person as well as others. Even religious people in their gatherings do not avoid backbiting. Worst of all is the fact that we do not even realize what backbiting is. Even when we suspect ourselves of this, we try to cover it up as narration of some event..

One of the Companions inquired from Muhammad (ص),

"What is backbiting?" He replied, "To mention something about your brother behind his back, which he would resent." The Companions then said, "And is it still backbiting if the thing mentioned about him is really true?" Muhammad (ﷺ) said, "In that case (if that which was mentioned is really true), it is precisely backbiting; but if what is mentioned is false; then you have in fact slandered him/her."

Once Muhammad (ﷺ) passed by two graves. He said, "On both the inmates of these graves, punishment is being inflicted in the grave. One is being punished because of backbiting, the other because of not having take precautions to become purified after urinating."

Muhammad (ﷺ) also said, "There are more than seventy degrees of evil in usury. The lowest form of it is comparable to committing incest with one's own mother; and taking one dirham of interest is a worse evil than having fornicated thirty five times. The worst and most evil degree of taking interest is the slandering of a Muslim."

Thirdly, we should be careful that the ears are kept away from listening to anything undesirable. It is equally unlawful to listen to anything that should not be said. Muhammad (ﷺ) has said, "In backbiting, both the backbiter and the one who listens to it are equal partners in wrongdoing."

Fourthly, the rest of the body should be kept away from wrongdoing and unlawful things. Neither should the hands touch it nor the feet walk towards it. With the stomach, special care should be taken, especially at the time of the post-sunset ending of the fast that no such thing enters it about which there is any doubt of it being lawful and legitimate. When a person fasts and, at the post-sunset ending of the fast, breaks the fast with unlawful food, that person is like a sick person who takes medicine as a cure, but also adds a little poison, which destroys him/her.

Fifthly, after having fasted, it is not advisable to fill the stomach completely even with lawful food at the post-sunset ending of the fast, because then the purpose of prescribed fasting is defeated. Prescribed fasting seeks to diminish one's carnal desires and increase one's faith and spiritual powers. For eleven months, we eat and drink freely enough. In Ramadan this should be cut down to a minimum. We have a bad habit of filling our bellies at the time of the post-sunset ending of the fast to make up for what was lost, and again at the pre-dawn meal in preparation for the day, thus actually increasing our average consumption. Ramadan for such people gives an edge to their appetite. Many such items of food are eaten that we normally do not eat at other times. This type of eating habit is completely against the spirit of Ramadan and the true spirit of prescribed fasting.

Al-Ghazzali asks the same question, "When the object of prescribed fasting is to conquer our carnal passions in opposition to our ego's desire, how can this possibly be done by eating excessively at the post-sunset ending of the prescribed fast?" Actually, in that case, we have only altered the times of eating and not really fasted. In fact, by having various types of delicacies, we consume even more than in normal times. The result is that, instead of lessening the carnal desires, they are considerably increased. The real benefit of prescribed fasting comes as a result of actual hunger in the true sense. Muhammad (ﷺ) said, "Negative influences and satanic temptations flow through the body of a person like blood; so, close up its path by remaining hungry," i.e. when the body is hungry, the spirit receives strength.

Apart from hunger, prescribed fasting gives us an opportunity to appreciate the condition of the poor and destitute, and thus engenders sympathetic feelings towards them. This, too, can be attained by remaining hungry and not by filling the stomach with delicious foods at the pre-dawn meal, so that one does not feel hungry until the post-sunset ending of the fast. Once a person went to a Sufi, whom he found shivering in the cold, in spite of having warm clothes lying at his side. That person inquired, "Is this a time for taking off the clothes?" The Sufi replied, "There are numerous poor and needy ones; I am unable to sympathize with them. The least I could do is to be in their condition." The Sufis plead for the same attitude in prescribed fasting as do the religious scholars.

A traditional book of advice says, "Do not eat excessively at the pre-dawn meal as this is a way to lose the object of pre-scribed fasting." A religious scholar writes, "When hunger is ready felt, the reward for prescribed fasting becomes definitely more. Similarly, a feeling is developed for the poor and hungry ones." Muhammad (ص) himself said, "God does not dislike the filling of anything to the brim more than He dislikes the filling of the stomach." On another occasion, he said, "A few morsels should suffice which can keep the back straight." The best way for a person is that one-third should be filled with food, one-third with drink, while the other third remains empty."

The sixth point is that, after prescribed fasting, one should always have some anxiety as to whether one's fast had been accepted by God or not. This should be the case with all forms of worship. One never knows whether some important part may have been left out, of which no notice was taken.

These above mentioned six things are compulsory for all truly righteous persons. As for the exceptionally pious ones, a seventh point is added. That is, during prescribed fasting, the heart should not be turned towards anyone except God, so much so that during the course of the prescribed fast there should be no worry as to whether there shall be something to eat for the post-sunset ending of the fast. Some Shaykhs even consider it a fault to think about food for the post-sunset ending of the fast, or that one should endeavor to acquire something, because this shows lack of faith in God's promise of being responsible for the granting of provisions. In the commentary on *The Revival of the Religious Sciences, (Ihya Ulum al-Din),* al-Ghazzali goes so far as to relate that, should something for the post-sunset ending of the fast arrive from somewhere before the time to break the fast, the Shaykh would give it to somebody else, for fear that for the rest of that day, the heart may be distracted from God by keeping it. This can of course only be carried out by the exceptionally pious ones. We cannot even imagine having such strong faith. Should we try to follow without it, we may destroy ourselves.

The Quran commands, *"Prescribed fasting has been made obligatory for you."* The commentators of the Quran say that from this verse it is deduced that prescribed fasting is made compulsory for every part of the body. Thus, fasting of the tongue means to avoid falsehood, etc.; fasting of the ears means not listening to negative talk; fasting of the eyes means not to look at any form of wrongdoing. Similarly, fasting of the self means to be free from all carnal desires. Fasting of the heart means casting out from it the love of worldly things. Fasting of the mind means avoiding thoughts about anything other than God.

6

PRESCRIBED FASTING
AND THE MEDICINE OF THE PROPHET

Muhammad al-Akili

The medicine of the Messenger, also known as *al-Tibbu Nabawi*, is based upon the Quranic revelation and the guidance of God's Messenger (ص). Interpretation of the vast collection of prophetic sayings (Traditions) by canonical scholars have adopted a successful and distinct style. In fact, several Muslim canonists, philosophers, jurists, theologians and historians, among others, have unsheathed their pen and gone to great lengths to elucidate prophetic guidance. They were successful in integrating Islamic medicine with the *materia medica* found in earlier medical systems.

Among the renown scholars in this area is Ibn al-Qayyim al-Jawziyya (b. AH 691/AD 1292). He was born in Damascus, Syria and studied under his father who was the local attendant of al-Jawziyya school. Later on he pursued his quest for knowledge at the hands of renowned masters and scholars of his epoch. He also studied the works and teachings of Sufi masters known in his time. His schooling centered around Islamic jurisprudence, theology, and the science of prophetic Traditions. He finally joined the study circle of Imam ibn Taiymiyyah

(1262-1329 AD) who kept him in his company as his closest student and disciple and later on became his successor. Among the works of Imam Jawziyya are *Zad al-ma'ad* (Provisions for the Hereafter) from which the Medicine of the Prophet is extracted. Prescribed fasting is considered to be a preventive measure for avoiding illnesses whether they be of the soul, heart, mind or body. In regard to the medicine of the hearts, he says:

"Medicine of the hearts can only be acquired through God's Prophets, upon all of whom be peace and blessings. To correct one's heart and wash it from impurities, one must recognize his Creator and Cherisher, His Divine Names and Attributes, observe His Actions, contemplate His Wisdom and adopt the criteria He instituted for His creation. Such hearts also must beseech His blessings by consenting to what He commands and loves and by abstaining from what He forbids and abhors, and one's heart will know no trueness or experience true life otherwise. Such knowledge can only be learned from the teachings of His Messengers, upon all of whom be peace, and thinking otherwise will be completely wrong and unfruitful. Therefore, should one think that he can do the opposite, it means that he merely fosters the health and strength of his animal mind, desire, lust, carnality and wantonness. His life will be meaningless and similar to that of animals while a true heart of piety is free from such base associations. One who cannot discern the difference between these two types of hearts should cry for his losses, for a true heart is alive and a heart that is blinded with carnality is dead. A true heart is filled with light while a dead heart is submerged in the abyss of darkness.

In regard to fasting, he says:

Fasting, or imposition of complete abstinence from food, is the best safeguard for the illnesses of the soul, the heart, the mind, and the body, and its benefits cannot be enumerated. Dietary fasting produces wondrous results in preventive medicine, and in softening and dissolving humoral excesses *(plethora)* which become obstructions the intestines cannot absorb, or which the body does not expel easily. Dietary fasting also helps control excessive desire for food and harmful substances, and such control helps to balance excessive desire (Arb. *nafs)* for food.

Fasting is best when observed in moderation, and in interrupted sequences, and is best when religiously required—that is, during the prescribed fasting of the lunar month of Ramadan. The body's need for such periodic complete imposition of abstinence from food *(nestitherapy)* is most natural and innate. Moreover, fasting helps adjust, moderate, and preserve humoral balance and muscular strength. Among its ancillary assets, fasting promotes the joy of the heart, both in this world and in the hereafter.

Fasting causes diseases to stand still, helps people of cold and moist temperaments, and produces extremely impressive results in health preservation. Fasting comes in the categories of spiritual medicine *(psychotherapy* < Gr. *psychichos,* of the soul, breath, spirit; Arb. *adwiya ruhaniyya),* and natural medicine *(naturopathy;* Arb. *adwiya tabi'iyya).*

Complete fasting *(limotherapy), is* one of the best treatments for most illnesses relating to excess food consumption, acute gastrointestinal obstructions, or severe constipation *(obstipation),* and it is better than immediate treatment with purgatives.

When a person who is fasting adheres correctly to the natural and spiritual requirements of abstinence, his heart rejoices and benefits greatly, and his abstinence will prevent access to adulterated, unnatural, easily corruptive foods, and indigestible foods. Hence, such temporary abstinence from food can eliminate gastrointestinal obstructions, and adjust humoral imbalance, among other benefits, all depending on the quality and correctness of one's fast.

As for the spiritual benefits, fasting also protects the believers from wrongdoing, guides their hearts to avoid possible trespassing, balances their minds, and helps them better perform other religious obligations including observing supererogatory prayers (Arb. *nafl),* reading the Quran and having a better understanding of it, among other benefits of nocturnal worship.

God Almighty says, *"Oh believers, fasting is ordained for you as it was ordained for people before you as your expression of piety"* (2:183). He also says, *"It is better for you (to fast)"* (2:184). God's Messenger said, "Fasting is a shield of protection," i.e., fasting is an act of piety, and piety is a most beautiful devotion that brings the servant to the nearness of his Lord and envelopes him in divine protection.

Hence, fasting is a diet of great benefits, and is intended to bring one's heart and total dependence before God Almighty, which act appeases the heart, the soul, the body, and the mind, and it educates them in love and obedience to their Lord and Creator.

The Messenger ended his daily fast with dates and water followed by *talbina* which is a soup made from bran flour, sweetened with honey. Ayisha, the wife of the Messenger, recorded that she heard him say, *"Talbina* enlivens the innermost heart of the sick and lessens sorrow."

Imam Bukhari explained that *talbina* is a light broth that resembles milk. Such basic, easily digestible, nutritional and sometimes meatless soup is filling and gives relief from stress and sorrow. The benefits of *talbina* come from the broth of barley flour which is cooked with its bran. The basic difference between this soup and that of the common barley broth is that in the latter, the barley is cooked whole and in *talbina* the barley is made farinaceous and this brings out is rich nutrients. In essence, when barley is cooked whole, its nutrients pass by the system and confer little of its benefits.

As for God's Messenger saying, "It enlivens the innermost heart," it denotes here the cardia of the stomach and it means that it comforts the body and softens the stomach. As for lessening the patient's sorrow, God knows best—for sorrow and grief cool the humors and weaken body defenses because one's spirit is leaning then towards the heart which is its natural abode. Drinking such broth warms up one's stomach, reanimates the body's defenses, and hence lessens the trauma brought about by one's sufferings. Others may say that the broth will lessen one's sufferings because it lifts the patient's spirits and because of refreshing substances some foods contain. It is also said that sorrow dries up one's body and particularly his stomach. Of course, lack of food has much to contribute to that. However, such hot broth will moisten the stomach, strengthen and nourish it and subsequently, the effects reach the heart. On the other hand, often, when under stress, the patient's stomach produces a higher level of gastric juices and accumulates phlegm and purulence; hence, taking the barley broth helps flush away such unnecessary accumulations as well as soothe the body, come to its defense, break the tension, balance the humors, raise the spirit, and help one to regain his poise.

It is also narrated that one should brush one's teeth when fasting. The Messenger said, "If I did not think that it would be burdensome to my followers, I would have ordered them to brush their teeth with a *miswak* before each prayer." Brushing with a *miswak* is good whether one is fasting or not, although it is more needed when fasting because it maintains oral hygiene and purifies the mouth. One of the Companions said, "I saw God's Messenger brushing his teeth with a *miswak* while performing the prescribed fast." Also, it is beneficial to properly rinse one's mouth during fasting and upon taking ablution. In this sense, when God Almighty spoke of appreciating the breath of a fasting person and treating it as if it were musk, He encouraged people to fast as a healthy expression of their devotion and in no way was He encouraging neglect of oral hygiene, for a fasting person to smell like musk.

Prescribed fasting only works as a preventive measure to keep away illnesses of the heart when accompanied by prayer. As to the benefits of prayer, Imam Jawziyya writes:

> As for the role of regular prescribed prayers in relieving the burdens of worries, depressions, anxiety,

stress from one's heart and in healing its ills, one must realize that there is nothing higher, more exalted, more redeeming, more rejuvenating, more satisfying, more gratifying, more comforting, more intelligent, and more beautiful than standing before one's Creator, bowing to Him, and connecting one's heart and soul with God's presence and nearness, rejoicing in the resonance of invoking His praises, immersing one's entire existence, consciousness, body, mind, soul, and functions in the most exhilarating spiritual and physical experiences of the prescribed prayers.

In prescribed prayers, one engages one's entire being, limbs, veins, arteries, bones, pores, and every cell of one's body in communion with the Creator, and one separates self, one's thoughts, attention, focus, gaze and regards towards everything but one's Lord. In prescribed prayers, one also turns off one's motor function of attachment to the world, its creation, business, concerns, infatuations, mundane conversations, and confusions, and one radiates with the effulgent light of one's Creator, turns on the inerrant magnet of devotion and worship, and stands before Him with one's entire being, one's heart, soul, and body, and gives each limb its rightful chance to worship its Lord, and to wash itself with the tears of love and yearning to meet Him, the tears of expiating one's sins, and the tears that draw God's love and compassion to forgive His servant his/her sins, and to raise him /her in station. Each limb will function according to its primordial attributes. The heart will become drawn to its Creator and Originator, and it will rest in the most momentous and magnificent peace of His presence. Such are the healing powers of prescribed prayer. It is food for the body and soul.

The peace, joy, happiness, comfort, satisfaction, and spiritual ecstasy are only some of the benefits a healthy heart is accustomed to partaking of. Sometimes, such noble and delicate nutrients may not even be suitable for a sick heart which acts just like a sick body. In its case, prescribed prayers are its best recourse to receive the needed help and to serve its interests in this world and in the hereafter. Prescribed prayer also helps the heart to repel the adversities in this world and those in the hereafter, and it acts as a shield against falling into wrongdoing. God willing, an unadulterated prayer can prevent physical illnesses, or even cure a physical illness. A true prayer sheds light on one's heart, lights one's face, refreshes one's body, awakens one's soul, blesses one's earnings, repels inequities, frustrates illicit thoughts, and neutralizes unlawful desires, and a true prayer also cools God's wrath, delivers His mercy, compassion, and forgiveness for His servant.

PART THREE: STRATEGISTS

7

STRATEGIES
FOR THE PRESCRIBED FAST

Pervez Hanif

The major goal of the believer is to learn to guard against wrongdoing (*taqwa*) or to attain piety. This is the only sign of superiority for those who submit to the Will of the One God. Attaining this goal requires the implementation of a certain set of strategies in one's daily life. The prescribed month of fasting allows the believer a time frame in which to practice the strategies with the hope that the strategies learned during this month long process will carry over into the other eleven months of the year.

The strategies to attaining the goal of being able to continuously and constantly sense the Presence of God in all that one does and thereby gain the state of piety (*taqwa*) are moral and spiritual ones and, therefore, to the modern world may appear strange. In the traditional perspective, however, it is these very basic traits which ensure happiness in both this world and the next.

According to this view, the human being is created with a nature originated by God. This nature is the innate disposition to the worship of the One God and it is the nurturing process which leads a person astray from this natural disposition.

Therefore, learned behaviors account for forgetfulness of God, not that God was not there to begin with. Changing these learned behaviors requires self-discipline in this view and through self-discipline and self-control, the servants of God are then able to better guard against wrongdoing by recalling and remembering God's Presence in all that they do.

These behaviors are only subsequently physical like the branches of a tree. The source is in the roots of the tree. Without contact with the roots, the branches soon whither and die. The roots are seen as moral and spiritual values or traits which allow the human form to grow towards perfection and completion much as a healthy tree grows from good roots.

Among the moral and spiritual values reinforced during the prescribed month of fasting are, at the social level, the spirit of brotherhood or sisterhood, being a fair and just person towards others. This spirit comes from being able to control one's passions through self-discipline. Self-discipline becomes easier when one strengthens one's will power and regulates the self to moderation or temperance. Will power is strengthened by eating less, having a light stomach which allows energies to flow to the spirit and soul rather than to the stomach. Moderation teaches one to be economical and not to overspend on food or attraction to pleasures. This, then, enhances a person's ability to be flexible and adapting to new situations. The ability to be more flexible arises from significantly changing one's behavior patterns at least one month out of twelve.

Flexibility and the ability to adapt to new situations arises for the believers from learned behaviors like patience and unselfishness, strengthening of one's conscience as to what best serves others versus what best serves self; devotion to God; the eternal absolute beyond the relative; hope in the expected response from the Absolute; and, finally, a sincere love which is able to say, "I do this for Your sake but even if You were to forsake me, I would love you no less. Even if You were to send me to the depths of hellfire, I would love You no less for it is Your will which is All-powerful and not mine." These traits or qualities are all aspects of wisdom in the traditional sense.

Outwardly the strategies of prescribed fasting are to refrain from eating, drinking, smoking and sexual intercourse from before dawn to just after sunset for one month, the blessed month of Ramadan. These outer strategies reinforce the inner ones fostering a sense of the real spirit of social belonging, of unity and brotherhood/sisterhood. This value arises from the feeling that one is joining with one's fellow worshippers throughout the world who are observing the same religious duty at the same time in the same manner for the same goal. While this is also true of the five daily prescribed prayers, with the prescribed prayers, worshippers are all performing the prescribed prayers together whereas with the prescribed fasting, worshippers are all abstaining form the same things together. That is, they are all learning self-control and control over their passions by strengthening their reasoning powers.

The natural function of reason is to preserve the eternal possibility of self. Guidelines for the development of reason have been sent through the prophets and takes the form of the Word as either a person—Jesus—or a Book—the Quran. The strategy of prescribed fasting is used by believers to strengthen reason. As reason grows stronger, it becomes better able to attract the spiritual heart, the center of Divine Light within towards itself and away from the passions. Reason is strengthened through will power to consciously deny the self its source of energy (food and sex). The parts of self which is being denied energy are the passions—lust and anger. As the power to reason grows stronger, the self learns self-control and self-mastery. It strengthens its ability to self stocktaking.

From self-control develops human dignity and freedom because when the devotee performs the prescribed fast, he or she learns to control the passions and discipline desires to resist wrongdoing. He or she is then freed from the control of negative behaviors and replaces them with inner peace.

When observing the prescribed fast, the believer grounds self in discipline which leads to a strengthening of will power and determination. This will power, guided by reason which rules over the passions, allows the devotee to further character and inner development. As Sayyid Qutb says, "Fasting is a field of activity whereby a definite and determined will is established and whereby the human being is attached to his/her Lord through complete obedience and willing submission. So, too, does it serve as an instrument for rising above all the needs of the body, bearing their pressure and weight—out of preference for God's pleasure and good rewards"[1]

The emphasis on the spiritual aspect of self calls for the lessening of emphasis on the stomach, allowing extra energies to flow towards the spiritual center of self, the "heart" and turn it away from natural desires. Sayyid Qutb continues, "All these factors are necessary for the training and preparing of souls to bear the hardships of a road covered with obstacles and thorns, at the sides of which desires and inclinations are strewn about, and along which are thousands of temptations beckoning its travelers.

Prescribed fasting proves to be a lesson in economics, as well, because one sees that one can survive with less food, thereby fostering the desire to give whatever extra one may have to those who are less fortunate.

Changing one's daily routine in such a drastic way through one's conscious decision helps the self develop courage to be able to be more flexible in new and unexpected circumstances. It is the reverse of instant gratification, teaching patience and understanding to the devotee. These values extend beyond self to understanding the predicament of others in the world who are daily confronted with less and responding to their needs more often. It creates a genuine empathy for others.

Prescribed fasting fosters the strategy of developing a sound and vigilant conscience because it is a vow between the person and God alone. No one else need know whether one is adhering to the prescribed fast or not. It is a conscious choice of conscience and free will enhancing devotion and nearness to God. It is done for God's sake alone. This, then, gives the devotee a sense of hope and a positive view of life in this world and the next. It is to prepare the mold of the body to receive Divine Grace if God so chooses to give. Finally, the prescribed fast reinforces the strategy of sincere love which, in turn, reinforces the ability to guard against wrongdoing, to develop piety and Godfearingness which, in turn, reinforces the remembrance of the real Beloved.

The believer also knows that God does not ask something of them that is too difficult. If a believer is unable to perform the prescribed fast for one reason or another, he or she must, in place of it, feed a needy person. As Sayyid Qutb explains, "At the beginning, fasting was very difficult for the Muslims. It was made obligatory in the second year after the migration to Madinah, s short while before defense through struggle (*jihad*) was ordained. Hence, relief was granted to those who could only fast with great difficulty. This is the significance of putting up with which connotes the exertion of maximum efforts. God grants this relief from fasting in return for feeding a needy person. God urges the idea of feeding needy people either voluntarily nor in atonement or in the form of exceeding the prescribed limit of atonement. As a Tradition states, 'He who does good of his own free will, goodness will accrue to him.'"2

Such a believer learns the same strategies by sensing the spirit of those around him or her. There is a hallowed respect in those who are not able to perform the prescribed fast. This respect for what believers see to be the right and best thing to do also strengthens their ability to guard against wrongdoing and to pray for a speedy recovery so that next year they might join in with their fellow believers in actually performing the prescribed fast.

8

PRESCRIBED FASTING ACCORDING TO THE FIVE SCHOOLS OF ISLAMIC LAW

Muhammad Mughaniyyah

Islam consists of both a Law and a Way. The Way, *Tariqah*, is that of mysticism or Sufism. The Law, *Shari'ah*, is the Divine Law which a person accepts by becoming a Muslim. It is the pattern upon which an individual bases his/her life and it binds the Muslim community (*ummah*) into a single community. It is the manifestation of the Divine Will which is manifested in different ways in different religions. In Islam, the Divine Will is manifested not only through general teachings but through concrete ones, as well. Not only is charity and humility or having a sense of justice emphasized, but how to be so in various life situations.

It is the concrete and all-encompassing nature of the Divine Law which has contributed to the lack of understanding of the significance for a Muslim. A Jew who believes in Talmudic Law can clearly understand what it means but it is difficult for most Christians to understand because in Christianity there is no clear division between the Law and the Way. Emphasis is more on universal teachings and principles rather than concrete laws. This difference is clearly explained by Seyyed Hossein Nasr in the following way:

The Christian view concerning law which governs man socially and politically is indicated in the well-known saying of Christ, 'Render therefore unto Caesar the things which are Caesar's'. This phrase has actually two meanings of which only one is usually considered. It is commonly interpreted as leaving all things that are worldly and have to do with political and social regulations to secular authorities of whom Caesar is the outstanding example. But more than that it also means that because Christianity, being a spiritual way, had no Divine legislation of its own, it had to absorb Roman Law in order to become the religion of a civilization. The law of Caesar, or the Roman Law, became providentially absorbed into the Christian perspective once this religion became dominant in the West, and it is to this fact that the saying of Christ alludes. The dichotomy, however, always remained. In Christian civilization law governing human society did not enjoy the same Divine sanction as the teachings of Christ. In fact this lack of a Divine Law in Christianity had no small role to play in the secularization that took place in the West during the Renaissance. It is also the most important cause for the lack of understanding of the meaning and role of the Shari'ah on the part of Westerners as well as so many modernized Muslims....Islam, on the other hand, never gave unto Caesar what was Caesar's. Rather, it tried to integrate the domain of Caesar itself, namely, political, social and economic life, into an encompassing religious world view. Law is therefore in Islam an integrated aspect of the revelation and not an alien element.[1]

The Islamic Divine Law is much closer to Judaism.

The Semitic notion of law which is universalized in both Judaism and Islam is the opposite of the prevalent Western conception of law. It is a religious notion of law where law is an integral aspect of religion. In fact, religion to a Muslim *is* essentially the Divine Law which includes not only universal moral principles but details of how the human beings should conduct his/her life and deal with his/her neighbor and with God; how he/she should eat, procreate and sleep; how he/she should buy and sell at the market place; how he/she should pray and perform other acts of worship. It includes all aspects of human life. It contains in its tenets the guide for a Muslim to conduct his/her life in harmony with the Divine Will. It guides the human being towards an understanding of the Divine Will by indicating which acts and objects are from the religious point of view prescribed or obligatory or lawful (*wajib*), which are meritorious or recommended (*mandub*), which are forbidden or prohibited or unlawful (haram), which are disapproved or reprehensible (*makruh*) and which indifferent (*mubah*). Through this balance the value of human acts in the sight of the Divine are made known to human beings so that they can distinguish between the Straight Path and that which will lead them astray. The Shari'ah provides for them the knowledge of right and wrong. It is by their free will that human beings must choose which path to follow.[3]

The following essay describes the Divine Law on the prescribed fast as it is followed by the five recognized schools of Islamic law: the Hanafi, Hanbali, Shafi'i, Maliki and Ja'fari, each being named after the person who compiled it. Each one is referred to as Imam. The first teacher was Imam Ja'far al-Sadiq, a descendant of the Messenger Muhammad (ﷺ), who was the teacher of Imam Abu Hanifah, the founder of the Hanafi school. Imam Malik is the founder of the Maliki school, Imam Hanbal, the founder of the Hanbali school and Imam Shafi'i, the founder of the Shafi'i school. In the Islamic world today, the Malikis are most extensive in North and West Africa. The majority of Muslims in Syria and Saudi Arabia follow the Hanbali school. The Shafi'is are most prevalent in Egypt while the Hanafis are in Malaysia, Indonesia, Turkey, Pakistan and India. The Ja'fari are in Iran, Iraq and Lebanon.

The Editor

Fasting in the month of Ramadan is one of the 'pillars' of the Islamic faith. No proof is required to establish its being prescribed and one denying it goes out of the fold of Islam, because it is obvious like the prescribed prayer, and in respect of anything so evidently established by both the learned and the unlettered, the elderly and the young, all stand on an equal footing. It was declared an obligatory duty in the second year of the migration upon each and every one capable of carrying out religious duties, i.e. a sane adult and breaking it is not permissible except for any of the following reasons:

1. *Hayd* and *nifas*: The schools concur that fasting is not valid for women during menstruation (*hayd*) and bleeding following childbirth (*nifas*).

2. Illness: The schools differ here. The Ja'faris observe that prescribed fasting is not valid if it would cause illness or aggravate it, or intensify the pain, or delay recovery, because illness entails harm and causing harm is prohibited (*haram*) More-. over, a prohibition concerning a rite of worship invalidates it. Hence if a person fasts in such a condition, his/her prescribed fast is not valid. A predominant likelihood of its resulting in illness or its aggravation is sufficient for refraining from prescribed fasting. As to excessive weakness, it is not a justification for not undertaking the prescribed fast as long as it is generally bearable. Hence the extenuating cause is illness, not weakness, emaciation or strain, because every duty involves hardship and discomfort.

The Hanafi, Hanbali, Shafi'i and Maliki schools state that if one who is fasting falls ill, or fears the aggravation of his illness, or delay in recovery, he/she has the option to fast or refrain. Fasting is not incumbent upon him/her. It is a relaxation and not an obligation in this situation. But where there is likelihood of death or loss of any of the senses, it is obligatory for the person not to perform the prescribed fast and doing so is not valid.

3. A woman in the final stage of pregnancy and nursing mothers: The Hanafi, Hanbali, Shafi'i, and Maliki schools say that if a pregnant or nursing woman fears harm for her own health or that of her child, her prescribed fasting is valid though it is permissible for her to refrain from fasting. If she opts for not fasting, the schools concur that she is bound to perform the missed prescribed fasts later. They differ regarding its substitute and atonement. In this regard the Hanafis observe that it is not at all obligatory. The Malikis are of the opinion that it is obligatory for a nursing woman, but not for a woman who is pregnant.

The Hanbalis and the Shafi'is say that giving the substitute is obligatory upon a pregnant and a nursing woman only if they fear danger for the child but if they fear harm for their own health as well as that of the child, they are bound to perform the prescribed fasts missed only without being required to give a substitute. The substitute for each day is one *mudd*, which amounts to feeding one needy person.

The Ja'faris state that if a pregnant woman nearing childbirth or the child of a nursing mother may suffer harm, both of them ought to break their prescribed fast and it is not valid for them to continue performing the prescribed fasting due to the impermissibility of harm. They concur that both are to perform the missed prescribed fasts as well as give the substitute, equaling the feeding of one needy person (one *mudd*), if the harm is feared for the child. But if the harm is feared only for her own person, some among them observe that she is bound to perform the missed prescribed fasts but not to give the substitute. Others say that she is bound to perform the missed prescribed fasts and give the substitute as well.

4. Travel, provided the conditions necessary for the overdue prescribed prayer of the traveler, as mentioned earlier, are fulfilled as per the opinion of each school. The Hanafi, Hanbali, Shafi'i and Maliki schools add a further condition to these, which is that the journey should commence before dawn and the traveler should have reached the point from where the prescribed prayer becomes overdue before dawn. Hence if a traveler commences the journey after the setting in of dawn, it is unlawful for him/her to break the prescribed fast, and if the

traveler does so, its making up for will be obligatory upon that person without an atonement.

The Shafi'is add another condition, which is that the traveler should not be one who generally travels continuously, such as a driver. Thus if a person travels habitually, he/she is not entitled to not perform the prescribed fast. In the opinion of the Hanafi, Hanbali, Shafi'i and Maliki schools, breaking the prescribed fast is optional and not compulsory. Therefore, a traveler who fulfills all the conditions has the option of performing the prescribed fasting or not. This is despite the observation of the Hanafis that performing the prescribed prayer as the shortened form during journey is compulsory and not optional.

The Ja'faris say that if the conditions required for praying the shortened form of the traveler are fulfilled for a traveler, his/her prescribed fast is not acceptable. Therefore, if he/she performs the prescribed fast, he/she will have to perform the missed prescribed fasts without being liable to atonement . This is if he/she starts the journey before midday, but if the journey begins at midday or later, the person will keep the prescribed fast and in the event of his/her breaking it , will be liable for the atonement of one who deliberately breaks the prescribed fast. And if a traveler reaches his/her hometown, or a place where he/she intends to stay for at least ten days, before midday without performing any act that breaks the prescribed fast, it is obligatory upon him/her to continue the prescribed fasting, and in the event of his/her breaking it, he/she will be like one who deliberately breaks the fast.

5. There is consensus among all the schools that one suffering from a malady of acute thirst can break the prescribed fast, and if the person can carry out its missed fasts later, it will be obligatory upon him/her without any atonement, in the opinion of the Hanafi, Hanbali, Shafi'i and Maliki schools. In the opinion of the Ja'faris, the person should feed a needy person by way of atonement. The schools differ in regard to acute hunger, as to whether it is one of the causes permitting breaking the prescribed fast, like thirst. The Hanafi, Hanbali, Shafi'i and Maliki schools say that hunger and thirst are similar and both make breaking the prescribed fast permissible. The Ja'faris state that hunger is not a cause permitting breaking the prescribed fast

except where it is expected to cause illness.

6. Old people, men and women, in late years of life for whom prescribed fasting is harmful and difficult, can break their fast, but are required to give a substitute by feeding a needy person for each fast day omitted. Similarly, the same is true for a sick person who does not hope to recover during the whole year. The schools concur upon this rule excepting the Hanbalis who say that giving a substitute is recommended and not obligatory.

7. The Ja'faris state that prescribed fasting is not obligatory upon one has fainted, even if it occurs only for a part of the day, unless where he/she has formed the intention of performing the prescribed fasting before it and recovers subsequently, whereat he/she will continue the prescribed fast.

EXCUSE NO LONGER NECESSARY
If the excuse permitting not performing the prescribed fasting ceases such as on recovery of a sick person, maturing of a child, homecoming of a traveler, or termination of the menses, it is recommended in the view of the Ja'faris and the Shafi'is to refrain from things that break the prescribed fast as a token of respect. The Hanbalis and the Hanafis consider refraining as obligatory, but Malikis consider it neither obligatory nor recommended.

CONDITIONS OF PRESCRIBED FASTING
As mentioned earlier, performing the prescribed fast in the month of Ramadan is obligatory for each and every sane adult. Hence the prescribed fast is neither obligatory upon an insane person in the state of insanity nor is it valid if he/she observes it. As to a child, it is not obligatory upon him/her, although valid if observed. Also essential for the validity of the fast are Islam and intention. Therefore, as per consensus, neither the prescribed fast of a non-Muslim nor the faith of one who has not formed the intention is acceptable. This is apart from the aforementioned conditions of freedom from menses, bleeding following childbirth, illness and travel.

As to a person in an intoxicated or unconscious state, the Shafi'is observe that the prescribed fast of such a person is not valid if the person is not in his/her senses for the whole period of the prescribed fast. But if he/she is in his/her senses for a part of this period, his/her prescribed fast is valid, although the unconscious person is liable for the missed prescribed fasts, whatever the circumstances, irrespective of whether his/her unconsciousness is self-induced or forced upon him/her. But the missed prescribed fasts is not obligatory upon an intoxicated person unless he/she is personally responsible for his/her state.

The Malikis state that the prescribed fast is not valid if the state of unconsciousness or intoxication persists for the whole or most of the day from dawn to sunset. But if it covers a half of the day or less and he/she was in possession of his/her senses at the time of making the intention and did make it, becoming unconscious or intoxicated later, making up for the prescribed fasts is not obligatory upon that person. The time of making the intention known for the prescribed fast in their opinion extends from sunset to dawn.

According to the Hanafis, an unconscious person is exactly like an insane one in this respect, and their opinion regarding the latter is that if the insanity lasts through the whole month of Ramadan, it is not obligatory to make up for the missed prescribed fasts and if it covers half of the month, he/she will perform the prescribed fast for the remaining half and make up for the prescribed fasts missed due to insanity.

The Hanbalis observe that it is obligatory for a person in a state of intoxication, irrespective of whether these states are self-induced or forced upon him/her, to make up for missed prescribed fasts. In the opinion of the Ja'faris, making up for missed prescribed fasts is only obligatory upon a person in an intoxicated state, irrespective of its being self-induced or otherwise; it is not obligatory upon an unconscious person even if the loss of consciousness is brief.

THINGS OBLIGATORY TO REFRAIN FROM DURING THE PRESCRIBED FAST

Those things from which it is obligatory to refrain during the prescribed fast, from dawn to sunset are:

1. Eating and drinking deliberately. Both invalidate the prescribed fast and necessitate making up for the prescribed fasts missed in the opinion of all the schools, although they differ as to whether atonement is also obligatory. The Hanafis and the Ja'faris require it, but not the Shafi'is and the Hanbalis.

A person who eats and drinks by an oversight is neither liable to making up for missed prescribed fasts nor atonement except in the opinion of the Malikis who only require its being made up for. Included in drinking is inhaling tobacco smoke.

2. Sexual intercourse, when deliberate, invalidates the prescribed fast and makes one liable to make up for missed prescribed fasts and atonement, in the opinion of all the schools.

The atonement is the freeing of a slave, and if that is not possible, prescribed fasting for two consecutive months; if even that is not possible, feeding sixty poor persons. The Ja'faris and the Malikis allow an option between any one of these; i.e. a sane adult may choose between freeing a slave, performing the prescribed fasting or feeding the poor. The Shafi'is, Hanbalis and Hanafis impose atonement in the above-mentioned order; i.e. releasing a slave is specifically obligatory, and in the event of incapacity prescribed fasting becomes obligatory. If that too is not possible, giving food to the poor becomes obligatory. The Ja'fari state that all the three atonements become obligatory together if the act breaking the prescribed fast is itself unlawful, such as eating anything usurped, drinking wine, or fornicating. As to sexual intercourse by oversight, it does not invalidate the prescribed fast in the opinion of the Hanafis, Shafi'is and Ja'faris, but does according to the Hanbalis and Malikis.

3. Seminal emission: There is consensus that it invalidates the prescribed fast if caused deliberately. The Hanbalis say that if seminal emission is discharged due to repeated sensual glances and the like, the prescribed fast will become invalid. The Hanafi, Hanbali, Shafi'i and Maliki say that seminal emission will necessitate making up for the prescribed fast without atonement. The Ja'faris observe that it requires both making up for it and atonement.

4. Vomiting: It invalidates the prescribed fast if deliberate, and in the opinion of the Ja'faris, Shafi'is and Malikis, also

necessitates making up for the fast. The Hanafis state that deliberate vomiting does not break the prescribed fast unless the quantity vomited fills the mouth. Two views have been narrated from Imam Hanbal. The schools concur that involuntary vomiting does not invalidate the prescribed fast.

5. Cupping: It invalidates the prescribed fast only in the opinion of the Hanbalis, who observe that both the cupper and his/her patient break the prescribed fast.

6. Injection invalidates the prescribed fast and requires the prescribed fast to be made up in the opinion of all the schools. A group of Ja'fari jurisprudents observe that it also requires atonement if taken without an emergency.

7. Inhaling a dense cloud of suspended dust invalidates the prescribed fast only in the opinion of the Ja'faris. They say that if a dense suspended dust, such as flour or something of the kind, enters the body, the prescribed fast is rendered invalid because it is something more substantial than an injection or tobacco smoke.

8. Application of collyrium invalidates the prescribed fast only in the opinion of the Malikis, provided it is applied during the day and its taste is felt in the throat.

9. The intention to discontinue the prescribed fast: If a person intends to discontinue his/her prescribed fast and then refrains from doing so, his/her prescribed fast is considered invalid in the opinion of the Ja'fari and Hanbalis; not so in the opinion of the other schools.

10. Most Ja'faris state that fully submerging the head, alone or together with other parts of the body, under water invalidates the prescribed fast and necessitates both making up for the fast and atonement. The other schools consider it inconsequential.

11. The Ja'fari observe that a person who deliberately remains in the state of prescribed impurity following sexual intercourse after the dawn during the month of Ramadan, his/her prescribed fast will be invalid and it is obligatory that the prescribed fast be made up as well as atoned for. The remaining schools state that his/her prescribed fast remains valid and he/she is not liable to anything.

12. The Ja'faris observe that a person who deliberately ascribes something falsely to God or the Messenger (i.e. if he/she speaks or writes that God or the Messenger said so and so or ordered such and such a thing while he/she is aware that it is not true), his/her prescribed fast will be invalid and he/she will be liable for making it up as well as for an atonement. A group of Ja'fari jurisprudents go further by requiring of such a fabricator the atonement of freeing a slave, prescribed fasting for two months, and feeding sixty poor persons.

THE PRESCRIBED FAST

All the schools concur that the prescribed fasts are those of the month of Ramadan, their being made up, the expiatory prescribed fasts performed as atonement, and those performed for fulfilling a vow. The Ja'faris add further two, related to the pilgrimage to Makkah and retreat to a mosque. We have already dealt in some detail with the prescribed fast of Ramadan, its conditions and the things that invalidate it. Here we intend to discuss its making up for and the atonement to which one who breaks it becomes liable.

MAKING UP FOR THE RAMADAN PRESCRIBED FAST

1. The schools concur that a person liable for the missed prescribed fasts of Ramadan is bound to perform it during the same year in which the prescribed fasts were missed, i.e. the period between the past and the forthcoming Ramadan. The person is free to choose the days intended to perform the prescribed fast, excepting those days on which prescribed fasting is prohibited. However it is obligatory upon the person to immediately begin making up for them if the days remaining for the next Ramadan are equal to the number of prescribed fasts missed in the earlier Ramadan.

2. If one capable of performing the prescribed fasts missed during the year neglects it until the next Ramadan, that person should perform the prescribed fast during the current Ramadan

and then perform the missed prescribed fasts of the past year and also give an atonement of feeding a needy person for each day in the opinion of all the schools except the Hanafi which requires the person to perform only the missed prescribed fasts without any atonement. And if the person is unable to perform the missed prescribed fasts such as when an illness continues throughout the period between the first and the second Ramadan, that person is neither required to make up for them nor required to give atonement in the opinion of the Hanafi, Hanbali, Shafi'i and Maliki schools, while the Ja'faris say that the person will not be liable to make up for the prescribed fasts missed but is bound to give food to a needy person as atonement for each prescribed fast day missed.

3. If one is capable of performing the missed prescribed fasts during the year but delays it with the intention of performing it just before the second Ramadan, so that the missed prescribed fasts are immediately followed by the next Ramadan, and then a legitimate excuse prevents that person from performing the missed prescribed fasts before the arrival of Ramadan, in such a situation the person will be liable only to make up for the missed prescribed fasts and not for atonement .

4. One who breaks a Ramadan fast due to an excuse, and is capable of later for making it up but fails to do so during his/her lifetime, the Ja'faris observe that it is obligatory upon his/her eldest child to perform the prescribed fasts missed on his/her behalf. The Hanafis, Shafi'is and Hanbalis state that charity of feeding one need person for each prescribed fast missed will be given on his/her behalf. According to the Malikis, his/her legal guardian will give to charity on his/her behalf if he/she has so provided in the will; in the absence of a will it is not obligatory.

5. In the opinion of the Hanafi, Hanbali, Shafi'i and Maliki schools, a person performing the prescribed fasts of Ramadan that were missed can change his/her intention and break the prescribed fast both before and after midday without being liable to any atonement provided there is time for him/her to perform the missed prescribed fasts later. The Ja'faris observe that it is permissible for him/her to break this prescribed fast before midday and not later because continuation of the pre-

scribed fast becomes compulsory after the passing of the major part of its duration and the time of altering the intention also expires. Hence if he or she acts contrarily and breaks the prescribed fast after midday, he or she is liable to atonement by giving food to ten poor persons; if he/she is incapable of doing that, he/she will perform the prescribed fast for three days.

PRESCRIBED FASTS OF ATONEMENT

The fasts of atonement are of various kinds. Here we shall discuss the rules applicable to a person fasting by way of atonement for not having observed the prescribed fast of Ramadan.

The Shafi'is, Malikis and Hanafis say that it is not permissible for a person upon whom fasting for two consecutive months has become obligatory consequent to deliberately breaking a Ramadan fast to miss even a single fast during these two months, because that would break their continuity. Hence, on his missing a fast, with or without an excuse, he should fast anew for two months. The Hanbalis observe: If he misses a fast due to a legitimate excuse, the continuity is not broken.

The Ja'faris state that it is sufficient for the materialization of continuity that he/she perform the prescribed fast for a full month and then a day of the next month. After that he/she can skip days and then continue from where he/she had left off. But if he/she misses a fast during the first month without any excuse, he/she is bound to start anew; but if it is due to a lawful excuse, such as illness or menstruation, the continuity is not broken and he/she will wait till the excuse is removed and then resume the fasts.

The Ja'faris further observe that one who is unable to perform the prescribed fast for two months, or release a slave or feed sixty poor persons, has the option either to perform the prescribed fast for eighteen days or give whatever he/she can as charity. If even this is not possible, he/she may give alms or perform the prescribed fast to any extent possible. If none of these are possible, he/she should seek forgiveness from God Almighty.

The Shafi'is, Malikis and Hanafis state that if a person is unable to offer any form of atonement, he/she will remain liable for it until he/she comes to possess the capacity to offer it, and this is what the rules of the Divine Law require .

The Hanbalis are of the opinion that if he/she is unable to give atonement, his/her liability for the same disappears, and even in the event of his becoming capable of it later, he/she will not be liable for anything.

The schools concur that the number of atonements will be equal to the number of causes entailing it. Hence a person who breaks two prescribed fasts will have to give two atonements. But if he/she eats, drinks or has sexual intercourse several times in a single day, the Hanafis, Malikis and Shafi'is observe that the number of atonements will not increase if the prescribed fast has been broken several times, irrespective of its manner.

The Hanbalis state that if in a single day there occur several violations entailing atonement, if the person gives atonement for the first violation of the prescribed fast before the perpetration of the second, he/she should offer an atonement for the latter violation as well, but if he/she has not given atonement for the first violation before committing the second, a single atonement suffices.

According to the Ja'faris, if sexual intercourse is repeated a number of times in a single day, the number of atonements will also increase proportionately, but if a person eats or drinks a number of times, a single atonement suffices.

THE DOUBTFUL DAYS

There is consensus among the schools that *imsak* is obligatory upon one who does not perform the prescribed fast on a doubtful day that later turns out to be a day of Ramadan, and he/she is liable to make up for it later. Where one performs the prescribed fast on a doubtful day that is later known to have been a day of Ramadan, they differ as to whether it suffices without requiring that it be made up. The Shafi'i, Maliki and Hanbali schools observe that this prescribed fast will not suffice and it is not obligatory to be made up. In the opinion of the

Hanafis, it suffices and does not require to be made up. Most Ja'faris state that its being made up is not obligatory upon him/her, except when he/she had performed the prescribed fast with the intention of Ramadan.

EVIDENCE OF THE NEW MOON

There is a general consensus among Muslims that a person who has seen the new moon is bound to act in accordance with this knowledge, whether it is the new moon of Ramadan or Shawwal. Hence it is obligatory upon one who has seen the former to perform the prescribed fast even if all other people do not and to refrain from performing the prescribed fast on seeing the latter even if everyone else on the earth is performing the prescribed fast, irrespective of whether the observer is trustworthy or not, man or woman. The schools differ regarding the following issues:

1. The Hanbalis, Malikis and Hanafis state that if the sighting of the new moon has been confirmed in a particular region, the people of all other regions are bound by it regardless of the distance between them; the difference of the horizon of the new moon is of no consequence. The Ja'faris and the Shafi'is observe that if the people of a particular place see the new moon while those at another place do not, in the event of these two places being closeby with respect to the horizon, the latter's duty will be the same; but not if their horizons differ.

2. If the new moon is seen during day, either before or after midday, on the 30th of Shaban, will it be reckoned the last day of Shaban (in which case, fasting on it will not be obligatory) or the first of Ramadan (in which case fasting is obligatory)? Similarly, if the new moon is seen during the day on the 30th of Ramadan, will it be reckoned a day of Ramadan or that of Shawwal? In other words, will the day on which the new moon is observed be reckoned as belonging to the past or to the forthcoming month?

The Ja'faris, Shafi'is, Malikis and Hanafis observe that it belongs to the past month and not to the forthcoming one.

Accordingly, it is obligatory to fast on the next day if the new moon is seen at the end of Shaban, and to refrain from fasting the next day if it is seen at the end of Ramadan.

3. The schools concur that the new moon is confirmed if sighted, as observed in this tradition of the Prophet, "Fast on seeing the new moon and stop fasting on seeing it." They differ regarding the other methods of confirming it.

The Ja'faris observe that it is confirmed for both Ramadan and Shawwal by the testimony of a sufficiently large number of people whose conspiring over a false claim is impossible, and by the testimony of two trustworthy people, irrespective of whether the sky is clear or cloudy and regardless of whether they belong to the same or two different nearby towns, provided their descriptions of the new moon are not contradictory.

The Hanafis differentiate between the new moons of Ramadan and Shawwal. They state that the new moon of Ramadan is confirmed by the testimony of a single man and a single woman, provided they are Muslim, sane and just. The Shawwal new moon is not confirmed except by the testimony of two men or a man and two women. This is when the sky is not clear. But if the sky is clear—and there is no difference in this respect between the new moon of Ramadan and Shawwal—it is not confirmed except by the testimony of a considerable number of persons whose reports result in certainty.

In the opinion of the Shafi'is, the new moon of Ramadan and Shawwal is confirmed by the testimony of a single witness provided he is Muslim, sane, and just. The sky's being clear or cloudy makes no difference in this regard. According to the Malikis, the new moon of Ramadan and Shawwal is not confirmed except by the testimony of two just men, irrespective of the sky's being cloudy or cloudless. The Hanbalis say that the new moon of Ramadan is confirmed by the testimony of a just man or woman, while that of Shawwal is only confirmed by the testimony of two just men.

4. There is consensus among the schools, excepting the Hanafi, that if no one claims to have seen the new moon of Ramadan, performing the prescribed fasting will be obligatory after the 30th day allowing 30 days for Shaban. According to the

Hanafis, fasting becomes obligatory after the 29th day of Shaban.

This was with respect to the new moon of Ramadan. As to the new moon of Shawwal, the Hanafis and the Malikis observe that if the sky is cloudy, 30 days of Ramadan will be completed and breaking the prescribed fast will be obligatory on the following day. But if the sky is clear, it is obligatory to perform the prescribed fast on the day following the 30th day by rejecting the earlier testimony of witnesses confirming the first of Ramadan regardless of their number. The Shafi'is consider ending the prescribed fast obligatory after 30 days even if the setting in of Ramadan was confirmed by the evidence of a single witness, irrespective of the sky's having been cloudy or clear. According to the Hanbalis, if the setting in of Ramadan was confirmed by the testimony of two just men, ending the prescribed fast following the 30 day is obligatory, and if it was confirmed by the evidence of a single just witness, it is obligatory to fast on the 31st day as well. In the opinion of the Ja'faris, both Ramadan and Shawwal are confirmed after the completion of 30 days regardless of the sky's being cloudy or clear, provided their beginning was confirmed in a manner approved by the Divine Law.

9

QURANIC COMMENTARY ON
"I ANSWER THE PRAYER..." (2:186)

Muhammad Husayn Tabataba'i

T he verse under discussion here falls between two verses relating to the prescribed fast in the month of Ramadan while it itself refers to supplication. As the commentator points out, this verse is unique in a second way, as well. It is the only verse in the Quran where God refers to Self in the first person singular seven times. Traditional commentators whether contemporary or not follow the Science of Commentary (*ilm al-tafsir*) which includes comparing the verse in question to other verses and then stating the relevant Traditions (*ahadith*, sing. *hadith*) or sayings and deeds of the Messenger (ص).

Supplication is a major strategy of a believer and the continuous practice of it is reinforced during the month of Ramadan. It is a major strategy to supplicate God during this blessed month but as the following detailed account of supplication shows, the response is only forthcoming if the seeker, the devotee, the believer believes the requested response will be given at some time, not necessarily when requested. The words in italics refer to the Quranic verses. The chapter and verse numbers precede or follow the quote verse.

The Editor

*A*nd when My servants ask you concerning Me, then verily I am near, I answer the prayer of the supplicant when
he calls on Me, so they should answer My call and
believe in Me, so that they may walk in the right way (2:186).

COMMENTARY

*And when My servants ask you concerning Me, then verily I
am near, I answer the prayer of the supplicant when he calls on
Me.* This is the best expression of the subject matter in a most
elegant and beautiful style. The whole verse is based on the
first person singular pronoun which shows the great importance which the speaker, i.e. God, attaches to this subject.
Then come the words *My servants* and not "people" or other
such words. This enhances its importance even more. The
reply (*then verily I am near*) starts dramatically just after the
question without any preamble like, "*then say that I am near.*"
The reply is emphasized with "*verily.*" The nearness of the
speaker is described with the adjective near and not with any
verb like "*I come near him.*" Thus it shows that He is already
near and will always remain near.... Then the answer (*I
answer the prayer of the supplicant*) is conditional upon *when
he calls on Me.* In reality it is not a condition separate from the
main cause. Both are one and the same thing. It serves to
emphasize that the prayer of the supplicant is answered without any condition or stipulation.

These points show how much importance has been
attached to the answering of prayers. In addition, this verse—
short as it is—repeats the first person singular pronoun seven
times; it is the only verse with this characteristic in the whole
of Quran.

Supplication (*du'a*) and calling (*da'wah*) refer to turning
the attention of the called one to the caller. Asking (*su'al*)
means to gain a benefit or advantage from the one whose
attention is drawn towards the seeker and before whom the

(seeker's) need is put. Therefore, asking is the final aim of calling. This meaning covers all types of asking like asking for the
removal of ignorance, asking with the meaning of reckoning,
asking in the sense of seeking beneficence, and so forth....

In short, God's ownership of His creatures .... gives Him
authority to answer any prayer which is put before Him by any
of His creatures, and to fulfill his or her need by accepting his
or her supplication..... It is not as though He has authority in
one eventuality and not in the other, as the Jewish scholars
say that when God created things and decreed their destinies,
His work was finished and now His hands are folded up, He
can not make any new decision. There is no abrogation (of previous laws), no change and no answering of prayer because
every affair is already finished....

The truth is that real ownership in its totality is by God
only and nobody owns any thing, unless and until He makes
him its owner and allows him to possess it. Therefore, whatever God wills and gives in possession and allows its coming into
being, comes into being. And whatever He does not will, and
does not give in possession and does not allow, does not come
into being, even if one strives his utmost to bring it into being.
God has said: *O people! You are they who are needy unto God,
and God is He who is the Self-sufficient, the Most Praised One*
(35:15). It is, thus, clear that this verse not only mentions a
fact, i.e., answering prayer, but gives its reasons also: Because
the supplicants are servants of God, He is near to them; and
because He is near to them, He answers their prayers without
any reservation. The unconditional answering of prayer means
that there is no condition imposed on prayer also. Whatever
prayer is addressed to Him, He shall answer it. Of course, it
seems that His promise, *"I answer the prayer of the supplicant,"* depends on the condition, *when he calls Me.* But this
condition is not something different from the main clause; and
such a mode of expression indicates that the main clause is
free from metaphor and analogy, that its meaning is what
appears from the words. For example, when we say, "Listen to
the sincere advisor when he sincerely advises you," or "Respect
the scholar if he be a scholar," it means that we want him to be

sure that the advisor is really sincere or the scholar is really a scholar so that listening to him or respecting him becomes necessary. In the same way, the condition when he calls on me shows that the promise of answering the prayer shall apply when the supplicant is a supplicant in reality; when he or she wants that thing according to his or her natural and deep-ingrained knowledge and when his or her heart is really in what his or her tongue is asking for.

The reality of prayer and supplication is what the heart desires and the tongue of nature asks for, not this tongue of flesh which moves as it is moved without caring whether the word spoken is a truth or a lie, a reality or a metaphor, a serious talk or a joke. It is because of this that God has even mentioned such prayer in which the tongue is not used at all. He said: *And He gave you of all that you asked Him; and if you count God's bounties, you will not be able to compute them; Verily, man is very unjust very ungrateful* (14:34). Humanity prays to Him and beseeches Him for bounties which they cannot count, but this asking is not done by the tongue of the mouth. It is done by the tongue of their neediness, the tongue of nature and existence. Also He said: *All those in the heavens and the earth do beseech Him; every day He is in a (new) splendor* (55:29). This verse more clearly proves what we have just said.

Therefore, the natural prayer addressed to God shall always be answered. If a prayer is not answered, then it lacks both or one of the two things mentioned in the verse: the prayer of the supplicant *when he calls on Me*. It may happen in the following ways:

First: There may be no prayer at all. It may only be a misunderstanding of the supplicant. For example, a person prays for an impossible thing (but he or she does not know that it is impossible), or for a thing which, if he or she knew the fact, would not have wanted at all. Let us say that someone was sick and died, but his friend is unaware of his death and prays for his recovery, while now the prayer should be for bringing him back to life. If he had been really sure that a dead body could be resurrected and had asked for its resurrection (as the prophets did), his life would have been returned to him; but he does not have such firm conviction and therefore the prayer is not answered. Or, let us say, he asks for a thing which, had he known it really, he would not have wanted. Therefore, it is not granted.

Second: There is indeed a prayer, but is it not addressed exclusively to God. For example, a person beseeches God for his or her needs, but his or her heart is looking towards its apparent causes or to some imaginary beings whom he or she thinks have the power to fulfill his or her needs. In this case, his or her prayer is not addressed exclusively to God. In other words, he or she did not beseech God at all because God, Who answers the prayers, is the One who has no partner in His affairs. He is not the one who works in partnership with apparent causes and imaginary beings. So these are the two groups of supplicants whose hearts were not sincere in their prayers even if their tongues were.

This is the gist of the subject of prayer according to the verse of the Quran. The meaning of all verses on this subject may be understood from this explanation. See, for example, the following verses: *Say: My Lord would not care for you were it not for your prayer; but you have indeed rejected (the truth), so soon you shall be in the grip* (25:77). *Say,: Think you that if the chastisement of God comes to you or the Hour comes to you, will you call upon other than God, if you are truthful .' Nay! Him you will call upon, so He clears away that for which you pray, if He pleases, and you will forget what you set up (with Him)'* (6:40-41). *Say: 'Who is it that delivers you from the (dread of the)darkness of the land and the sea (when) you pray to him (openly) humiliating yourselves and secretly:.' If He delivers us from this, certainly we shall be of the grateful ones. Say: 'God delivers you from them and from every distress, yet again you associate (others) with Him '* (6:63-64).

These verses prove that the human being has been created with a natural propensity to prayer and inner beseechment which is silently addressed to his or her Lord. But when he or she spends his or her life in ease and prosperity, his or her soul becomes blinded by apparent causes and he or she treats them as partners to his or her Lord. Thus he or she becomes confused and thinks that he or she does not ask his or her Lord for anything and does not beseech Him, while the fact is that he or she does not beseech anyone other than God, because this prayer (to God) is ingrained into his or her nature, and there is no change in the creation of God.

Later comes the hardship and the apparent causes become divorced from the expected effects. Those whom he or she treated as partners of God, or intercessors before Him, disappear completely. Then he or she realizes that there is no one to fulfill his or her needs and to answer his or her prayers except God. Thus, he or she returns to his or her natural monotheism and forgets every other cause and turns his or her face towards the Beneficent Lord. The Lord clears away his or her hardship and fulfills his or her wants and places him or her under the shade of opulence. But as soon as he or she regains his or her prosperity and happiness, he or she goes back to the previous polytheism and forgetfulness....

There are other relevant verses, and all of these contain the pillars of prayer and explain the manner of the supplication. The most important of all is to keep the prayer exclusively for God. It will come true when the feeling of the heart conforms with the words spoken by the tongue, when one abandons reliance on all apparent reasons other than God and depends exclusively upon God. Also among them are: fear of God; hope in His answering; His love and reverence; humility and humbleness; as well as perseverance in prayer; remembrance of God; good deeds; true faith; presence of heart at that time; and similar things.

So they should answer My call and believe in Me. This sentence branches out from the previous one. God is near to His servants. Nothing comes between Him and their prayer. He cares for them and for the things they ask for. That is why He invites them to call upon Him and He is of such high attributes. Therefore, they should accept this invitation of their Lord and should advance towards Him, and have faith in Him about this attribute, having firm belief that He is near and He answers their call; so that they may be guided rightly in praying unto Him.

TRADITIONS

Followers of all five schools of Law have narrated from the Prophet that "Prayer is the armament of the believer." It is narrated in a Sacred Tradition (*hadith al-qudsi*): "Oh Moses! Ask from Me all that you need, even fodder for your goat and salt for your dough." The Prophet said, "Calling (upon God) is better than reciting the Quran, because God (Powerful and Great is He!) said, 'Say, My Lord would not care for you were it not for your prayer'."....

The Prophet said, "God said, 'No creature seeks refuge in another creature, leaving Me, but that I cut off all the means in the heavens and the earth for him (or her). Then if he (or she) asks from Me, I do not give him (or her) and if he (or she) calls on Me, I do not answer him (or her). And no creature seeks refuge in Me, leaving My creatures, but that I make the heaven and the earth responsible for his (or her) sustenance; then if he (or she) calls on Me, I answer him (or her) and, if he (or she) seeks pardon from Me, I forgive!"

The aim of the above two traditions is to emphasize that the supplication must be purely for God. It was not meant to negate the positive causes which God has created as instrumental links between the things and their needs. But these instruments are not independent causes. The Independent Cause is only God. The human being has an inner feeling of this fact. He or she feels by his or her nature that there is a Perfect Cause who fulfills his or her needs and who can never fail in bringing about the desired effect. On the other hand, he or she knows that all the apparent causes which are expected to produce an effect, sometimes fail to do so. Thus he or she knows that the First Cause, Who is the Source and Origin of everything and upon whom every need relies and depends for its fulfillment, is other than these apparent causes. Once he or she realizes it, he or she will never entirely rely on these causes, forgetting the Real Cause. The human being may appreciate this fact after just a little thinking....

The Prophet said, "Call upon God and you can be confident that it will be answered." In a Sacred Tradition, God said, "I am near the expectation of My servant about Me so he (or she) should not expect from Me except good."

It is because if one prays and at the same time is pessimistic or doubtful about its outcome, then it shows that the prayer is just a formality, the supplicant has no real intention of asking for it. And the traditions forbid asking for a thing which one is sure will not come about.

The Prophet said, "Resort to God in your needs; and seek refuge in Him in your misfortunes. Humiliate yourselves before Him and beseech Him, because, verily, supplication is the essence of worship. And no believer calls upon God but He answers him (or her). It is either speeded up to him in this world or is kept in reserve for him (or her) for the next one, or his (or her) sins are forgiven in proportion to his (or her) supplication, provided he or she does not pray for a sinful thing." Ali ibn Abi Talib (the fourth rightly guided caliph) wrote in his will to his son, Husayn ibn Ali, "Then He placed the keys of His treasures in your hands in the sense that He allowed you to ask Him. Therefore, whenever you wish, you may open the doors of His bounties with prayer and receive the heavy rains of His Mercy upon you. Delay in acceptance of the prayer should not disappoint you, because the granting of prayer is according to the measure of your intention. Sometimes the answering of your prayer is delayed so that it brings a greater reward to the seeker and a better granting to the expectant. Sometimes you ask for a thing and it is not given to you, but a better thing is given to you, immediately or later or a thing is diverted from you for some greater good for you, because often you ask for a thing which would have destroyed your religion had it been given to you. Therefore, your prayer should be for things whose beauty should last for you and whose evil should remain away from you. As for wealth, it will not last for you, nor will you last for it." [Nahj al-balaghah].

The answer, then, is given according to the call. The supplicant is granted whatever he or she asks for from God with the firm conviction of his or her conscience and with his or her heart, and not what is asked for in words.

There are eight similar traditions narrated by a number of the companions, like Salman, Jabir, 'Abdullah ibn 'Umar, Anas ibn Malik and Ibn Abi Mughith from the Prophet; and all of them mention raising of the hands in the prayer. Therefore, it is meaningless to reject raising of hands in the prayer as someone has done saying that "it is suggestive of the belief that God has a body," because the raising of the hands towards the sky is an indication that He is there— Holy and Sanctified is He from it. But this statement is wrong. All acts of worship performed by the body are in reality the heartfelt sense of gratitude and inner attention which is reduced to the level of symbolic appearance. Spiritual realities are demonstrated in the molds of the body, as one may see in the prescribed prayers, the prescribed fast, the pilgrimage to Makkah, etc., and their parts and conditions. Had it not been so, there would not have been any justification for worship by the body.

And supplication is such a form of worship. It is the attention of the heart and the inner supplication demonstrated by the symbol of the begging of a wretched pauper coming near a powerful and wealthy person, raising and extending his hands towards him and asking his needs from him, humiliating himself before him and imploring him to grant him his requirements. It is narrated that the Prophet used to raise his hands when he prayed and beseeched God as a pauper begs for food. .... There are other traditions with this meaning and the reason is that there is in reality no prayer and supplication with forgetfulness and inattention.

The Torah says that God says to His servant, "Verily, when you pray against one of my servants because he was unjust to you, then at the same time there may be another of my servants praying against you to because you were unjust to him. Now, if you so wish, I shall grant your prayer and also his prayer against you; and if you so wish, I shall postpone the cases of both of you for the Day of Resurrection."

If someone prays for something then it means that he or she is pleased with it and this pleasure naturally extends to all those things which are similar to it in all respects. He or she prays for punishment of his or her oppressor. He or she prays against that person because of his or her oppression and injustice. It means that he or she is pleased with the punishment of the unjust. Now, if he or she oppresses another person, then the same prayer against his oppressor shall become a prayer against himself or herself. God said, *"And the human being prays for evil as he ought to pray for good, and the human being is ever hasty "* (17:11).

The Messenger of God said to Abu Dharr, "Abu Dharr! Should I not teach you some words by which God will benefit you?"

Abu Dharr)said, "Surely! O Messenger of God."

He said, "Guard the commands of God, and God will guard you. Keep the remembrance of God, and you will find Him before you. Make the acquaintance of God in opulence, He will know you in hardship. And when you ask, ask from God; and when you seek help, seek help from God, because whatever is to happen up to the Day of Resurrection has already been written, and if all the creatures together strived to benefit you with what God did not write for you, they would not be able to do so."

His words, "Make the acquaintance of God in opulence, He will know you in hardship," mean, "Call upon God in opulence and do not forget Him, so that He will answer your call in hardship and will not forget you." Anybody who forgets his Lord in opulence is as if he believes that the apparent causes are the total and real cause of his opulence. Then comes the hardship and he starts calling on his Lord. His action indicates that he believes in the Lordship of God only when he is afflicted with hardship. But God is not so. He is the Lord in every condition and every situation. Therefore, if he calls on a lord whose lordship is limited to the time of hardship only, he does not call on the True Lord....

Let us look at the example of the human being. Whatever one does, is done with one's limbs and organs: one gives with one's hands, sees with one's eyes and hears with one's ears. Now, if one asked one's Lord to fulfill one's needs neglecting its causes and means, it would be as if one asked someone to give one something without using one's hand, or to look at one without using one's eyes or to listen to one's pleas without using one's ears.

On the other hand, if one relies on the nominal causes without remembering God, it would be as though one thinks that it is the human being's hand which gives, one's eyes which see and one's ears which hear, and forgets that the real doer of these actions is the human being. Such a person is stupid and a simpleton.

The above explanation does not mean that the Power of God is limited, or that His Authority is conditional. No, His Power and Authority are All-encompassing and without limit. In the same way the limitations are meant to apply to the deeds not to doers. Obviously, it is the human being who has the power to give, see and hear, though one gives with one's hand, sees with one's eyes and hears with one's ears. Likewise, God is All-powerful, but the specification depends on intermediate causes. So and so is a creation of God, and he was born through the union of his parents in a certain place on a certain day when certain conditions were fulfilled and certain obstacles removed. Now, if even one of these causes be missing and one of these conditions be not fulfilled, there would be no so and so. Thus the existence of so and so depends on the fulfillment of all these causes and means; but what depends is the creature, i.e., so and so, not the Creator....

Also, Ibn 'Umar narrates from the Prophet, "Whenever the door of prayer is opened for anyone among you, the doors of Mercy are opened for him." Another Tradition says, "When the door of prayer is opened for anyone among you, the doors of the Garden Paradise are opened for him." Also there is a tradition from Ma'adh ibn Jabal from the Messenger of God, "Had you known God, as He should be known, verily the mountains would have been moved by your prayer."

If a person does not know the dignity of the Creator and the power of His Lordship, and if one relies upon the causes, then one believes that these causes have real influence upon the result and that events cannot happen without their normal and apparent causes. Sometimes one does not believe that these causes have any real effect upon the outcome, still one thinks that they are essential in order to bring a thing into existence. For example, we see that movement and walking brings one nearer to one's destination. And even when we do not believe that movement has any real effect on the nearness, we go on believing that movement is a means, though it is God who is the Real Cause, of that nearness, and in this way we go on believing that the middle causes are essential, at least as a means, if not as the Real Cause. Thus, we think that if there is no movement, we cannot come near our destination. In short, we believe that the effect cannot be separate from its causes, even if these causes are just apparent means and not the Real Cause.

But such a belief is below the dignity of God; it does not conform with divine authority which is total and perfect. It is this belief which creates the idea that effects cannot come into being without their normal causes, e.g. a body cannot be without a weight and gravity; movement is necessary for bringing two things nearer; eating and drinking is essential for satisfying the hunger and thirst, etc. etc. We have already mentioned in the discussion of miracles that the system of cause and effect is an inescapable fact; but it does not mean that the 'cause' is confined to the normal causes only. Reason as well as the Quran and the Traditions prove that while everything depends upon a cause, that cause is not confined within the limits of normal ones. The Creator may create causes for it, quite different from the normal ones. So, while it is true that the effect depends upon a cause, it is not true that it depends upon a particular cause.

In short, when you properly know God, you will believe that the prayer for what is not impossible by reason, even if normally it does not happen, will be answered. A major portion of the miracles of the prophets was basically the answer to their calls.

10

THE QURAN AND ITS RECITATION DURING RAMADAN

Muhammad Husayn Tabataba'i

It was during the month of prescribed fast that the Quran was revealed all at once according to 2:18 (?) as a guide to humanity and then individually, verse by verse, over a period of twenty-three years as a guide to humanity. This Book of Guidance is the eternal Book of the community (*ummah*) of believers. It is the guidance which takes the believer from darkness to light. It is in gratitude for this revelation that the believer may perform the prescribed fast. The following essay describes the Quranic revelation and its major concepts.

The Editor

GENERAL BELIEFS OF MUSLIMS CONCERNING THE REVELATION OF THE QURAN

More than any other revealed book, especially the Torah and the New Testament, the Quran describes the details of the revelation, the transmission and even accounts of the experience of the revelation. The general belief of Muslims concerning the revelation, based on the Quran, is that the text of the Quran is the actual speech of God transmitted to the Prophet by one of His chosen angels.

The name of this angel, or heavenly being, is Gabriel or the Faithful Spirit. He transmitted the word of God over a period of twenty-three years to the Prophet. He would bring the divine instructions to the Prophet, who would relate them faithfully to the people using the same words in the form of a verse.

The Prophet thus used the meaning of the verses to call the people to an understanding of faith, of belief, of social laws and of individual duties. These instructions from God to His messenger are known as the prophecy, or the message; the Prophet transmitted this message without making any addition to or detraction from it in any way.

THE VIEW OF CONTEMPORARY NON-MUSLIM WRITERS CONCERNING THE REVELATION AND PROPHECY

Most contemporary writers who take an interest in different religions and ideologies adopt the following view of the Quran: they say the Prophet was a social genius who appeared to save society from the throes of decline into savagery and to raise it up in the cradle of civilization and freedom. They claim also that he called people to his own ideas of pure and sincere behavior by giving them a comprehensive religious form and order. They affirm that he had a pure soul and tremendous ambition; that he lived in a particularly dark and ignorant age, where only the law of force and foolish singing of verse, social chaos and selfishness, stealing, marauding and savagery were to be seen.

They describe how he was troubled by witnessing such things and, sometimes when overcome by the pain of such sights, he would withdraw from people and pass days alone in the cave in the Tihamah mountains; he would marvel at the sky and its shining stars, the earth, the mountains, the sea, the desert and all the precious means placed at the disposal of the human being by the Creator; he would be grieved at the bad behavior and ignorance of those around him, who had thrown away a life of well-being and happiness for a tormented succession of bestial habits.

This feeling was always present with the Prophet; he bore this pain and vexation up to his fortieth year when, according to these contemporary non-Muslim writers, he formed a plan to save his fellow-men from their miserable state of nomadic wandering, rebellious independence, selfishness and lawlessness.

This plan, called the religion of Islam, was the most suitable one for the times. The Prophet being of pure and sincere character, realized that his chaste thoughts were the Word of God and Divine Revelation which were infused in him through his virtuous nature. His good will and benevolent spirit, from which his thoughts exuded and established peace in his heart, was called the Spirit of Trustworthiness and Gabriel, the angel of revelation.

Furthermore, according to this contemporary view of Muhammad, he perceived the forces of good and happiness in nature as Angels and all the forces of bad as Satan and the *jinn* (invisible entities). He called his own task, which he had undertaken according to his own conscience, prophethood and himself, the deliverer of the divine message.

This explanation, however, comes from those writers who affirm the existence of God or at least some kind of nature-force, and attach a certain importance to the religion of Islam, albeit in the name of just and unbiased assessment. Those, however, who deny outright the existence of a Creator see Prophecy, revelation, divine duties, reward and punishment, the fire and the garden as mere religious politics, a lie in the name of religion to further one's own ends.

They say that the prophets were reformers who brought about social change in the name of religion. They argued that since people of past ages were drowned in ignorance and superstitious worship, the prophets contained the religious order within a framework of superstitious beliefs about the origin of Creation and the day of reckoning in order to further their prospects of reform.

WHAT THE QURAN ITSELF SAYS CONCERNING THIS MATTER

Scholars who explain the power of revelation and prophecy using the above explanation, attach great importance to the Science of nature and the visible world, and claim that everything in the world works according to the laws of nature. They view historical events, right up to the present-day, as the developing and constantly changing face of nature.

Likewise, they view all revealed religions as social manifestations. Thus they would agree that if one of the geniuses of history, like Cyrus, Darius or Alexander, had announced himself as having been chosen by God as an executor of divine commands, their explanation would have been no different than that given above.

We do not intend here to establish the existence of the unseen, of the world beyond the visible world of nature; we are not saying to other scholars or scientists that any one science may only be discussed by remaining within the strict limits of that particular science. We are not suggesting that the modern sciences which investigate the properties and effects of the material world, (whether or not they be positively or negatively disposed to the creation), do not have the right to enter into an investigation of the metaphysical.

What we are saying is that any explanation they propose must be in accordance with the explanation of society, existence, nature and the cosmos given by the Quran. The Quran is an authentic document of prophecy and is the basis of all social, metaphysical and scientific discussion; the explanation of the Quran contain proofs against their arguments which we can enumerate and reflect upon. These proofs are connected to different Quranic verses discussed below.

DIVINE REVELATION

According to the explanation of modern non-Muslims and atheists, the Prophet's nature was pure through which came to him the word of God, meaning that the divine system of thought was alive in his own thoughts; the idea of divinity manifested itself in his thoughts because he was pure and holy; it was natural (in the minds of these scholars) for prophets to attribute these thoughts to God for, in this way, they ennobled and exalted their own task.

The Quran, however, strongly and convincingly denies that it is the speech or the ideas of the prophet or, indeed, of any other man. In chapters 10:38 and 11:13 the Quran declares that if it is the word of the human being then detractors of Islam should produce similar words about every subject treated in the Quran, namely, belief in the after-life, morals, laws, stories of past generations and other prophets, wisdom and advice. The Quran urges them to seek help anywhere if they do not realize that it is the word of God and not of the human being, but adds that even if *jinn* and the human being joined forces together they would not be able to produce a Quran like it.

In chapter 2:23 the Quran challenges those who consider it merely the speech of Muhammad to produce a book similar to it or even just one chapter like it. The force of this challenge becomes clear when we realize that it is issued for someone whose life should resemble that of Muhammad, namely, the life of an orphan, uneducated in any formal sense, not being able to read or write, who grew up in the unenlightened age of the the age of ignorance before Islam.

In 4:82 the Quran asks why no inconsistencies or changes appeared in the verses considering that neither the wording nor the meaning of the verses has altered despite being revealed over a period of twenty-three years. If it was the word of the human being and not the word of God, then it would have certainly been affected by change like all other things in the temporal world of nature and matter.

It is clear that this challenge and these explanations are not mere empty words of exultation; rather they present the Quran for what it is, namely the Word of God. The Quran establishes its own miraculous nature in hundreds of verses. This miracle is still unexplained by normal literacy standards used to "grasp" a text. Indeed, previous prophets established their prophethood through similar verses revealed by God. If prophecy was merely the call of an individual conscience or the inspiration of a pure and sincere soul, then there would be no sense in claiming it as divine proof or seeking help in its miraculous nature as the Prophet, in fact, did.

Some writers interpret the many miracles of the Quran in terms of undisguised mockery. When we investigate the subject of their mockery we inevitably discover that the Quran means something other than that which they have understood.

It is not our intention to try and prove the miraculous nature of the Quran nor to demonstrate the soundness and authenticity of its narration; rather, we would point out that the Quran clearly describes the miracles of the past prophets, like Salih, Abraham, Moses and Jesus. The stories related in the Quran can only be understood and interpreted in the light of miraculous guidance.

Why, we may ask, if the prophets were mere men, inspired by the purity of their character, was it necessary to establish the existence of this miraculous guidance?

THE ANGEL GABRIEL

According to the explanation of the above-mentioned writers, the prophet referred to his own pure soul as the "Faithful Spirit" or the giver of revelation. The Quran, however, does not support this view and names Gabriel as the deliverer of the verses.

God says in chapter 2:97, *"Say: (0 Muhammad), to humanity): Who is an enemy to Gabriel for it is he who has revealed (this book) to your heart by God's permission."* This verse refers to the Jews who wanted to know who had revealed the Quran to the Prophet. He replied that it was Gabriel. They said, *"We are enemies of Gabriel as he it was who gave us (the tribe of Israel) the laws and legal punishments and as we are enemies to him, we do not believe in the book which he has brought."* Thus God replies to them in the verse that Gabriel revealed the Quran to the Prophet by God's permission. God further says that the Quran is to be believed in, and that it is not the speech of Gabriel. It is important to note that the Quran, in the words of the above verse, was revealed "to the heart" of the Prophet Muhammad by Gabriel.

In another verse [26:193-4] we read that it was transmitted by the Faithful Spirit, *"which the Faithful Spirit has brought down upon your heart."'* By comparison of these two verses it becomes evident that it is the angel Gabriel who is meant here by the words, "Faithful Spirit."

In chapter 81:19-23 God describes the transmission of revelation: *"That this is in truth the word of an honored messenger (Gabriel), Mighty established in the presence of the Lord of the Throne, one to be obeyed and trustworthy and your comrade (the Prophet) is not mad. Surely he saw him on the clear horizon."*

These verses show that Gabriel was one of the intimates of God, possessing great power and trust. Again in chapter 60:7 we read, *"Those who bear the power, and all who are around Him, praise their Lord and believe in Him and ask forgiveness for those who believe."* Such characteristics as belief in God and seeking forgiveness from him are only to be expected from independent, sentient creatures.

In chapter 4:172-173 we read, *"The Messiah will never disdain to be a servant of God, nor will the favored angels. Whoever disdains His service and is proud, He will gather them all to Himself, then as for those who believe and do good, He will pay them fully their rewards and give them more out of His grace, and as for those who disdain and are proud, He will punish them with a painful doom. And they will not find for themselves besides Allah a guardian or a helper."*

It is clear that although the Messiah, Jesus, and the favored angels do not disobey the commands of God they are, nevertheless, warned of a painful punishment on the day of reckoning if they were to commit a wrong. The possibility of neglect of their duties or committing wrong action is necessarily dependent on their being sentient beings, possessed of free will and entrusted with the task of transmitting the revelation of God.

Thus we learn from the Quran that Gabriel is the Faithful Soul: he is trustworthy and to be obeyed because he is obeyed by angels in his task. An indication of these obedient angels comes in the verse, *But truly it is a warning—so let whoever will pay heed to it, on honored leaves exalted, purified (set down by scribes) noble and righteous* (80: 11-16).

THE ANGELS AND THE DEVILS

According to the explanation of contemporary non-Muslim writers, angel is the name given to forces in nature which represent goodness, and happiness and devils are forces in nature representing evil and unhappiness. What we understand from the Quran, however, is that they are beings existing beyond our sense-range, who possess feelings and an independent free-will. To the verses above, (indicating that angels possess independence and free will), may be added many other verses which confirm these same qualities.

The refusal of Satan to prostrate himself before Adam and the dialogue between Satan and God occurs several times in the Quran. Satan, after having been expelled from intimacy with God, says in chapter 38:82-83, *"I surely will lead every one of them astray except your sincere slaves among them. "*And God replies *"I shall fill hell with you and with those who follow you together"* [38:85].

It is clear that punishment can only take place if the punished understand the reason for the punishment. God in chapter 34:20, says in confirmation of Satan's warning to the human being, *"And Satan indeed found his calculation true concerning them, for they follow them, all except a group of true believers."* Likewise, we read in chapter 14:22, *"And Satan said when the matter had been decided: Indeed! God promised you a promise of truth; and I promised you and failed you. And I had no power over you except that I called to you and you obeyed me. So do not blame me but blame yourselves. "*

Blame is a matter which can only be associated with those who possess the power of reason and free-will. We quote these verses to show that Satan, like the rest of the angels, is a thinking independent being rather than a force in nature.

Just as verses occur in the Quran concerning the angels and the devils, there also are verses which clearly and vividly describe the *jinn* (elemental spirits or invisible beings, either harmful or helpful). In chapter 46:18 reference is made to those who, invited to believe in Islam, spurn it as just another ancient fable or superstition: *"Such are those in whom the word concerning nations of the jinn and humanity which have passed away before them has effect. Indeed they are the losers."*

We may understand from this verse that the *jinn,* the invisible entities, like humanity, live in different nations, pass a period of time in their different societies and finally die.

In the same chapter, verses 29-32 we read, *"And when we inclined toward you (Muhammad) certain of the jinn who wished to hear the Quran and when they were in its presence said, 'Listen! 'and, when it was finished turned back to their people warning. They said: 'O our people! Truly we have heard a book which has been revealed after Moses, confirming that which was before it, guiding to the truth and a right road. O my people! respond to God's Summoner and believe in Him. He will forgive you some of your wrong actions and guard you from a painful doom.' And whoever does not respond to God's Summoner, he can in no way escape in the earth, and you (can find) no protecting friends instead of Him. Such are in clear error."*

These verses clearly confirm that the *jinn,* like people, live in groups, are thinking individuals possessing free will and charged with duties, Moreover, there are other verses dealing with the day of rising which affirms these same qualities in the *jinn.*

THE CALL OF CONSCIENCE

According to the explanation of certain modern writers prophethood is the rising up of a person from amongst his people in order to undertake social reform in accordance with the call of his conscience. The Quran, however, gives a different meaning to the prophethood. In 91:7-8 we read, *"And a soul and Him who perfected it, and inspired it (with conscience of) what is wrong for it and (what is) right for it. "*

In this verse God demonstrates that each individual perceives from his own conscience and God-given nature the difference between good and bad action; and, that the potential for reform and the bettering of one's self is contained within each person; some listen to their conscience and act correctly while others pay no heed and so act wrongly.

Thus in the following verses of the same chapter God says: *"He is indeed successful who causes it to grow and he is indeed a failure who stunts it."* If prophethood manifests itself as a result of the conscience, which everyone possesses, then everyone in theory may become a prophet. God, however, has reserved this duty for certain men only.

Thus He says in chapter 6:124, *"And when a sign comes to them, they say: we do not believe until we are given that which God's messengers are given. God knows best with whom to place His message. "*

THE REALITY OF THE PROPHET'S MISSION

We should repeat at this point that we do not intend to prove or disprove here the truth of Islam or the validity of the Prophet's invitation of the people to Islam. Rather, we simply want to state that the second of the modern non-Islamic explanations is also not in accordance with the explanation given in the Quran.

According to it, the Prophet succeeded in convincing people to believe in a set of superstitions framed in a politico-religious framework; he was aided in this, so they say, by the fact that his own people were tribesmen having no advanced culture of their own. In the name of public good and the well-being of society harsh punishments were promised to those who did not obey the religious laws; the Prophet instilled a fear of the Day of Reckoning and promised rewards for those who obeyed.

Thus fervor for the promised paradise and fear of the Day of Reckoning created a society based on a religious foundation. The history of the lives of other prophets has, for the most part, been lost in time, but the life of the Prophet Muhammad (ص) is well documented. Anyone who researches into it will not be left in the least doubt that he had total faith and inner certainty in his mission. If religious beliefs were mere superstitions or a means to unify and subdue a society, then all the proofs expounded in the Quran concerning the Hereafter, the existence of a Creator of the World, Divine Unity, His attributes, belief in a prophecy and the reckoning of a human being's actions after death would have absolutely no meaning.

WHAT THE QURAN SAYS ABOUT
THE MEANING OF REVELATION AND PROPHECY

The Quran clearly states that it is a book revealed to the Prophet and that revelation is a kind of divine utterance beyond the understanding or communication of the material world; revelation is unperceived by sense or intellect but apprehended by other faculties which, by God's will, are present in certain individuals. Instructions from the unseen are received through revelation and their acceptance and implementation is called prophethood. To clarify this matter we may make the following points.

THE HUMAN BEING'S INNATE NATURE

In the beginning of this book we explained that each created entity, whether mineral, plant or animal, is endowed with an inherent force which enables it to develop in accordance with its own innate design and nature.

Thus we read in chapter 20:50, *"Our Lord is He who gave everything its nature, then guided it correctly, "* and again in chapter 87:2-3 *"Who creates, then disposes, who measures then guides."* We also know that the human being is not excluded from this general law, that is, he has a direction and an aim towards which he develops, having been endowed with faculties which allow him to fulfill this aim. All his happiness lies in achieving this aim; his sorrow, grief and misfortune are the result of his failure to achieve this aim. He is guided to this special purpose by his Creator.

As God says in chapter 76:3, *"Indeed, we have shown him the way whether he be grateful or disbelieving."* Likewise we read in chapter 80:1-2, *"From a drop of seed, He creates him and proportions him. Then makes the way easy for him. "*

THE HUMAN BEING'S PATH
IN TRAVERSING THE ROAD OF LIFE

The difference between the animal and plant kingdoms and the human being is that the former react according to their inherent knowledge or instinct, while the human being, also possessing an inherent knowledge, is equipped with an intellect and the capacity to use or recognize wisdom. Even if the human being is capable of undertaking a certain action, he/she weighs the good or the bad, the benefit or harm, contained in that action and implements it only if he/she estimates that the benefit outweighs the harm.

Thus he/she follows the instruction of his/her intellect in every action; the intellect dictates the necessity of an action. The intellect causes one to abandon an act if it is likely to bring with it an unacceptable degree of trouble and hardship; it not only instructs one on the feasibility of an action, but it also takes into account the dictates of sentiment and feeling.

Indeed the perception of sentiment with regard to the relative good or bad in matter is so closely connected with the decision of the intellect as to be considered one and the same thing.

THE HUMAN BEING AS A SOCIAL BEING

No one would deny that human beings are social beings who co-operate with each other to better meet their daily needs. We may wonder, however, whether human beings desire this co-operation from their natural feelings; are they naturally inclined to undertake an action with others and share an interest in something as a social project?

On one level, human beings' needs, feelings and desires cause them to act for their own benefit and without regard for the needs and wishes of others. Human beings use every means to fulfill their own needs: they use every kind of transport to reach their destination; they use the leaves, stems and fruit of plants and trees; they live upon the meat of animals and their products, and takes advantage of a multitude of other things to complement their own deficiencies in certain respects. Can the human being, whose state is such that they use everything they find to their own ends, be expected to respect another human being? Can they extend their hand to another in co-operation and turn a blind eye to their own desire for the sake of mutual benefit?

The answer in the first instance must be no. It is as a result the human being's countless needs, which can never be fulfilled by themselves alone, that they recognize the possibility of fulfilling them through the help and co-operation of others. Similarly, they understand that their own strengths, desires and wishes are also shared by others, and just as they defend their own interests so others defend theirs.

Thus, out of necessity, they co-operates with the social nexus and gives a certain measure of their own efforts to fulfill the needs of others; in return they benefit from the efforts of others in order to fulfill their own needs. In truth they have entered into a market-place of social wealth, always open to traders and offering all the benefits obtained by the collective work of the society. All these factors are placed together in this marketplace of pooled human resources and each person, according to the importance society attaches to their work, has a share in these benefits.

Thus human beings first nature incites them to pursue the fulfillment of their own needs using others in the process and taking advantage of their work for their own ends. It is only in cases of necessity and helplessness that they lend a hand to co-operate with society.

This matter is clear when we observe the nature of children: anything children want they demand in an extreme way; they emphasize their demand by crying. As they grow older, however, and become a part of the social fabric, they gradually put an end to their excessive demands. More evidence for the truth of this may be seen when a person accumulates power which exceeds that of others and they reject the spirit of cooperation and its restrictions of society; such individuals use people and the fruits of their labors for themselves without giving anything back in return.

God refers to the necessary spirit of natural cooperation in society in chapter 43:32, "*We have apportioned among them their livelihood in the life of the world, and raised some of them above others in rank that some of them take labor from others .*

This verse refers to the reality of the social situation in which each individual has a different capacity and different talent: those who are superior in one domain engage the cooperation or employ of others for their eventual mutual benefit.

Thus all members of society are linked together in the ways and wants of the fabric of one single social unit. Those who do not see the obvious necessity of mutual cooperation are condemned by God in chapter 14:34, *"Truly the human being is surely a wrong-doer, (a* tyrant)"*and, in chapter 33:72, "Indeed he has proved a tyrant and a fool."* These verses refer to the natural instinct of human beings which, unless checked, drives him to take advantage of their fellow beings and in doing so to overstep the rights of others.

THE MANIFESTATION OF SOCIAL DIFFERENCES AND THE NECESSITY OF LAW

Human being in their dealings with their fellow human beings are obliged to accept a social life based on cooperation; in doing so they effectively forgoes some of the freedom enjoyed within their own sphere of work. Merely taking part in a society based on injustice and gaining social differences is not enough to satisfy the basic needs of the average human being. In such a society, taking advantage of the efforts of others leads to corruption and a loss of the original purpose of removing glaring differences between people and bettering their lives.

It is clear that a framework of laws, understood and respected by all, must govern the different members of society. If there are no clear laws governing even the most basic of transactions (like buying and selling), transactions will cease to function correctly. Laws are necessary to preserve the rights of individuals. The power and wisdom of the Creator, who has guided the human being towards his/her well-being and happiness, has also guaranteed the success and happiness of society.

Guidance in the form of social law is mentioned by God in 80:19-20, *"From a drop of seed He creates him and proportions him. Then makes the way easy for him."* This making of life easy for the human being is an indication of the social guidance which God has given to the human being in the form of laws and instructions.

THE INTELLECT IS NOT SUFFICIENT IN GUIDING MAN TOWARDS RESPECT OF THE LAW

The guidance we are considering here is that which emanates from the wisdom of the Creator; this wisdom has created the human being and allotted him/her the goal of well-being just as it has assigned a path and goal to all creation. This goal of happiness and well-being is the path of self-fulfillment based on correct behavior in a social setting. It is clear that, of necessity, there can be no inconsistencies or shortcomings in the work of the Creator.

If, at times, one cannot discern His aim or it seems hidden from normal perception, it is not through lack of reason or cause on the part of God, but rather that the cause is linked to other causes which obscure the one in question. If there were no hindrances to a clear perception of the causal chain of events, two given actions would never appear inconsistent or contradictory to the harmony of creation. Nor would the work of the Creator appear (as it sometimes does to those whose perception is hindered by the intricacy of the causal chain of events), inconsistent and imperfect.

Guidance towards the law, whose function is to remove differences and conflict between individuals in society, is not a matter for the intellect since it is this very intellect which causes the human being to dispute with others. It is the same intellect which incites the human being to profit at the expense of others and to preserve, first and foremost, his/her own interest, accepting justice only when there is no alternative.

The two opposing forces, one causing difficulties and one doing away with them, are qualities of the human being's character; they do not obviously exist in the Creator: the countless daily transgressions and violations of the law, in effect, all result from those who use their intellect incorrectly; they themselves are the very source of their own difficulties.

If the intellect was truly a means of removing wrong action

from society and was itself a trustworthy guide to the human being's well-being, it would recognize the validity of the law and prevent human beings from violating it. The intellect's refusal to willingly accept what is obviously given for the well-being of the human being is confirmed when we realize that its acceptance of a society based on just laws is only out of necessity. Without this compulsion, it would never accept to know the law.

Those who transgress the law do so for many reasons: some oppose it without fear, because their power exceeds that of the law; others, because they live outside the reach of the law, through deceit or negligence on the part of the authorities; others are able to invent reasons which make their wrong actions appear lawful and acceptable; some make use of the helplessness of the person they have wronged. All, however, find no legal obstacle in their wrong aims; even if an obstacle appears, their intellect, rather than guiding them to an acceptance of the law, renders the obstacle right and ineffective.

From these examples we are left in no doubt that the intellect, far from controlling, restricting or guiding the human being, merely uses its influence to its own purpose. We must include, therefore, that it is incapable of guiding the human being towards a social law which guarantees the rights, freedom and well-being of all the members of society.

God says in chapter 96:6-7 *"Indeed the human being truly rebels when he thinks himself independent. "* The independence referred to here includes the independence of those who imagine that they can claim their rights through other than the path of legality.

THE ONLY WAY TO GUIDANCE
IS THAT OF REVELATION

Human beings, like the rest of creation, naturally seek their own well-being and happiness as they live out their life. Since, by their very make-up, they have a variety of natural needs, they have no alternative but to live in society in order to fulfill these needs; their own well-being and search for the fulfillment of their natural character takes place in the wider framework of society's well-being.

Thus, the only acceptable pattern of existence, regulated by a comprehensive law common to all people, is the one which guarantees both the well-being of society and of the individual in a balanced and just fashion. It is also clear that the human being, like the rest of creation, must endeavor to achieve his/her well-being and undertake whatever preparation is necessary for achieving this by allowing himself/herself to be guided by his/her Creator.

It is but a logical next step in our analysis to say that any guidance from the Creator must be towards this comprehensive law, common to all and, at the same time, in accord with the individual's well-being. Intellect is not enough to guide the human being to the law since it does not always decide in favor of cooperation with others nor in favor of the common good.

The path, the way, which fits perfectly the requirements of the human being is the way taught by the prophets and messengers of God. It is the way brought to them by God through revelation and established as undeniably true and valid, by the example of their own lives and their intimate knowledge and contact with God.

In chapter 2:213, God says, *"Humanity was one community and God sent (to them) prophets as bearers of good news and as warners and revealed to them the book with the truth that it may judge between humanity concerning that in which they differed."* Here we understand "one community" to mean a society at peace, its members living without dispute or difference. After a period of time, human beings differed with one another and as a result God sent the prophets.

Again He says in 4:163-165, *"Indeed we have inspired you as we have inspired Noah . . . Messengers of good news and a warning in order that humanity might have no argument against God after the Messenger."* Intellect alone does not make the human being accountable to God and this is why he/she must be awakened to the reality of his/her inner condition by other means.

The first of the above-mentioned verses recognizes the way of revelation and prophecy as the only way of removing differences between human beings. The second shows revelation and prophecy to be the complete and absolute proof to humanity of the truth of God's message.

THE PATH OF REVELATION IS PROTECTED AGAINST MISTAKES

The path of revelation is part of the Creator's program. He never makes mistakes, neither in His Creation nor in the system of belief and the laws of the *shariah,* which are delineated for the human being through revelation.

God says in 72:26-28, *"(He is) the Knower of the Unseen and He reveals His secret to no one except to every messenger He has chosen and He makes a guard go before him and a guard behind him, that He may know that they have indeed conveyed the message of their Lord. He surrounds all their doings and He keeps count of all things."*

From this we understand that the prophets and messengers of God must be infallible both in receiving the revelation and in preserving it against alteration and attack. They are as instruments at the disposal of the Creator's wisdom. Were they to make an error in receiving or teaching the message of the revelation or be led astray by the whispering of evil persons, were they themselves to commit wrong or deliberately change the message they had to deliver, then the wisdom of God would be unable to perfect its program of guidance. God confirms in chapter 16:9 that He is in total control of the human being's guidance by means of his messenger, *"And God's is the direction of the way, and some (words) do not go straight."*

THE HIDDEN REALITY OF REVELATION

The reality of revelation is hidden from us. What is clear is that the aim of the program of life, outlined for human beings by the Creator, cannot possibly have been put together by the intellect; there must be another way of understanding, of perceiving, (other than through reflection and thought), by which human beings learn of the duties incumbent on them and their fellow human beings. This understanding may only be encompassed by the path of revelation.

There are, however, only a limited number of human beings who possess this kind of understanding since receiving revelation requires an understanding based on purity, sincerity and freedom from all corruption and bad thoughts. It requires people whose spiritual qualities do not change; people who are psychologically balanced in their judgments and who possess real depth of understanding. It must be admitted that these qualities are rarely to be found amongst people.

The prophets and messengers mentioned in the Quran are people of precisely these qualities. The Quran does not mention their number; it only names a few (namely Adam, Noah, Hud, Methusaleh, Abraham, Lot, Ishmael, Elisha, Ezekiel, Elias, Jonah, Enoch, Isaac, Jacob, Joseph, Shu'ayb, Moses, Aaron, David, Solomon, Job, Zachariah, John, Jesus and Muhammad; others are indicated but not named).

We, as ordinary human beings, do not share at all their qualities and so we cannot taste the reality of their perception. Prophecy, as an experience, remains unknown to us. Moreover, few of the past revelations have reached us and we have only a limited view of the reality which is revelation and prophecy. It may be that what has reached us in the form of revealed books is exactly as the revelation we are familiar with, that is the Quran. Nevertheless, it is possible that other revelations (completely unknown to us) may have contained information and instructions of which we have no knowledge.

HOW THE QURAN WAS REVEALED

Quranic revelation, according to the Quran itself, is an utterance on behalf of God to His Prophet; the Prophet received the speech of God with all his being, not just by way of learning. In 42:51-52 God says, "*And it was not to be for any man that God should speak to him unless (it be) by revelation or from behind a veil or (that) we send a messenger to reveal what He will by His leave. Truly He is exalted, wise. And thus We have inspired in you (Muhammad) a spirit of Our Command. You did not know what the Book, nor what the Faith was. But We have made it a light whereby We guide whom We will of our slaves. And truly you surely guide to a right path."*

On comparison of these two verses we discover three different ways of divine utterance. Firstly, God speaks without there being any veil between Him and the human being. Secondly, God speaks from behind a veil: like the tree on the mountain from behind which Moses heard God speaking. Thirdly, God's speech is brought to the human being by an angel who had previously heard the revelation from Him.

The second of the two verses above show that the Quran has reached us by means of the third of three possible ways. Again God says in 26:192-5, *"(A revelation) which the Faithful Spirit (Gabriel) has brought down upon your heart, that you may be (one) of the warners, in plain Arabic Speech,"* and in chapter 2:97 *"Who is an enemy to Gabriel! For it is he who has revealed (this book) to your heart. "*

From these verses we understand that the Quran was transmitted by way of an angel named Gabriel, or the "Faithful Spirit," and that the Prophet received the revelation from him with all his being, all his perception and not merely by listening. The verse says *"on your heart,"* which in Quranic terms means perception or awareness. In 53:10-11 we read, *"And He revealed to His slave that which He revealed. The heart did not lie (in seeing) what it saw,"* and in 98:2 reception of the revelation is indicated as a reading of *"pure pages"* by God's Messenger.

11

REMEMBRANCE OF GOD

Munir Abu Salman

One of the most important strategies of Ramadan is supplication and prayer because prayer reinforces the remembrance of God for the believer. Many prayers have come through the Word of God (Quran) and the words and deeds of Muhammad (Traditions) which the believer may recite. Among the prayers of special interest for a harmonious interfaith dialog, are the prayers of Adam and Eve, Abraham, Bilqis, the Queen of Sheba, Moses, Asiyah, the wife of Pharaoh, Hannah, the mother of Mary, Jesus and Muhammad. The following is a brief compilation of such prayers, as revealed in the Quran.

ADAM AND EVE'S PRAYER

The Quran relates the story of Adam and Eve in the following way: *"And when your Lord said to the angels, 'I am setting in the earth a vicegerent,' they said, 'What, will You set therein one who will do corruption there and shed blood while we proclaim Your praise and call You Holy?' He said, 'Clearly I know what you know not.'*

And He taught Adam the Names, all of them. Then He presented them to the angels and said, 'Now tell Me the Names of these, if you speak truly.' They said, 'Glory be to You! We know not except what You have taught us. Surely You are the Knower, the Wise.'

He said, 'Adam, tell them their Names.' When he had told them their Names, He said, 'Did I not tell you I know the unseen things of the heavens and earth? And I know what things you reveal and what you were hiding.'

And when We said to the angels, 'Bow yourselves to Adam', so they bowed themselves except Iblis. He refused and was proud and so he became one of the unbelievers.

And We said, 'Adam, dwell you and your wife in the Garden and eat thereof freely where you desire but do not near this tree for fear that you be wrongdoers.'

Then satan caused them to slip therefrom and brought them out of where they were and We said, 'Get you all down, each of you an enemy of each and in the earth a temporary stay shall be yours and enjoyment for a time' (2:30-36).

Adam and Eve both prayed, *"Our Lord! We have wronged ourselves; if You forgive us not and have not mercy upon us, indeed, we shall be among the lost"* (7:23).

PRAYERS OF ABRAHAM

Abraham, known to the believers as the Friend of God, a monotheist who passed all the tests put to him, remains a key figure as the father of the Judeo-Christian-Islamic Tradition through his two sons, Ishmael, his first born whose mother was a slave woman, Hagar, and Isaac, his second son from his first wife, Sarah. Abraham is frequently referred to in the Quran which mentions his contemplation upon creation; the development of an unshakable faith in the One God; his destroying the idols of the Babylonians, being cast into a fiery furnace by the tyrant Nimrod and his miraculous escape; his migration to Canaan; his willingness to sacrifice his son as a result of a dream he had; his reconstructing the Kabah in Makkah with his son, Ishmael, and conveying the Divine Message to the people. Muslims often pray, "Oh God! Shower Your blessings upon Muhammad and the followers of Muhammad even as You showered Your blessings upon Abraham and the followers of Abraham."

Abraham's prayer for himself and his father, an idol carver, was: *"My Lord! Give me wisdom and join me with the righteous. Appoint me a tongue of truthfulness among posterity. Make me one of the heirs of the Garden of Bliss. Forgive my father, for he is one of those astray. Abase me not on the Day when they will be raised up, the Day when neither wealth nor sons shall avail except unto him who comes unto God with a pure heart"* (2:83-89)

Once he had destroyed the idols, he was persecuted by his people. He prayed, *"Our Lord! in You we trust. To You we turn. To You is the homecoming. Our Lord! Make us not a temptation to those who disbelieve and forgive us. Our Lord, You are the Powerful, the Wise"* (60:4-5).

When Abraham was about to leave his people and as he was childless, he prayed, *"Behold! I am going to my Lord. He will guide me. My Lord, give me one of the righteous"* (37:99-100). Soon thereafter he was given his first son, Ishmael. Ishmael's mother, Hagar, was Abraham's concubine whose marriage Sarah had approved. Once Hagar became pregnant, Sarah could not bear it as she was childless so she told Abraham that Hagar had to leave. Abraham had a dream that he should take her to Makkah which he did. Abraham left Hagar and Ishmael in Makkah and returned to live with Sarah. God then blessed Sarah with the birth of Isaac. Hagar became the founder of the city of Makkah. Many years later when Ishmael had grown up, Abraham returned to Makkah and he and Ishmael rebuilt the Kabah which had been destroyed in the flood.

Abraham prayed for Makkah, *"Our Lord, Make this a land secure and provide its people with fruits such of them as believe in God and the Last Day"* (2:126). Then father and son prayed for God's blessings upon the completion of the Kabah, *"Our Lord! receive this from us. You are the All-hearing, the Knower. Our Lord, make us submissive to You and of our seed, a nation submissive to You. Show us our rites and turn towards us. Surely You turn and are the Compassionate. Our Lord! do You send among them a Messenger, one of them, who shall recite to them Your signs and teach them the Book and the Wisdom and purify them. You are the Powerful, the Wise"* (2:127-129).

Abraham then prayed for Makkah and its people, *"My Lord, make this land secure and turn me and my sons away from serving idols. My Lord, they have led astray many people. Then whoso follows me belongs to me and whoso rebels against me, surely You are the Forgiver, the Compassionate. Our Lord, I have made some of my seed to dwell in a valley where is no sown land by Your House. Our Lord, let them perform the prescribed prayer and make hearts of people yearn towards them and provide them with fruits. Haply they will be thankful. Our Lord, You know what we keep secret and what we publish. From God nothing whatever is hidden in earth and heaven. Praise be to God who has given me, though I am old, Ishmael and Isaac. Surely my Lord hears the petition. My Lord, make me a performer of the prayer and of my seed. Our Lord, receive my petition. Our Lord, forgive me and my parents and the believers upon the Day when the reckoning shall come to pass"* (14:35-41).

PRAYERS OF MOSES

The Quran refers to Moses in various chapters and makes mention of his birth, how he was saved from Pharaoh's decree, how he grew up in Pharaoh's palace, about his speech impediment, how he accidentally kills an Egyptian, escaping to Midian, marrying one of the daughters of Shu'aib, seeing the burning bush, speaking with God, receiving prophethood and God's Commands and the power to work nine miracles. Moses is known as the one who spoke to God.

There are differences with Judaism and Christianity in regard to his early life. There is no reference in the Quran to Pharaoh's daughter, but rather to Pharaoh's wife, Asiyah, who brought him up. Asiyah is known as one of the four most righteous women. It is said in the Quran that Moses accidentally killed an Egyptian when he struck him with his fist and not that he purposefully did so. There is no reference to Jethro and his seven daughters, but rather to the old man of Midian and Moses' marrying one of his two daughters.

Moses, a descendant of Isaac, was born in Egypt where the Jewish people were in bondage to Pharaoh. Pharaoh had been warned that a male child of the Jewish people would arise against him. He ordered all male children under a certain age to be killed. Moses was saved when he was found by Pharaoh's wife who took him to the palace where she raised him. One day when Moses had grown up he came across two men fighting. One was Jewish and the other was Egyptian. Moses struck the

Egyptian with his fist, accidentally killing him. He then prayed, *"My Lord! Behold I have wronged my soul; therefore, forgive me"* (28:16). When he was forgiven by God, he said, *"My Lord! Since You have favored me I shall never again be a supporter of the wrong-doers"* (28:17).

The Egyptians resolved on killing Moses as he had killed one of them. Knowing their intention, Moses escaped, praying, *"My Lord! Deliver me from the oppressive people"* (28:21). He came to the wells of Midian. He found two daughters of the leader of Midian, an old man, waiting to water their sheep. He helped them and then prayed, *"My Lord! Behold I stand in need of whatever good You send down to me"* (28:24).

When prophethood and the mission was actualized in Moses, he prayed, *"Glory be to You! Unto You do I turn repentant and I am the first of the true believers"* (7:143). Moses asked to see god, praying, *"My Lord! Show me (Your Self) that I may behold you"* (7:143).

God then commanded Moses to go to Pharaoh and to deliver the message of the One God. Moses prayed, *"My Lord, open my breast and make my task easy. Unloose the knot upon my tongue that they may understand my words. Appoint for me of my folk a familiar, Aaron, my brother. By him confirm my strength and associate him with me in my task. So shall we glorify You and remember You abundantly. Surely You see into us"* (20:25-35).

Pharaoh and his people did not cease persecuting Moses. Moses prayed, *"Our Lord! Behold, You have given Pharaoh and his chiefs splendor and riches in worldly life, our Lord, that they may seduce people from Your way. Our Lord, confound their riches and harden their hearts for they will believe not until they see the tormenting punishment"* (10:88). When Moses triumphed over the Pharaoh's magicians and they became believers, Pharaoh threatened to crucify all of them. The followers of Moses prayed, *"Our Lord! Pour out patience to us and cause us to die among those who submit to Your Will (muslim)"* (7:126).

When the Jewish people were led out of Egypt, Moses was called by God to the mountain to receive the Divine Law. In his absence, the people made a golden calf which they began to worship. When Moses came down from the mountain he saw this and prayed, *"My Lord! Forgive me and my brother. Receive us into Your mercy for You are the Most Merciful of those who show mercy"* (7:151).

Moses chose seventy men from among his people and took them to the mountain where God used to speak to him. Knowing the disbelief and diseased heart of these men, God sent thunder and lightning and would have destroyed them if Moses had not prayed, *"My Lord! If You had willed You could have destroyed them and me as well. Will You destroy us for that which the foolish among us have done? It is naught but Your trial whereby You will mislead whom You will and guide whom You will. You are our Guardian. Therefore, forgive us and have mercy upon us. You are the best of those who forgive. Write down for us that which is good in this world as well as in the Hereafter. Behold! Unto You we are directed"* (7:155-156).

They came down from the mountain and Moses said to his people that God has commanded them to sacrifice a cow. The people did not believe him and he prayed, *"I seek refuge in God lest I should be of the foolish"* (2:67).

Moses called his people to enter the holy land which God had predestined for them. They refused to obey Him. Moses prayed, *"My Lord! Behold I have control over none save myself and my brother. Therefore, do You distinguish between us and the wrongdoers?"* (5:25).

THE PRAYER OF ASIYAH, PHARAOH'S WIFE

Asiyah had saved Moses from the Pharaoh's decree. A righteous woman, she was an example of a woman who rightfully rebelled against her husband who was a tyrant and oppressor. She was severely punished by Pharaoh for following Moses and believing in his teachings to worship the One God. When she was dying from this torture, she prayed, *"My Lord! Build me a home near You in Paradise and deliver me from Pharaoh and his work. Deliver me from the wrongdoers"* (66:11).

THE PRAYER OF BILQIS, THE QUEEN OF SHEBA

The land of Sheba was famous as being one of the most wealthy countries in the world. It included Yemen and a part of

Abyssinia. The queen, who lived about 1000 BC, was said to have been beautiful, prudent and diplomatic. She ruled through consultation with her ministers. She and her people worshipped the sun until she met Solomon. He invited her to visit his kingdom and she had hoped to impress him with her wealth. She had not reckoned his supernatural powers for he had been taught "the language of the birds." When Bilqis was asked to enter Solomon's hall, the floor of which had been made of glass, she thought she was walking on water and raised up her skirt. Realizing her mistake, she prayed, *"My Lord! Behold I have wronged my soul and I surrender with Solomon unto God, Lord of the worlds" (27:44).*

THE PRAYER OF HANNAH, THE MOTHER OF MARY

Hannah, barren and old of age, begged God for a child. God granted her prayer. Hoping that she was bearing a son, she dedicated the unborn child to the service of God and God bestowed Mary upon her. Hannah's prayer where she vowed her offspring to God was, *"My Lord! Behold I vow unto You that which is in my womb for Your service. Therefore, accept it from me. Behold! It is You Who are the All-hearing, the Knower "* (3:35). And then when Mary was born, she prayed, *"My Lord! Behold I have brought forth a female,"* —God knew very well what she had brought forth—a male is not as a female—"and behold I have named her Mary and behold I commend her to Your protection and also her offspring from satan, the outcast" (3:36). Prophet Muhammad has been reported to have said that everyone who comes into the world is touched at birth by satan. Since Hannah had prayed for Mary and her offspring, Iblis could not touch either Mary or Jesus (see Bukhari).

THE PRAYERS OF MARY AND JESUS, SON OF MARY

The Chapter entitled "Mary" in the Quran, tells of the birth of Jesus. *"And mention in the Book Mary when she withdrew from her people to an eastern place and she took a veil apart from them. Then We sent unto her Our Spirit that presented himself to her, a man without fault. She said, "I take refuge in the All-merciful from you! If you fear God...' He said, 'I am but a Messenger come from your Lord to give you a boy most pure.'*

She said, 'How shall I have a son whom no mortal has touched, neither have I been unchaste?'

He said, 'Even so your Lord has said: "Easy is that for Me and that We may appoint him a sign unto people and a mercy from Us; it is a thing decreed."'

So she conceived him and withdrew with him to a distant place. And the birthpangs surprised her by the trunk of the palm-tree. She said, 'Would I had died rather than this and become a thing forgotten!'

But the one that was below her called to her, 'Nay, do not sorrow; see, your Lord has set below you a rivulet. Shake also the palm-trunk and there shall come tumbling upon you dates fresh and ripe. Eat therefore and drink and be comforted. And if you should see any mortal, say, "I have vowed to the All-merciful a fast, and today I will not speak to any person"'

Then she brought the child to her folk, carrying him and they said, 'Mary, you have surely committed a monstrous thing! Sister of Aaron, your father was not a wicked man nor was your mother a woman unchaste.'

Mary pointed to the child then but they said, 'How shall we speak to one who is still in the cradle, a little child?' He (Jesus) said, 'Lo, I am God's servant. God has given me the Book and made me a Prophet. Blessed He has made me, wherever I may be and He has enjoined me to pray and to give alms so long as I live and likewise to cherish my mother. He has not made me arrogant, unprosperous. Peace be upon me the day I was born and the day I die and the day I am raised up alive!'

That is Jesus, son of Mary, in word of truth concerning which they are doubting. It is not for God to take a son unto Him. Glory be to Him! When He decrees a thing, He but says to it 'Be,' and it is. Surely God is my Lord and your Lord so serve you Him. This is a straight path.' (19:16-22; 27-35).

In another place, the Quran tells the story of the birth of Jesus in the following verses: *"And when the angels said, 'Mary, God has chosen you and purified you. He has chosen you above all women. Mary, be obedient to your Lord, prostrating and bowing before Him' (that is of the tidings of the unseen, that We reveal to you for you were not with them when they were casting quills which of them should have charge of Mary. You were not with them when they were disputing).*

When the angels said, 'Mary, God gives you good tidings of a Word from Him whose name is Messiah, Jesus, son of Mary. High honored shall be he in this world and the next, near stationed to God. He shall speak to people in the cradle and of age and righteous he shall be.' '

Lord,' said Mary, 'how shall I have a son seeing no mortal has touched me?' '

Even so,' God said, 'God creates what He will. When He decrees a thing, he Does but say to it "Be," and it is. And He will teach him the Book, the Wisdom, the Torah, the Gospel, to be a Messenger to the Children of Israel saying, "I have come to you with a sign from your Lord. I will create for you out of clay as the likeness of a bird; then I will breathe into it and it will be a bird, by the leave of God. I will also heal the blind and the leper and bring to life the dead, by the leave of God. I will inform you too of what things you eat and what you treasure up in your houses. Surely in that is a sign for you, if you are believers. Likewise confirming the truth of the Torah that is before me, and to make lawful to you certain things that before were forbidden unto you. I have come to you with a sign from your Lord, so fear your God and obey you me. Surely God is my Lord and your Lord so serve Him. This is the Straight Path."' When Jesus asked who his helpers would be, his disciples prayed, *"We will be helpers of God. We believe in God. Witness our submission. Lord, we believe in what You have sent down and we follow the Messenger. Inscribe us therefore with those who bear witness.'* (3:42-49).

When the disciples of Jesus asked him whether His Lord was able to send down for them a table spread with food from heaven. Jesus prayed, *"Oh God! Our Lord! Send down a table unto us from heaven that it may be a festival unto us, unto the first of us and the last of us and a sign from You and provide for us sustenance for You are the best of providers"* (5:114).

PRAYERS OF MUHAMMAD IBN ABD ALLAH (ص)

While there are many prayers in the Quran which a believer learns to recite at various times, we can isolate seven prayers that are specific to the Prophet Muhammad (ص). This is not to include those supplications which are complete chapters in themselves and which are recited in the five daily prescribed prayers by the believers just as they were recited by the Prophet.

According to the Traditions, Prophet Muhammad (ص) said in regard to supplication, "Whenever anyone of you invoke God for something, be firm in asking. You should not say, 'If You wish, give me...' for none can compel God to do something against His Will" (*Bukhari*, vol. 9, *hadith* no. 556). He also said in another Tradition, "None of you should say, 'O God! Forgive me if You wish,' or 'Bestow Your Mercy upon me, if You wish,' or 'Provide me with means of subsistance if You wish,' but you should be firm in your request for God does what He will and nobody can force Him (to do anything)" (*Bukhari*, vol. 9, *hadith* no. 569).

One of the most fervent supplications of Prophet Muhammad (ﷺ) is, *"My Lord, increase me in knowledge"* (20:114). In the verses preceding this verse, Prophet Muhammad (ﷺ) is told that whenever a verse is revealed to him, he should supplicate with this prayer.

It has been narrated in the Traditions that Prophet Muhammad (ﷺ) said, "The example of guidance and knowledge (that is, the Quran and the *sunnah*) with which God has sent me is like abundant rain falling on the earth, some of which was fertile soil that absorbed rain water and brought forth vegetation and grass in abundance. Another portion of it was hard and held the rain water and God benefitted the people with it and they utilized it for drinking, making their animals drink from it and for irrigation of the land for cultivation. And a portion of it was barren which could neither hold the water nor bring forth vegetation (then that land gave no benefits).The first is the example of the person who comprehends God's religion (submission to the Will of God, islam) and receives benefit from the knowledge which God has revealed through me (Prophet Muhammad (ﷺ)) and learns and teaches others. The last example is that of a person who does not care for it and does not take God's guidance revealed through me (that is, that person is like barren land). (*Bukhari*, vol. 1, *hadith* no. 79).

The second prayer or supplication we are studying here is one which was revealed just before Prophet Muhammad (ﷺ) migrated from Makkah to Madinah. The prayer is, *"My Lord! Cause me to enter (Madinah) with a true entry and to come forth (from Makkah) with a true forthcoming and provide me from Your Presence a helping power"* (17:80).

Those who seek self-transformation, see the migration as

historic as well as symbolic of the greater jihad—the struggle with self which begins with a migration from "the city of unbelievers" (as Makkah was at that time) to "The City" of the Messenger (Madinah). It is also seen as symbolic of the migration of the real self, in the sense that it is a prayer to move from individual development (the Makkan period) to social development and the establishment of the Muslim community (the Madinah period).

Third, *"Say (Muhammad), 'As for me, my Lord has guided me to a straight path, a right religion, the creed of Abraham, a man of pure faith (*hanifa, *monotheist, someone who practices* hilm *or the moral reasonableness of a religiously cultured person*); he was no idolater.' Say (Muhammad), 'My prescribed prayer, my ritual sacrifice, my living, my; dying—all belong to God, the Lord of all Being. No partner has He. Even so I have been commanded and I am the first of those that surrender' "* (6:161-163).

Two interesting Traditions are related to these verses. In the first Tradition, Prophet Muhammad (ﷺ) met Zayd ibn Amr ibn Nufayl at the end of the valley of Baldah before he had received any revelation. A meal was presented to Muhammad (ﷺ). He refused to eat it. Then it was presented to Zayd who said, "I do not eat anything which you slaughter in the name of your stone idols. I eat nothing but those things on which God's Name has been mentioned at the time of slaughtering." Zayd used to criticize the way the Quraysh used to slaughter their animals. He used to say, "God has created the sheep and He has sent water for it from the sky and He has made the grass grow for it from the earth, yet you slaughter it in other than the Name of God.'" He used to say this because he rejected the practice and considered it to be something abominable.

Zayd went to the area known as Sham (Syria, Palestine, Lebanon and Jordan) asking about a true religion to follow. He met a Jewish religious scholar and asked him about his religion. He said to the Jewish scholar said, "I intend to embrace your religion so tell me something about it." The Jewish scholar said, "God would be angry with you if you were to embrace my religion." Zayd said, "I run from God's anger and I will never cause it to appear if I have the power to avoid it. Can you tell me about some other religion?" The Jewish scholar said, "I know of no other religion except that of the *hanif*s (monotheists)." Zayd asked, "What is a *hanif*?" The said, "A *hanif* is a follower of the religion of Prophet Abraham who was neither a Jew nor a Christian. He used to worship none but God."

Zayd left and continued his journey. He met a Christian scholar and told him the same thing he had told the Jewish scholar. The Christian scholar said, "God would be angry with you if you were to embrace my religion." Zayd gave the same answer, "I try to avoid God's anger and I will never cause it to appear if I have the power to avoid it. Can you tell me about some other religion?" The Christian scholar replied, "The only other religion I know is that of the *hanfi*s." Zayd asked, "Who are they?" The scholar replied, "That is the religion of the followers of Abraham who was neither a Jew nor a Christian and he used to worship none but God."

When Zayd heard what they had to say about the religion of Abraham, he left that town and went to the outskirts where he raised both his hands and said, "O God! I make You my witness that I am a follower of the religion of Abraham."

The daughter of Abu Bakr, Asma, related that she saw Zayd standing with his back against the Kabah and saying, "O people of the Quraysh! By God, none of you follows the religion of Abraham except me." Zayd used to save the lives of little girls. If somebody wanted to kill his daughter (as was the practice in pre_islamic Arabia to bury girl children alive), Zayd would say to that person, "Do not kill her for I will feed her on your behalf." He would take her and when she grew up, he would say to her father, "Now if you want her, I will give her to you and if you wish, I will feed her on your behalf" (*Bukhari*, vol. 5, *hadith* no. 169).

The second Tradition which relates to this supplication of the Prophet Muhammad (ﷺ) is that he said, "Every child is born with a true faith (*fitrat Allah*) of worshipping none but God alone, but the child's parents convert the child into Judaism, Christianity or Zoroastrianism just as an animal delivers a perfect baby animal and yet you find it mutilated.

Then the recorder of this Traditions recited, *"Fitrat Allah with which He has created humanity. No change let there be in the creation of God. That is the Straight religion, but most of them know not"* (30:30) (*Bukhari*, vol. 2, *hadith* no. 441).

The fourth and fifth supplications were recited when the disbelievers disputed the Truth concerning God and His Messenger Muhammad (ص). Prophet Muhammad (ص) would pray, *"My Lord! Judge You with truth"* (21:112). The fifth, *"My Lord! If You should show me that (punishment) which they (the disbelievers) are promised, then my Lord! include me not among the wrongdoers"* (23:94-95).

In order to seek refuge from Satan and satanic temptations, Prophet Muhammad (ص) was taught the prayer, *"My Lord! I seek refuge in You from the satanic temptations of the satans and I seek refuge in You, my Lord! lest they approach me"* (23:97-98). In the Tradition are related to this verse, two men abused each other in front of Prophet Muhammad (ص). One of the two abused his companion furiously and his face became red. Prophet Muhammad (ص) said, "I know a sentence the saying of which will cause him to relax. He should say, 'I seek refuge with God from satan, the out-cast.' They then asked the man who was furious if he had heard what the Messenger (ص) had said. The man answered, 'I am not mad'" (*Bukhari*, vol. 8, *hadith* no. 136).

The last two prayers are, *"Our Lord! We believe, therefore forgive us and have mercy upon us for You are the Best of those who show mercy"* (23:109) and *"My Lord! Forgive (me) and have mercy for of the merciful, You are the Best"* (23:118). The humility of the approach of these two prayers in echoed in the supplication that Prophet Muhammad (ص) is recorded in the Traditions to have recited when daily ending the prescribed fast of Ramadan. He would say, "O God, I fasted for Your sake. I believed in You and relied on You and I break my fast with Your provisions."

In the Traditions relating to the prayers in 23:109 and 23:118, Prophet Muhammad (ص) said, "None is more patient than God against the harmful saying. He hears from the people.

They ascribe a son (or offspring or children) to Him, yet He gives them health and provisions" (*Bukhari*, vol. 8, *hadith*, 121). And, "I heard God's Messenger saying, 'God has divided Mercy into 100 parts and He kept 99 parts with Him and sent down one part to the earth. Because of this, this one single part, His creatures are merciful to each other so that even the mare lifts up its hoofs away from its small colt lest it should be trampled on'" (*Bukhari*, vol. 8, *hadith* no. 29).

Only a few examples of the beautiful supplications of Prophet Muhammad (ﷺ) in the Quran as well as those of other men and women have been presented here. None of this is exhaustive but a glimpse at the words which act as a healing for the believer.

The supplications looked at here are either historic and situation oriented or spiritual and strengthening of belief oriented and of course, we need to remind ourselves that the English renderings presented here pale in comparison to the original Arabic, the language in which they were revealed. While believers are certain that God answers their supplication in whatever language presented, it is also clear that reciting them in the original Arabic is closer to the *sunnah* of Muhammad ibn Abd Allah (ﷺ), Muhammad, man of God.

PART FOUR:
MORAL HEALERS

12

MORAL HEALING THROUGH FASTING

Laleh Bakhtiar

The self (*khudi*) in the traditional perspective is described as a circle of unity. The center from which the circle emerges is known as the heart. From this center—the heart— emerges a threefold division. The uppermost segment is known as cognition, intellect or reason, the *nafs lawwamah* (the soul which blames, reproaches self for wrongdoing). It symbolizes that aspect of self which God blew into the human form. By doing so, God created Adam in His image. This upper segment is the human angelic quality.

The bottom two segments, known collectively as the animal soul (*nafs ammarah*), are referred to as avoidance of harm/pain and attraction to pleasure. These two segments and aspects of self make up what are called the passions. Attraction to pleasure is the center of lust or desires while avoidance of pain is the center of anger. These two are the human animal qualities.

The purpose of creation in this view is for the human self to struggle (*jihad*) to attain the highest human perfection possible. This struggle is known as the greater struggle (*jihad al-akbar*). It is a struggle between reason and the passions for the attention of the heart. If reason succeeds in attracting the heart to itself, the self is turned towards the spiritual and external world. If the passions succeed, the self is turned towards the material and impermanent world. This struggle is a significant one for the goal-setting believer's strategies because it reinforces those values which the model human being—Muhammad (ص)— manifested. That is, when reason succeeds in attracting the heart towards itself, the self gains control and mastery over the passions—lust and anger. Gaining mastery, the self can then process values to which it has been guided by revelation and turn away from the disvalues which guidance through revelation has discredited.

This struggle—a continuous kind of tension—is a more difficult one requiring one's constant attention to remember and recall the purpose of life. Forgetfulness and heedlessness, seen as aspects of satanic-ego temptations, are as strong a natural force which when in control of self, allow for the responses of lust and anger to take over the self. It is then that the animal qualities within rule over the angelic or, in other words, the passions rule over reason.

Traditional prescribed fasting, which is always accompanied by prescribed prayer and supplication, serves to cut off the energies to the passions, weakening their response. This, in turn, strengthens the powers of reason. There are three kinds of fasts for the believer: prescribed, recommended and disapproved. One of the recommended fasts is that practiced by Zachariah and the Virgin Mary. It is a fast of silence. As regards the recommended fast of the Virgin Mary, God says to her once Jesus has been conceived, "*So eat and drink and be glad and if you see any human being, say, 'Verily I have vowed a fast to the Compassionate so I shall not speak to any human being this day.'*"

The Traditions relating to this verse all reinforce the idea that once one makes a vow or promise to follow a command of God, one should keep one's promise. One Tradition says, "The Messenger said, 'The best amongst you people are those living in my generation, then those coming after them, and then those coming after the second generation.' I do not know whether the Messenger mentioned two or three generations after his, but he then added, 'There will be some people after you who will be dishonest and will not be trustworthy and will bear witness without being asked to bear witness and will vow but not fulfill their vows and obesity will appear among them.'"[1]

The Sufi Sayf al-Din,[2] describes the role of the prescribed fast in subduing the ego.

> The prescribed fast during the month of Ramadan further enhances the possibility of reason to win the struggle with the passions because of its duration. As the passions are weakened and the heart is attracted towards reason and the spiritual, the heart begins to see the mysteries of the universe. These mysteries are veiled from the heart during normal times by satanic whisperings or human ego desires which are symbolized by shadows covering the heart. Holding to the vow to the prescribed fast once made helps to remove the shadows over the heart. This is confirmed for the believer by the Tradition, 'If the satans did not swarm around the hearts of the children of Adam, they would look at the dominion of the heavens.'[3] The instruments used by the satanic forces in leading the self astray and misguiding it are the passions—anger and lust.
>
> > Could Adam have been brought down
> > > from the Garden
> > had the peacock and serpent
> > > not guided Iblis?
> > Your anger and lust
> > > are peacock and serpent—
> > The first helps satanic forces
> > > The second the animal soul.[4]
>
> Further elucidating this analogy, Sayf al-Din says, "Through hunger the substance of anger and lust is weakened.' Thereby satan becomes thin since, 'The satan of the person of faith is emaciated.' When satan has no instrument or weapon left, it cannot whisper. The Seal of the Prophets—the Merciful's blessings be upon him—explained this meaning as follows, 'Satan runs in the child of Adam like blood. So constrict his running places through hunger and thirst.' Hence Jesus—God's blessings be upon him—counseled his disciples by saying, 'Keep your bellies hungry, your

bodies naked, and your livers thirsty so that perhaps
your hearts may see God.'
        The cause of anger and lust
            is a bite of bread,
        the blight of mind and wisdom
            is a bite of bread.
   However, excessive hunger also causes harm. It car-
ries the danger of madness, corruption of the brain
and other illnesses. In short, a middle course is desirable in all things. The seeker must always keep 'the
best of affairs is their middlemost' before their eyes.
'Both sides of moderation in affairs are blameworthy.'
This alerts you to a universal law. And from God, aid
is sought.[5]

Mastering, controlling the passions is traditionally known
as moral healing. Anything that reinforces and strengthens the
power of reason to attract the heart, the center of self, towards
the Real, the Truth, serves to morally heal and balance the self.
Prescribed fasting is one of the best disciplines to reinforce values about what is right or wrong for the believer.

For the believer, remembrance of the afterlife and the eternal possibility of self gives life meaning and connection to the
unseen world. It is this 'eternal possibility of self' which, for the
believer, needs to control 'the preservation of the species' or lust
and 'the preservation of the individual' or anger. If a person
does not believe what he or she is doing is the right thing to do,
is a reinforcement of the eternal possibility of self, there will be
inner conflict. This inner conflict will cause two effects: either a
weakening of will power which will, in turn, undermine the
believer's ability to attain the goal he or she set forth to perform
the prescribed fast in the month of Ramadan or secondly, the
believer may fast, but it will be an even greater struggle than it
has to be. Once the values of the believer are clarified, resulting
in a relaxing of the tension between attachment to this world
vs. attachment to the eternal world, the struggle within the self
becomes more manageable and with greater chance of success.
The prescribed fast then becomes a means for the believer to
express gratitude for the blessings one has received. This is

brought out in a Tradition related by Ayisha, the Messenger's wife. While the Messenger was in a state free of negative traits, yet his prescribed prayers, fasting and supplications were intense. One day she said, "Oh Messenger of God, God has forgiven your sins, but you still invite this discipline upon yourself." He immediately replied, "Should I not be grateful?"[6]

13

ATTACHMENT TO THIS WORLD

Muhammad al-Ghazzali

Muhammad al-Ghazzali (d. 1111 CE) is one of the greatest synthesizers of Islamic thought in the history of Islam. The following essay from his masterpiece, The *Revival of Religious Sciences* (*Ihya ulum al-din*) is a classic work. In this particular section, al-Ghazzali describes one of the major purposes behind the Divine command to perform the prescribed fast and that is for the believer to detach himself/herself from the world. Sufis have been criticized throughout Islamic history for this position. The criticism is unfounded in the case of many Sufis like al-Ghazzali who, while emphasizing the need to detach oneself from the world, stress the need for balance and moderation. It is simply a reminder that this life is passing and that one should not forget the next life, but not that one should withdraw from it completely because that would not be the middle way. Al-Ghazzali uses extensive Traditions in this essay from the Messenger which refer to previous prophets including Jesus (ع), Moses (ع) and Solomon (ع) and their emphasis upon not becoming too attached to this world.

The Editor

Ah praise is due to God who discloses the merits and demerits of the world to His friends. They weighed its benefits.... If you do good to the world for one hour, it does you harm for one year. If you carry on business with worldly people, you gain no benefit but loss. He who seeks the world faces many dangers and difficulties which cannot be enumerated. Whoso wants it, it flees away from him; and whoso does not want it, it goes to him.

THE WORLD CAN BE AN ENEMY OF GOD

The cause is that the world undercuts the way of serving God. For this reason, God keeps an eye on it since He created it. The world is an enemy of the friends of God. The cause is that it presents itself with its best finery just like an unchaste woman dressed with various beautiful dresses. The world is also an enemy of the enemies of God. The cause is that the world entraps them in a net of love after deceiving them and opens its door of love to them. They are deceived by its love and become attached to it. The result is that they are dishonored and disgraced. When they leave it, their hearts are pierced because of the separation and fortune bids them farewell forever. There is no limit to their remorse. Therefore seek refuge in God. They have purchased this world in exchange for the next. When the harms of the world are many, we should know its snares and charms and then save ourselves from its deceptions and love.

NEGATIVE EFFECTS OF ATTACHMENT TO THIS WORLD

There are innumerable verses of the Quran regarding the evils of the world. The goal of the Messenger was to turn away the people from the evils and harms of the world and so there is no necessity of collecting verses from the Quran about it. I shall mention only some Traditions.

(1) It has been narrated that the Messenger was once passing by a dead goat and said to his companions, "Learn from this dead animal. Its owner is now looking at it with hate. By One

in whose hand there is my life, just as this dead goat is more an object of hated to its owner, the world is likewise more an object of hatred to God. If the value of the world would have been like the wing of a mosquito, He would not have given a drought of water to an unbeliever to drink."

(2) The Messenger said, "The world is a prison to a believer and a paradise to an unbeliever."

(3) He said, "The world is cursed and all the things in it are cursed."

(4) He said, "One who loves the world injures one's hereafter and one who loves the hereafter injures one's world. So take what will last forever by giving up what will not last."

(5) He said, "Love of the world is the root of all wrongdoing."

(6) A Companion reported, "We were once with Abu Bakr (a Companion and the first rightly-guided caliph). He ordered water and honey which were brought to him. He lifted them to drink but began to weep. On being asked the reason he said, "This is the world. It came to me with beautiful face. I said, 'Be off.' The world said, 'You have saved yourself from me, but those who will come after you will not be safe from my hand.'"

(7) The Messenger stood by a place full of human bones and said to the people, "Do you like to look at the world?" He then took a rotten cloth and crumbled bone and said, "This is the world." He said that the wealth and pleasures of the world will be ruined like the rotten cloth and all the people will be crumbled like the crumbled bone.

(8) The Messenger said, "This world is sweet and fresh and God made you His representatives therein. He is observing how you act therein."

(9) When the children of Israel were given enormous wealth and when they were engrossed therein, they were attached to worldly pleasures, love of women and precious scents and clothes.

(10) Jesus (ع) said, "Don't take the world as your lord. If you do so, it will make you its slaves. Hoard up your wealth with the One Who will not destroy it. Guards of wealth of this world cannot be relied on, but you can rely on the guards of God." He also said, "Oh my disciples, I have leveled the world with earth

for you. Don't take it up after me." One of the evils of the world is that the people commit wrongdoings therein. Another evil of the world is that the next world cannot be acquired unless this world is given up. So take care and think that the world has passed away and don't live therein with happiness. Know that the root of all evils is attachment to this world. Many a time the present greed becomes the cause of a person's calamities.

(11) Jesus (ع) also said, "The world lies behind you and you take a seat thereon. Therein the kings and women stand as stumbling blocks against you. Don't dispute with the kings regarding this world as they will not stand in your way if you give up connection with them and their affairs. Save yourselves from women with prescribed fasting and prayers." He also said, "The world searches for the people and the people search for the world. The world searches for one who searches for the next world until one's provision does not become complete. The next world searches for one who searches for the world until death. Thereafter it catches one's neck and climbs upon one." He also said, "God created nothing so obnoxious as the world. He did not look at it on the day He created it."

(12) It has been reported that Prophet Solomon (ع) was roaming in air and birds were giving him shade and people and *jinn* were on his right and left sides. He met a hermit of the Israel tribe on the way and the hermit said to him, "O son of David, Almighty God has given you reign and power." At this Solomon said, "One phrase in praise of God in the book of deeds of a believer is superior to my reign because what has been given to the son of David will end but the praise of God will remain."

(13) The Messenger (ص) said, "Excessive wealth has made you forgetful." The son of Adam said, "My wealth, my wealth. Do you have any other wealth than what you have eaten and ended, what you have put on and gotten old? What you have given in charity that remained lasting?"

(14) The Messenger (ص) said, "He who has no abode takes the world as his abode. He who has no wisdom makes enmity for it. He who has no power of doing justice, covets it. He who has no sure faith makes efforts for it."

(15) He said, "He who gets up at dawn with the world as his object of thought is not God-fearing. Four attitudes develop: (a) such anxiety as has no end, (b) such engagement as has no limit, (c) such poverty as can never make him rich and (d) such hope which has no end."

(16) It has been recorded, "The Messenger said to me, 'Oh Abu Hurayrah (a Companion and recorder of Traditions), shall I show you what obnoxious things are here in this world?' I said, 'Oh Messenger of God, show me.' Then he caught my hand and took me to a valley of China and showed me a place full of carcasses, stool and urine, rotten clothes and bones and hides. He said, 'Oh Abu Hurayrah, there were in their heads greed like your greed and hopes like your hopes, but today those are with the rotten remains. All those will be consumed by earth after some days. All these are of the world. If you can weep at the sad plight of the world, then weep. Then we began to weep.'"

(17) It has been reported that it is written in the Scripture of Abraham (ع), "Oh world, how ignoble you are to religious people. You have presented yourself to them with your finery, but hatred has been cast at you in their hearts and for that they have turned away from you. There is nothing so obnoxious to Me as you. Every act of yours is mean and comes to destruction. I have recorded for you on the day I created you that you will not stay with anybody forever and that the one who loves you will be the miser. Thanks to those pious people who seek Me with pleasure in their hearts, those in whose hearts there is truth and who stand on the right path. Happy are they as they will receive rewards for what their hands have acquired. When they will come to Me from the graves, light will move forward in front of them and the angels will surround them. They will receive mercy as they all hoped from Me."

(18) The Messenger (ص) said, "There will appear such persons on the Resurrection Day whose merits will be high like the hillock of Tohama but they will be ordered to go to hellfire." The Companions asked, "Oh Messenger of God, did they offer prayers?" He replied, "Yes, they observed prescribed prayers and fasting and prayed also at night, but whenever anything of the world came to them, they jumped at it." The Messenger said

in his sermon, "Believers will live with two fears. One fear is for their fate which is past and they does not know what was recommended therein. Another fear is to gather sufficient provision for themselves from the world for their next world, from their life for their death, from their youth for their old age because the present world has been created for your good and you have been created for the next world. By One in whose hand there is my life, there is on field for labor except paradise and hellfire and there is no abode after the world."

(19) Jesus (ع) said, "Love of both this world and the next cannot remain united in the heart of a believer just as water and fire cannot remain united." Gabriel asked the Prophet Noah, "O one having a very long life, how have you found the world?" Noah said, "It is like an abode having two doors. I have entered through one door and come out of another."

(20) Jesus (ع) was asked, "Why do you not construct a house to live in?" He said, "The abode of our predecessors is sufficient." The Messenger said, "Beware of the world, as it is a sorcerer greater than Harut and Marut."

(21) Hasan al-Basri (an early Sufi) said, "Once the Messenger came out to his Companions and said, 'Who amongst you who does not wish bright eye sight after his blindness? Beware, the more he is attached to the world and the greater are his hopes, the more God blinds his heart and the more he gives up the world and the more he curtails his hopes, God gives him more wisdom without education and guides him more without guidance. Beware, there will come such a people after you whose kingdom will not be without massacre and oppression, who will not acquire wealth without pride and miserliness and who will not love except for passion. Beware, whoever reaches that age and remains patient with poverty even though he can acquire wealth and remains patient with hatred even though he can earn love, and remains patient with dishonor even though he can earn honor and he has no other object for these things than the satisfaction of God, will receive the rewards of fifty truthful men."

(22) It has been reported that Jesus (ع) began to search for refuge having fallen in a storm, lightning and thunder, until he

found a tent. He went to it, but when he found a beautiful woman inside, he turned away. Thereafter he came to a cave where there was a tiger. Then he placed his hand upon the ground and said, "O Lord, you have given shelter to everything, but not to me." God then revealed to him, 'Your shelter is God's mercy. I shall get you married on the Resurrection Day with one hundred houris whom I have created with My hands. "Your marriage ceremony will continue for four thousand years, one day of which is equal to the age of this world. I will order a proclaimer to proclaim, 'Those who were religious and ascetics will join this marriage ceremony.'"

(23) Jesus (ع) said, "Alas for those people who are addicted to the world. How can they die after leaving the world and its fortunes? How the world deceives them and they put their trust in it? The world plays treachery with them, but they live out its fear. What is not loved comes to them. What they love moves away from them. What has been promised to them must come. Alas for those whose only object of thought is this world and whose actions are wrongdoings. How can they appear tomorrow with their wrongdoing?"

(24) It has been reported that God revealed to Moses (ع), "Oh Moses, what necessity do you have in the abode of the wrongdoers (world)? It is not your abode. Drive out your thoughts from it and remain aloof on the strength of your wisdom. What a bad house it is! It is a good abode for one who does good therein. O Moses, I am searching for one secretly commits oppression therein so that I may take his virtues and give them to the one who is oppressed."

(25) It has been reported that the Messenger (ص) once sent a Companion to the province of Bahrain. He went there and returned with enormous wealth from the inhabitants and placed it before the Messenger. The Helpers came to know of it and assembled for the morning prescribed prayer to the mosque. After the prescribed prayer the Messenger said, "You have perhaps heard about the riches brought by Abu Ubaydah (a Companion)." Then he said, "I don't fear for your poverty, but I fear for your enormous wealth just as previous nations had. They received enormous wealth and engaged in quarrels with

one another. As they were destroyed by this wealth, you will likewise be destroyed by it."

(26) The Messenger (ص) said, "I fear that you will be given the plenties of the world." He was asked, "What are the plenties of the world?" He said, "Riches and treasures of the world." The Messenger said, "Don t keep your mind engaged in the thoughts of the world."

(27) Jesus (ع) said to his disciples, "In order to get peace of this world as well as in the next, it is more preferable to eat bread with only salt, to wear a gunny sack and to sleep in stables."

(28) It has been reported that the Messenger (ص) had a she-camel named Ajwa which defeated all camels. A desert Arab came with a camel which defeated Ajwa. The Muslims were grieved to see this and the Messenger said, "It is a duty of God that He does not raise up a thing without lowering it."

(29) Jesus (ع) once said, "Who is there who constructs a house in the currents of sea? It is the world. Don't take it as your permanent abode. "

(30) Jesus (ع) was once asked, "Give me such short advice by virtue of which God will love us." He said, "Hate the world and God will love you."

(31) The Messenger (ص) said, "If you had known what I know, you would have laughed little and wept much. Hate the world and love the next world."

(32) A Companion said, "Had you known what I know from the Messenger, you would have come out to every elevated place and wept for the salvation of your soul, given up the riches and treasures of the world except what is essentially necessary for you."

(33) Jesus (ع) said, "Oh my disciples, be satisfied with little of worldly riches but with greater divine service, as the worldly addicted person remains satisfied with little of divine service but greater worldly riches."

(34) Jesus (ع) said, "It is a greater virtuous act to give up the world for those who search the world for religion."

(35) The Messenger (ص) said, "The world will be broadened

for you after me but it will consume your faith in such a way as fire consumes a dry wood."

(36) God sent revelation to Moses (ε), "Oh Moses, don't be addicted to the world as you will not come to Me with a greater wrongdoing than this."

(37) Once Moses (ε) passed by a man who was weeping. He found the man in the same condition when he was returning. Then Moses (ε) prayed to God, "Oh Lord, your servant is weeping for fear of you." God said, "Oh son of Imran, if his tears flow over his head and he keeps his hands raised up until they fall down, I shall not forgive him because he loves the world."

WISE SAYINGS

Ali ibn Abi Talib (the first cousin of the Messenger and fourth rightly-guided caliph) said, "He who has six virtues leaves nothing in his search for paradise and salvation from hellfire: obeying God after knowing Him, following truth after knowing it, disobeying the devil after knowing him, saving himself from falsehood after knowing it, giving up the world after knowing it, and searching for the next world after knowing it."

Hasan al-Basri said, "God shows mercy on him who competes with another in matters of religion. He throws one on his neck who corrupts you in matters of the world."

Luqman advised his son, "Oh dearest one, the world is a deep sea and many people are drowned therein. Make piety your boat, faith your oar, reliance upon God your sail so that you may receive salvation or else I don't see that you will be saved."

The saint Fazil said, "We should ponder deeply over the Quranic verse, *I have made adornments for the world. I have created them with the object that I will see who among them is great in good works.*"

A hermit was questioned, "What do you think about time?" He said, "Time destroys the body, creates new hopes, takes death near and removes light distant."

A sage said, "Success in the world means failures, cleanliness therein means uncleanliness and its dwellers remain in fear of loss of wealth, of calamity and impending death."

One man said to the saint Abu Hazern, "I have no abode in the world, yet I complain to you about my attachment to the world." He said, "Look to what God granted you regarding wealth. Don't take except what is lawful. Don't lawfully spend except for things for which you should spend. If you conduct yourself in such a way, attachment for the world will not harm you."

The saint Fazil said, "If the transient world was made of gold and ever-lasting and the next world of clay, it would have been our duty to love the clay-made next world than the world made of gold. How futile is it to love transient earth-made world in comparison to the everlasting gold-made next world."

The wise Luqman (a slave who became a Prophet) said to his son, "Oh dearest one, sell your world in exchange this for the next world. You will then receive benefit in both the worlds. Don't sell the next world in exchange for this world. You will then be a loser in both the worlds."

Ibn Abbas (the Messenger's uncle) said, "God divided the world into three parts: one part for the believers, (2) one part for the hypocrites, and (3) one part for the infidels. A believer gathers his provision therein, a hypocrite adorns it and an infidel makes enjoyments therein."

Baheli said, "After the Messenger became the Messenger of God, the armies of the devil came to him and said, 'One Messenger has appeared and one nation has come out. What shall we do now?' The devil said, 'Do they love the world?' They said, 'Yes.' The devil said, 'I do not worry about them even though they do not worship idols provided they love the world. I will come to them morning and evening with three pieces of advice: (1) acquire wealth unjustly, (2) spend money in improper places, and (3) be miser in places where expenditure is necessary. All wrongdoings are based on these three.'"

Ali ibn Abi Talib was once asked about the world. He said in short that accounts will be taken of lawful things in the world and punishment will be given of unlawful things.

A Sufi said, "When there is the next world in the mind of a person, the world stands before him/her. When there is the world in his/her mind, the next world does not come in, as the next world is honorable but the world is an object of hatred."

Malek ibn Dinar said, "The thoughts of the world will leave your mind in proportion to your sorrows for the next world."

An early Sufi said, "I saw such men to whom this world was more an object of hatred than trodden mud. They paid no attention to whom it went, to whom it rested and from whom it set in."

Once when Umar ibn al-Khattab (a Companion of the Messenger and the second rightly-guided Caliph) was the caliph, he went to visit Syria when Abu Ubaydah was its governor. He came riding on a she-camel to receive the caliph. The she-camel had a rope tied to her nose. Umar conversed with him and then went to Abu Ubaydah's governor's mansion, but found nothing therein except a sword, a shield and a wooden stand for placing the Quran therein. The caliph asked him, "Why have you not kept other necessary things in your house?" The governor said, "Oh Commander of the Faithful, these things will carry me to the place of questions and answers (grave)."

The wise Luqman said to his son, "O dearest one, you are drifting away from this world from the day in which you were born and advancing towards the next world. The abode to which you are proceeding is better than the abode from which you are drifting away."

The saint Farnil said, "Wonderful is the person who roams merrily even though he/she knows that death is inevitable. Wonderful is the person who laughs even though he/she knows that hellfire is a truth. Wonderful is the person who remains satisfied with the world even though he/she knows that it is transient. Wonderful is the person who keeps himself/herself engaged in earning wealth even though he/she knows that fate is true."

Hasan Basra said, "The life of a person will not leave the world but repentance for three things: (1) that he/she could not enjoy with satisfaction what he/she hoarded, (2) he/she could not fulfill what he/she hoped for, and (3) he/she could not do actions which ought to have been done for the next world."

A certain sage was asked, "For whom is this world?" He said, "For those who give up this world." He was asked, "For whom is the next world?" He said, "For those who want it."

The saint Ihya ibn Ma'az said, "Wise people are of three types: (1) one who gives up the world before the world gives that person up, (2) one who keeps self prepared for the grave before one enters it, and (3) one who keeps God satisfied before one meets Him."

Hasan Basra once wrote to the caliph Abdul Aziz, "This world is transient, not everlasting. Adam was sent to the world as a sort of punishment. O Commander of the Faithful, fear the world. Giving up the world means gathering provision from this world for the next world. To remain in want in the world means to possess wealth in the Hereafter. Every moment of the world destroys a person. One who honors the world is humiliated by it. One who hoards up for the world is thrown into want. The condition of the world is like poison. One who does not know it, eats it and therein there lies one's destruction. Live in the world like the person who treats his/her wound and bears hardship for a time for fear of long suffering and is patient towards bitter pills for fear of too many medicine. So fear this abode of deception, deceit and treachery. Treasures of the world were presented to our Messenger. Had he accepted them, he would not have received honor like the wing of a fly."

There is in Sacred Tradition in which God said to Moses, "When you see wealth coming to you, tell it, 'Punishment of sin will soon come.' When you see poverty coming to you, say, 'Welcome to you, thanks to the sign of the religious men.'"

If you like, follow Jesus as he used to say, "Hunger is my curry. Piety is my sign. Wool cloth is my dress. The sun's rays in winter is my provision. The morning is my lamp. My feet are my conveyances. What the earth grows is my food. I pass nights having nothing and I pass my days having nothing. Who is a richer man than I am?"

Uhab ibn Hunabal said, "When God sent Moses and Aaron to Pharaoh, He said, 'Don't fear him. His forelock is in my hand. He cannot move his tongue nor breathe without My permission.'"

Ali ibn Abi Talib said in a sermon, "O people, know that you are dead and you will be raised up after you are dead. Let not the life of the world deceive you. This world's life is surrounded by dangers and difficulties. Its destruction and its treachery are well known to all. What is therein will pass away along with the world and the world will roam in the midst of its votaries."

ILLUSTRATIONS OF THE WORLD

First illustration. The world is moving towards destruction. The world promises that it is lasting, but it breaks its promise immediately after that. Look to the world. It is motionless and steady, but in reality it is always moving.

Second illustration. The world is like the shade. Shade outwardly appears to be steady, but in reality it is moving and constantly drifting.

Third illustration. The world is like a dream of night and like the different ideas in a dream. The Messenger said, "The world is like a dream and like happiness and punishment in a dream." Yunus ibn Ubayd said, "I found myself like a sleeping man in the world. He sees what he likes and does not like and then he wakes up from sleep in this condition. Similarly the people are asleep and rise up at death."

Fourth illustration. Know, dear readers, that a person has three possibilities: One condition is that he/she was nothing at one time and that was before birth. The second possibility is that he/she will not see the world after death until the resurrection. The third possibility is the time between these two times—the time of life. This is the time of life's span. Now compare this short time with the endless time before and after. Jesus (ع) said, "The world is like a bridge. Cross it but do not live in it." This is a clear illustration as this world's life is drifting towards the next world. The beginning of this bridge is the birth place and the end is the grave. To construct houses on the road and to adorn them is foolishness in the extreme as it shall have to be crossed.

Fifth illustration. At first, it seems that there is joy and happiness in the world but it is difficult to get out of it safely. Ali ibn Abi Talib wrote to Salman Farsi, "The world is like a snake which is smooth to touch but whose poison is destructive. So be careful of what seems therefrom liking to you. When you are certain that you shall have to part from it, you should give up all thoughts about it. The more you enjoy the objects of happiness in the world, the more it will be the cause of your sorrows."

Sixth illustration. The Messenger said, "The person who is addicted to the world is like one who walks upon water. Can he walk upon water without getting his/her feet wet in the water? This is a lesson for those who think that their soul is pure although their body is in worldly happiness. Worldly attachment becomes a stumbling block to receiving pleasure from divine services." Jesus said, "I tell you with truth, the person addicted to this world does not receive pleasure from divine service just as a diseased person does not receive any taste from delicious foods. I tell you with truth, if you do not your riding animal hold under control, its nature will change and you will feel difficulty in riding on it. Similar is the condition of the mind. If you cannot keep the mind under control by constant Divine services and remembrance of death, it will become hard and harsh." The Messenger said, "There are difficulties and dangers in the world. The good work of any of you is like a pot. It is upper portion is clean, its inner portion is also clean and if its upper portion is unclean, its inner portion also is unclean."

Seventh illustration. The Messenger said, "The world is like a torn cloth from its beginning to end. The end of the cloth is hanging up with a thread which will soon be torn."

Eighth illustration. Jesus (ع) said, "The searcher for the world is like one who drinks the water of the sea. The more he/she drinks the salty water of the sea, the more his/her thirst will increase and ultimately he/she will meet with his/her end.

Ninth illustration. The temptations and greed of the world attract one to happiness as the greed for food is enjoyable to the belly. Everyone will see his/her greed of the world as an object of hatred at the time of his/her death as the delicious foods become obnoxious in the stomach. The more the food is delicious and tasteful, the more the stool gives out obnoxious smell. Similarly the more the temptations are delicious to the heart, the more it will become troublesome at the time of death. The more a person has worldly riches, the more are his/her pangs of separation at the time of death. What is the meaning of death except the leaving of worldly riches? The Messenger said, "God likened the world to the food of people and likened the food to the world."

Tenth illustration. The Messenger said, "What is this world in comparison with the next world? This world is like that scanty water which a finger catches when it is put into sea."

Eleventh illustration. This world is like a guest or rest house built for the travelers and not for permanent residence therein. The rest house is to be enjoyed only temporarily. This world is similarly a rest house for the travelers of the next world who will take benefit therefrom for their permanent residence.

SPECIAL KNOWLEDGE OF THE WORLD

What is the world? Which portion of the world is to be accepted and which to be rejected? Which is good in the world and which is bad? This world and the next world are two conditions of your mind. Everything before death is the world and everything after death is the next world. The things which gives you pleasure before death increase your greed and give you a taste for this world while the things which will give you pleasure after death are of the next world.

Three kinds of things are not this world: First, the things that will go to the next world with a person are knowledge and actions. The objects of knowledge are God, His Attributes, His Actions, His sovereignty over heaven and earth, and so forth. Actions mean the actions done for the sake of God and His satisfaction. The learned person is one who possesses these two attributes. To this person, knowledge of the former is greater, for which he/she gives up food, drink and even marriage as the happiness of the former is greater than that of the latter. This knowledge is a position of the world, yet it cannot be called world. It is included within the next world. A certain sage said, "I fear death as it will destroy my night prayer." Another sage said, "Oh God, give me strength in the grave to pray, to bow and prostrate." The Messenger said, "Three things of the world are dear to me: woman, perfume and prayer." Even prayer was considered as belonging to the world. The things which can be perceived by the five senses are of this world. Prayer is done by the movement of the bodily organs and therefore it is included within the world.

Second, these things are also not included within the world and these are such things as are absolutely necessary for a person in this world. What is not absolutely necessary is this world. What is not done for the next world is attachment to this world and not the next world, just as to enjoy lawful things in excess of necessity, to enjoy silver and gold, horse, cattle, landed property, houses and buildings, clothes and delicious foods of various kinds. Umar ibn al-Khattab reported that he had appointed Abu Darda as governor of the province of Hems. The governor erected a latrine at the cost of two dirhams. Umar wrote to him on hearing this news: "From Umar, Commander of the Faithful, to Abu Darda. You have ample worldly adornments in the palaces of Chosroes and Byzantines, but God purposes to destroy them. When this letter of mine reaches you, you and your family must come to Damascus and stay there until death." Umar thought it even unnecessary.

Third, the things of the third kind are in the intermediary between the above two classes. This is to work with the object of doing next worldly actions, such as taking food and drink only to save life, to wear coarse cloth only to cover one's private parts and to do such works from which there is no escape. So what is necessary of food and drink to save life and health is not world.

Three things will go with a person at the time of his death, purity of heart, satisfaction arising out of the remembrance of God, and engagement of mind in divine love. Purity of mind cannot be attained if one cannot control oneself from worldly passions and temptations. Satisfaction cannot be gained unless there is constant remembrance of God and keeping patience therein. These three things will be the cause of satisfaction. By death the existence of the human being does not end but one returns to God after separation from things dear to that person in the world. From this, it is known that a traveler towards the next world must necessarily possess three qualities—remembrance of God, good thoughts and meditation and pious actions which prevent the person from worldly greed. To such a person, the pleasures of the world are bitter. If there is no health, these qualities cannot be attained and health cannot be gained without a little quantity of food, dress and an abode for habitation. So these things are also necessary. If a person takes these things to the proportion of necessity with the object of the next world, that person cannot become addicted to the world. For such a person, the world is a seed ground for the future.

There are two classes of these things: Lawful and unlawful. Unlawful things lead to the punishment in the next world and lawful things stand as blocks to higher ranks. To wait for rendering account on the Day of Resurrection is a sort of punishment. The Messenger said, "There are accounts for the lawful things of the world and punishment for the unlawful things." He also said, "There is also punishment for the lawful things but this punishment is lighter than that of unlawful things."

So everything in the world is cursed, small or great, lawful or unlawful. The proportion of a thing which helps one gain piety is not world. One whose inner knowledge of God is strong takes great care of the world. Jesus (ε) once was sleeping, placing his head on a stone. The devil came to him and said, "You have become attached to the world." At this, he threw the stone at Satan. Prophet Solomon (ε) entertained his people with various dishes, but himself ate the husk of wheat. The Messenger was presented the treasures of the world, but he kept himself hungry for some days and bound stones around his belly to reduce the pangs of hunger. For this reason, the prophets and friends of God were given the most severe trials, so that they may enjoy eternal happiness in the next world. So what is not done for the sake of God is called this world and what is done for His sake is not this world.

Question. What are the things for the sake of God?

Answer. All things are divided into three classes. First, what is not done for the sake of God, such as wrongdoings or prohibited things and unnecessary lawful things. These are the things of the world. Second, what is done for the sake of God. Third, worldly actions done for the sake of God, such as food and drink, marriage etc. The second class of things are again sub-divided into three classes. First, remembrance about the creation of God, second, remembrance of God, and third, abstaining from worldly greed and passions. When these things are done for the sake of God and not for show, they appertain to the third class. They are food, drink, marriage etc. If they are done for the sake of God, they are next worldly actions, but if they are done to satisfy lust, they are worldly actions. The Messenger said, "One who searches lawful things of the world to show glory or boast will meet with God in His enraged condition, but one who searches the world to abstain from begging and to save oneself will come on the Resurrection Day with face bright as the full moon." God says, *"He who restrains himself from vain desires will have paradise as his destination"* (19:40.

Passion or vain desire is composed of five things. God says of them in the following verse, *"Know that this world's life is a mere sport, vain plays and adornment, mutual boast and increase in wealth and children"* (57:20). In another verse, seven things have been counted as vain desires (3:14): *"Men have been given the vain desires of women, children, hoarded wealth of silver and gold, horses of good quality, quadrupeds and crops. These are things of this world's life"*

Now you have come to know what is world and what is not world. Food, clothes and abode to the extent of utmost necessity and if done to please God are not world. What is in excess of these things is called world. There are things which are absolutely necessary and things which are simply necessary. There is the middle course between these two kinds which is best and the middle course keeps near the border line of absolute necessity.

The saint Uways Qarni was regarded by his countrymen as a mad as he subjected himself to the strictest rigors of life. They constructed for him a hut which he visited once a year or once in two or three years. He used to go out before the call for morning prescribed prayer and returned home after the night prescribed prayer. His food were the stones of dried grapes. He used to put on the torn pieces of cloth after sewing which he gathered from heaps of refugees in markets. Often the boys threw stones at him. He said to the boys, "Throw small stones as my ablution might break for bleeding if large stones are thrown at me." The Messenger sensed his actions with honor and said, "I am feeling the breath of God from the land of Yemen." This is a hint of the existence of Uways Qarni.

Haran ibn Hayan said, "When I heard this from Umar ibn al-Khattab. I came to Kufa and searched far Uways Qarni and found him at noon washing cloths in the bank of the Tigris. I found him strong and stout, with bald head, thick beard, and broad face." I asked him, "How are you, O Uways?"

He replied, "O Haran, son of Hayan, how are you? Who told you my address?"

I said, "God."

I wondered how he came to know my name when he had not seen me before. I asked him, "How have you come to know my name and the name of my father?"

He said, "The Almighty gave me this information. My soul recognized your soul when I talked with you. Similarly a believer can recognize another believer."

I said, "Tell me a Tradition of the Messenger."

He said, "I never met the Messenger (ﺹ), but I saw some of his Companions and heard some Traditions from them." Then he recited the Quranic verse, *"I have not created the heavens and earth and what is between them out of sport. I created them with truth, but most people do not know"* (44:39).

When he had recited this, he raised a loud shriek and said. "O Haran, your father Hayan has died and you will soon die. Adam, his wife Eve, prophets Noah, Abraham, Moses, David and even Muhammad, the world Messenger, died. Abu Bakr died and my friend Umar also has just expired. Alas, O Umar, alas, h Umar."

I said, "Umar has not died. I saw him alive when I left him."

He said, "My Lord has just now given me the news that Umar has died."

Then he said to me, "Walk in the path of God's Book and the

believers and pious believers. The news of your and my death have come. Don't be unmindful even for a twinkling of an eye. When you will return to your people, give sermons to them. Don't go a single steps from the community of the Muslims. Invoke for me and for you. Haran, I entrust you to God. May God shower mercy on you. You will not see me again. I am going this way and you go that way."

MEANING OF THIS WORLD AND THE NEXT WORLD

It will be clear to you from what has been described above that the things on which the sun casts its rays and the things which the earth grows are all included within the limit of this world, and the things if done for the sake of God and the things contrary to the above are the next world. Whatever is absolutely necessary to gain strength for Divine service is an action of the next world if taken in accordance with the wishes of God. If a pilgrim is on his way to pilgrimage and takes care of things necessary for his pilgrimage, such as provisions for himself/herself and his/her conveyance, the pilgrimage is not nullified because of this. He/she is engaged then in the actions of pilgrimage. Similarly the body is the carrier of soul and walks along the distance of life. So efforts to gain and preserve the strength of body to be able to acquire knowledge and good works are not called the world, but included within the next world. The saint Tanafusi said, "I was attached to the door of Banu Shaiba of the Kabah for seven days. On the eighth day, I heard an unknown voice say, 'Be careful, God makes the internal eye of one blind who takes from the world things in excess of what is necessary for him.'"

REAL KNOWLEDGE OF THE WORLD

Know dear readers, that the meaning of the world is: the things which exist in the world, the things to which people are connected, and the things for the adornment of which people are engaged.

The things which exist in the world are the earth and the things that are on it. God says, "*I have created whatever is in the earth as adornment in order to try who among them is best in action.*" The earth is a bed for the children of Adam and for their rest. Whatever is grown is divided into three classes: mineral substances, plants and animals. Animals include human beings, birds and beasts. Human beings want to subdue birds, beasts and even other human beings and call them slaves. They also want women for enjoyment. These are the world. Men love women, children, gold and silver, crops and quadruped animals.

Human beings have two connections with these things: internal and external. The meaning of internal connection is to love these things with the heart, to engage with them in enjoyments and to turn all thoughts to them. One's heart then becomes addicted to the world like a slave. For this reason, all evils, such as pride, treachery, show, hatred, name and fame, flattery, love of wealth enter the heart. This is the internal connection with the world.

The meaning of outer connection is that of the body to take recourse to business and industry. So there is the connection of mind with love and connection of body with the things. All the things are for food of the body, but food of the soul is the intention with which food is taken for the sake of God. The person who forgets his/her goal and soul living in the world is like the pilgrim who remains always engaged with his/her conveying animal and forgets his/her pilgrimage. The pilgrim towards the next world remembers his/her goal and does only what is necessary to take him/her to the destination.

Causes of engagement in the world: The three causes are to gather food, clothes and abode. Food is for preservation of the body, clothes are for the protection of the body from heat and cold, and an abode is for protection of the body and to keep away the causes of destruction of lives and wealth. God created these things for the benefit of humanity.

There are five necessary things for people which are the basis of industry and main causes of his engagement: cultivation, grazing, hunting, weaving and construction. Cultivation is for growing crops and food stuffs. Grazing is for maintaining beasts and quadrupeds. Weaving, is for making cloth and dresses and construction is for making houses for habitation. For smooth living, administrative works, judicial works and military works are necessary. So mankind is divided into three classes from the point of view of these works: cultivators and industrialists, soldiers, and officers of government.

Religious people are of different classes. One class of religious people think that this world is a house of dangers, difficulties and labor and think also that they will be owners of fortune in the next world irrespective of their actions being good or bad. Another class of religious people think that natural passions must be uprooted for salvation and it is not sufficient only to bring them under control. Another class think that it is impossible to observe religious rules and that God has no necessity for the divine service of people. Another class think that Divine service is not necessary as it is sufficient to have knowledge of God. Another class of religious people rightly think that there is salvation in following the prophets especially the last Messenger of Arabia, Muhammad ibn Abd Allah (ص). They do not give up the world nor uproot their passions. They take from the world whatever is absolutely necessary for them. The Messenger said that out of many parties, only one party will receive salvation. The Companions asked, "O Messenger of God, who are they?" He said, "People who follow the *sunnah* and the community." The Messenger was asked, "Who are the people of the *sunnah* (i. e., those who follow the Divine Law) and community?" He said, "Those who tread my path and the path of my Companions. They did not take the world for its sake but for religion. They did not give up the world, but in reality they pulled back from the world. They adopted the middle course in their actions and did not go to extremes."

14

ON SPIRITUAL FASTING

Muhyiddin Abdul Qadir Gilani

T he author of this essay, Shaykh Muhyiddin Abd al-Qadir Gilani (d. 1166) is one of the foremost Sufi masters. At the age of eighteen, he went to Baghdad in search of inner knowledge. This was the same year that al-Ghazzali left Baghdad and government employment work in quest of the same inner knowledge. Shaykh Gilani is the founder of the Qadiriyyah order of Sufism. In this essay, the Shaykh emphasizes the fasting of truth which is to go beyond what the average person does when he or she performs the prescribed fast.

The Editor

T he fasting prescribed by religion is to abstain from eating, drinking and sexual intercourse from dawn to sunset, while spiritual fasting is, in addition, to protect all the senses and thoughts from all that is unlawful. It is to abandon all that is disharmonious, inwardly as well as outwardly. The slightest breach of that intention breaks the prescribed fast. Religious fasting is limited by time, while spiritual fasting is forever and lasts throughout one's temporal and eternal life. This is true fasting.

Muhammad (ﷺ) says, "There are many of those who perform the prescribed fast who get only hunger and thirst for their efforts and no other benefit." There are also those who break their prescribed fast when they eat, and those whose fast continues even after they have eaten. These are the ones who keep their senses and their thoughts free of evil and their hands and their tongues from hurting others. It is for these that God Most High promises, "Fasting is a deed done for My sake, and I am the one who gives its reward." About the two kinds of fasting Muhammad (ﷺ) says, 'The one who fasts has two satisfactions. One is when he breaks his fast at the end of the day. The other is when he sees his Lord."

Those who know the outer form of the religion say that the first satisfaction of the one who performs the prescribed fast is the pleasure of eating after a day of fasting, and the meaning of the satisfaction 'when he sees his Lord' is when someone who performed the prescribed fast the whole month of Ramadan sees the new moon marking the end of the prescribed fast and beginning the festivities of the holiday. The ones who know the inner meaning of the prescribed fast say that the joy of ending the prescribed fast is the day when the believer will enter paradise and partake of the delights therein. The meaning of the greater joy of seeing is when the faithful sees the truth of God with the secret eye of the heart.

Worthier than these two kinds of prescribed fasting is the fast of truth which is prevents the heart from worshipping any other than the Essence of God. It is performed by rendering the eye of the heart blind to all that exists, even in the secret realms outside of this world, except the love of God. For although God has created all and everything for the human being, He has created the human being only for Himself. He says, "The human being is My secret and I am his/her secret." That secret is a light from the Divine Light of God. It is the center of the heart made out of the finest of matter. It is the self which knows all the secret truths. It is the secret connection between the created one and his/her Creator. That secret does not love nor lean towards anything other than God.

There is nothing worthy to wish for, there is no other goal, no other beloved in this world and in the hereafter, except God. If an atom of anything other than the love of God enters the heart, the fast of truth, the true fast, is broken. Then one has to make it up, to revive that wish and intention, to return back to His love, here and in the hereafter, for God says, *"Prescribed fasting is only for Me, and only I give its reward."*

PART FIVE:
ENERGIZERS

15

THERAPEUTICS
OF PRESCRIBED FASTING

Shahid Athar

Like other Muslims, I perform the prescribed fast during the month of Ramadan. I do so not because of its medical benefits or for losing weight. I fast because God has so commanded us to. The Quran says, *"Oh you who believe, fasting is prescribed for you, as it was prescribed for those before you so that you may earn self restraint."* (2:183)

It is my experience that within the first few days of Ramadan, I begin to feel better even before losing a single pound. I work more and pray more; physical stamina and mental alertness improve. As I have my own lab in the office, I usually check my chemistry, that is, blood glucose, cholesterol, triglyceride before the commencement of Ramadan and at its end. As I am not overweight, thank God, weight loss is minimal. The few pounds I lose, I regain soon after fasting in Ramadan will be a great blessing for the overweight whether with or without mild diabetes (Type II). It benefits those also who are giving to smoking or nibbling. They can rid themselves of these addictions in this month.

PHYSIOLOGY OF EATING AND FASTING

Food is needed by the body to provide energy for immediate use by burning up carbohydrates, that is, sugar. Excess of carbohydrates which cannot be used are stored up as fat tissue in muscles, and as glycogen in the liver for future use. Insulin, a hormone from the pancreas, lowers blood sugar and diverts it to other forms of energy storage, that is, glycogen. To be effective, insulin has to be bound to binding sites called the receptors. Obese people lack receptors; therefore they cannot utilize their insulin. This leads to diabetes.

When one performs the prescribed fast or decreases carbohydrate intake drastically, it lowers his/her blood glucose and insulin level. This causes the breakdown of glycogen from liver and of fat from adipose tissue to provide glucose for energy needs.

EFFECTS OF SEMI-STARVATION DIETS

On the basis of human physiology described above, semi-starvation (ketogenic) diets have been devised for effective weight control. These diets provide calculated amounts of protein in divided doses with plenty of water, multi-vitamins, etc. These effectively lower weight and blood sugar, but because of their side effects, they should be used only under supervision of physicians.

EFFECTS OF TOTAL FASTING

Total fasting reduces or eliminates hunger and causes rapid weight loss. In 1975, Allan Cott in his *Fasting as a Way of Life* noted, "Fasting brings a wholesome physiological rest for the digestive tract and central nervous system and normalizes metabolism." It must be pointed out, however, that there are also many adverse effects of total fasting.

PRESCRIBED FASTING IN RAMADAN

Prescribed fasting is different from any of the above diet plans. Prescribed fasting has beneficial features of both plans. Its unique medical benefits are due to the following factors.

As compared to other diet plans, in performing the pre-scribed fast during Ramadan, there is no malnutrition or inad-equate calorie intake since there is no restriction on the type or amount of food intake during the post-sunset ending of the fast nor the pre-dawn meal. This was confirmed by M. M. Hussaini during Ramadan 1974 when he conducted dietary analysis of Muslim students at the State University of North Dakota at Fargo. He concluded that calorie intake of Muslim students during fasting was at two-thirds of NRC-RDA.

Prescribed fasting in Ramadan is voluntarily undertaken. It is not a prescription imposed by a physician. In the hypothala-mus part of the brain there is a center called "lipostat" which controls the body mass. When severe and rapid weight loss is achieved by a starvation diet, the center does not recognize this as normal and, therefore, reprograms itself to cause weight gain rapidly once the person goes off the starvation diet. So the only effective way of losing weight is slow, self-controlled and grad-ual weight loss by modifying behavior and one's attitude about eating while eliminating excess food. Ramadan is a month of self-regulation and self-training in terms of food intake thereby causing, hopefully, a permanent change in lipostat reading.

God does not want to punish Muslims, as in the case of total fast; nor does He want to subject them to a diet of selective food only (i.e. protein only, fruit only types of diets). God wants them to enjoy every lawful thing. As breakfast, medically is the most important meal of the day, the pre-dawn meal is recommended by the Messenger. Likewise, the post-sunset breaking of the prescribed fast is needed in the evening when the prescribed fast is broken. Hypoglycemia (low blood sugar) which is normal at the end of the prescribed fast, is wisely treated with some-thing sweet such as dates or juice.

THERAPEUTIC EFFECTS OF THE SPECIAL PRAYER

In order to utilize (metabolize) the extra amount of food eaten during the post-sunset ending of the fast and dinner, additional prayers are prescribed which are twenty cycles. Using a calorie counter, I counted that ten extra calorie output is used for each cycle of the special night prayer. Thus, the special night prayer should burn up ten times twenty or 200 calories. Moreover, the night prayer is a better form of physical exercise than aerobic exercises because it is mild and uses all the muscles and joints of the body.

Prescribed fasting in Ramadan is actually an exercise in self-regulation and training. For those who smoke continuously, nibble food al the time or drink coffee every hour, it is the best time to reprogram themselves into moderation.

MENTAL EFFECTS
OF RAMADAN PRESCRIBED FASTING

Muhammad (ﷺ) advises us, "If one slanders you or aggresses against you, say, 'I am performing the prescribed fasting.'" (al-Hakim). There is a peace and tranquillity of mind in Ramadan. Personal hostility is at a minimum and crime rates decrease. These effects are not only spiritual, but also due to metabolic factors. Sometimes abnormal behavior is related to outbursts of hormones like epinephrine or too much or too little thyroid and testosterone and low or high blood sugar. All these parameters are made more even in their secretions instead of the wide fluctuations which occur in one's day-to-day life. It may be hoped that peace and tranquillity as a psychological state of mind will, after a month's training in Ramadan, tend to become a normal part of life.

PRESCRIBED FASTING AND MEDICAL PATIENTS

Insulin dependent diabetics and those taking heart and blood pressure medicines should not perform the prescribed fast unless approved and supervised by their physicians; otherwise, their condition will get worse. They can perform the prescribed fast after making some adjustments in their medicine, that is, instead of Inderal four times a day, one can use long acting Inderal (Inderal LA 80) or eliminate Regular Insulin and lower the dose (by 1/3) of intermediate insulin.

QUESTIONS AND ANSWERS

I have been asked questions by Muslim patients, a few of

which I share with you here.

Question 1: I am pregnant. Should I perform the prescribed fast or not? How do I know if I am causing any damage to my baby if I do so?

Answer: This is not an easy situation. Pregnancy is not a medical illness, therefore, the same exemption does not apply. There is no mention of such exemption in the Quran. However, the Messenger said that pregnant and nursing women do not perform the prescribed fast. This is in line with God not wanting anyone, even a small fetus, to suffer. There is no way of knowing the damage to the unborn child until the delivery and that might be too late. In my humble opinion, during the first and third trimester (three months) women should not perform the prescribed fast. If, however, Ramadan happens to come during the second trimester (4th-6th months) of pregnancy, a woman may elect to perform the prescribed fast provided that, first of all, her own health is good and second, it is done with the permission of her obstetrician and under close supervision. The possible damage to the fetus may not be from malnutrition provided the post-sunset ending of the fast and the pre-dawn meal are adequate, but from dehydration, from prolonged (10-14 hours) abstinence from water.

Question 2: I'm diabetic. Should I perform the prescribed fast and if so, how should I adjust my insulin dosage?"

Answer: Diabetics who are controlled by diet alone can perform the prescribed fast and hopefully with weight reduction, their diabetes may even be cured or at least improved. Diabetics who are taking oral hypoglycemic agents like Orinase along with the diet should exercise extreme caution if they decide to perform the prescribed fast. They should reduce their dose to one-third and take the drug not in the morning, but with the post-sunset ending of the fast. If they develop low blood sugar symptoms in the daytime, they should immediately break their prescribed fast.

Diabetics taking insulin should not perform the prescribed fast. If they do, at their own risk, they should do so under close medical supervision and make drastic changes in the insulin dose. For example, eliminate regular insulin altogether and take only NPH in divided doses after the post-sunset ending of the fast or before the pre-dawn meal. Diabetics, if they perform the prescribed fast, should still take a diabetic diet during the post-sunset ending of the prescribed fast and the pre-dawn meal and dinner. The sweet snacks eaten in Ramadan are not good for their illness.

Question 3: I have high blood pressure and I am taking several medications that need to be given every 4-6 hours. Should I perform the prescribed fast and if so, how should I adjust my medication?

Answer: Those who have mild to moderate high blood pressure along with being overweight should be encouraged to perform the prescribed fast since it may help to lower their blood pressure. They should see their physician to adjust medicines. For example, the dose of the water pill (diuretic) should be reduced for fear of dehydration and long acting agents like Inderal LA or Tenormin can be given once a day before the pre-dawn meal. Those with severe hypertension or heart disease should not perform the prescribed fast at all.

Question 4: I have noted that prescribed fasting aggravates m;y migraine headache. What should I do?

Answer: Even in tension headache, dehydration or low blood sugar will aggravate the symptoms, but in migraine during prescribed fasting, there is an increase in blood free fatty acids which will directly effect the severity or precipitation of migraine through release of catecholamines. Patients with migraines are advised not to perform the prescribed fast.

Question 5: While performing the prescribed fast, I caught a bad flu. Should I continue with prescribed fasting or break it to take medication?

Answer: During flu, rest is the best treatment and medications are not of much proven value. One should be his or her own judge of the condition and decide if he or she is sick enough to break the prescribed fast and to take antihistamines, aspirin or whatever is necessary.

In summary, medical patients are not encouraged to perform the prescribed fast, but if they want to, they should first consult their physician.

I want to end this article with a saying from the Messenger, "If one does not abandon falsehood in words and deed, God has no need for his abandoning his food and drink." (*Bukhari*)

16

MEDICAL BENEFITS OF PRESCRIBED FASTING

Ebrahim Kazim

S cience is in a state of continuous evolution and discoveries follow one upon another. There is a large flow of information, recently computerized, coming like a spring from symposia and medical journals yet few are studying traditional religious methods of maintaining well-being which this author does.

The Editor

H omeostasis or the normal steady state of the body is maintained during the prescribed fast in the month of Ramadan because it lasts approximately fourteen hours. of being a result of co-ordinated physiological mechanisms. Those disturbances due to changes in the human being's external or internal environment are automatically adjusted and normalcy is evidenced in the following values:

1. There is no significant alteration in routine hematology or serum electrolytes.[1]

2. Liver function tests, including SGOT, SGPT, Alkaline Phosphates, Thymol Turbidity and cephalin-cholesterol floccu-

lation tests are normal. Serum albumin, globulin and total serum proteins are normal. The constancy of the serum globulin level during fasting ensures any tendency to deficient antibody formation.[2]

3. Plasma cholecystokinin and gastric levels are normal.[3]

4. The basal metabolic rate is normal.[4] The protein-bound iodine is normal.[5] (Only when fasting is prolonged does the basal metabolic rate fall as does voluntary physical activity, thus conserving calories, and this ensures that loss of weight is not excessive. With the fall in BMR, the pulse rate and the blood pressure also fall. The concentrator of T3 also falls.[6] Serum angiotensin-converting enzyme activity (ACE) is reduced during fasting. However, it may be the low T3 level in fasting that produces a fall in B.P. rather than the reduced ACE.[7]

5. Weight is unaffected depending on the intake and expenditure of energy. In fact, some Muslims put on weight during Ramadan, due to excess food intake.

6. Glomerular filtration rate is normal, and the urine specific gravity remains constant throughout:[8] Blood urea nitrogen is normal.

7. Blood glucose concentration is maintained normally at 80 mgms.% with hepatic production of glucose Squalling utilization, mainly by the brain, which oxidizes approximately 100 Gms. glucose per minute to CO_2 and H_2O. The brain alone consumes 1/3 to 1/4 of the total calories, or about 500 Kcal./day. Even the most concentrated brain work causes no extra demands on caloric output. After 12 hours of fasting, the glucose level in the capillary blood approximates to that in the venous blood.[9]

During the first few hours of a fast, the increased glucagon and the decreased insulin secretion result in stimulation of hepatic gylcogenolysis, and the gradual depletion of the hepatic glycogen store. As the level of glucose falls, the rate of insulin secretion decreases and that of glucagon rises. The secretory pattern of these two islet hormones is actually pulsatile rather than continuous, the pulse interval being approximately 10 minutes in humans.[10] The rate of hepatic glucose production is dynamically changing in synchrony with the pulsing hormonal signals. Under normal circumstances, the plasma glucose falls more slowly during the transition from the fed to the fasted state and stabilizes at levels well above 50 mgms.%. Muscle, fat and the brain are the main glucose consumers.

8. During fasting, the secretion of ACTH and cortisol is normal.[11] The peak of the circadian rhythm in human plasma cortisol concentration normally occurs approximately at the time of waking in the morning, and the nadir occurs near the onset of sleep, in subjects maintained on a normal day/night schedule. Reversal of the phase of lighting schedule results in a reversal of the corticosteroid rhythm. (However, when fasting acts as a stress, ACTH is secreted, leading to a discharge of adrenal corticoids. Glucocorticoids stimulate gluconeogenesis and regulate the blood sugar level during fasting. Glucocorticoids help to maintain normal glomerular filtration rate and blood pressure. They protect the body against the harmful effects of antigen-antibody reaction).

9. The fasting stomach is empty and contracted. The rate of bile secretion is low and the pressure in the bile duct is correspondingly small.[12]

ADVERSE CIRCUMSTANCES

However, if there are adverse circumstances surrounding the prescribed fast in Ramadan such as (a) dehydration due to excessive sweating because of hot weather or exercise, (b) if too little food or water was available at the pre-dawn breakfast, or (c) if fasting was prolonged for any reason, the following changes may be observed: If the diet is otherwise normal, the renal blood flow remains unchanged even after 4 days of complete deprivation of water. There would be no decrease in plasma volume and no hemoconcentration, because the interstitial reserves will be called upon. Then the urinary output will be reduced to approximately one ounce/hour.[13] In water deprivation, the posterior lobe of the pituitary gland secretes antidiuretic hormone which reduces urine flow to a minimum, thus conserving water. The total water content of the body decreases due to loss of extracellular water. Urinary acidity is increased.

BODY PHYSIOLOGY IN PROGRESSIVE STARVATION

During fasting, the subject must live on his own body tissues for energy purposes. In a 70 Kgm. man, stored carbohydrate totals about 2000 Kcal., available from 100 Gms. of liver glycogen, 380 Gms. of muscle glycogen and 20 Gms. of glucose in extracellular fluid. In contrast, 140,000 Kcal. are available as stored fat, and the remainder in proteins. Energy is stored in adipose tissue as triglyceride, with glucose serving as the main source formed during glycolysis in the fat cells.

The blood sugar is maintained at a steady level during fasting, the glucose being formed in the liver from glycogen and from neutral fats which have been mobilized in adipose tissue. The main source of energy is glucose derived from glycogenolysis in the liver followed by ample energy source from fat reserves. Even if no physical work is done, about 2000 Kcal. will be needed daily, although the average requirement of a man doing light work is about 3000 Kcal. Even without activity, 500 Gms. of glycogen can maintain the body for 24 hours. The available energy from fat and protein reserves of the body will be sufficient to maintain life for approximately a month or so. In the prescribed fast of 14 hours or so, the body proteins are not used up, as the glycogen stores are the first to be used up at the beginning of the fast.

The function of the brain is critically dependent on an adequate level of glucose in the blood above 50 mgms. Thus at any time during the fast, a balance is reached at a plasma, glucose level sufficient to prevent excessive depletion of stored nutrients. [14] The gradual decrease of plasma glucose is the primary signal causing decrease of insulin secretion. The decrease of insulin level goes hand in hand with a moderate increase of glucagon level during fasting.[15] Together, insulin and glucagon increase the release of both stored and newly synthesized glucose into the blood. The decline of insulin also decreases glucose uptake by muscle and increases the plasma level of free fatty acids, which spare the glucose for the brain. Under the relatively low concentrations of insulin and glucose that prevail in the fasted state, especially during the afternoons of the prescribed fast, little glucose is metabolized by the muscle and the predominant fuel are the free fatty acids. After a meal such as the post-sunset meal when plasma insulin and glucose increase, the liver and the muscle may take up most of the glucose circulating in the blood. Insulin stimulates glycogen, fat and also protein synthesis. Some of the excess glucose transported into the muscle after the post-sunset meal undergoes glyc. ysis, especially during the Special Night Prayer (*tarawih*). If there is a lot of glucose circulating in the blood, it may spill into the urine, especially after the pre-dawn meal, probably because we eat the pre-dawn meal faster.

However, if there is at all a tendency to hypoglycemia, the adrenal medulla immediately secretes increased amounts of catecholeamines, viz. adrenaline and noradrenaline, which prepare the body for "fight or flight." Adrenaline increases hepatic glycogenolysis. Both adrenaline and noradrenaline increase coronary artery blood flow. These amines act on organs supplied by the sympathetic nervous system, and help the body to withstand any state of emergency. Secretion of adrenaline from the adrenal medulla in response to a fall in blood sugar leads to the breakdown of liver glycogen to glucose and a compensatory rise in the blood sugar.

Adrenaline mobilizes liver glycogen and provides glucose for the active tissues, especially the brain where glucose utilization has to continue during fasting; the blood sugar is maintained by suppression of insulin secretation.

If the rate of fall of plasma glucose was very rapid, say to below 50 mgms.%, the glucoreceptors in the CNS and spinal cord are activated, and this will stimulate the sympathetic nervous system outflow to the liver, adipose tissue, muscle and adrenal medulla.[16] The local release of noradrenaline and increased level of circulating adrenaline cause increased coronary blood flow, relax smooth muscle of the gastrointestinal tract while contracting the sphincters. They also relax bronchiolar smooth muscle. The metabolic effects of catecholamines are:

(a) Liver : increased glycogenolysis and gluconeogenesis.

(b) Muscle : increased glycogenolysis.

(c) Adipose tissue: increased lipolysis and heat production.

(d) Kidneys : release renin and increase systolic blood pressure.

(e) Pancreas :

(1) A cells: increases glucagon release and plasma glu cose is increased.

(2) B cells. Depresses insulin release and hence plasma glucose is increased.

If the period of starvation is unduly prolonged, which does NOT occur with the prescribed fast of Ramadan, unless the subject takes negligible amounts of post-sunset and pre-dawn meals, the following changes occur: The catecholamines activate the lipolytic pathway in adipose tissue and the glygenolytic pathway in muscle.[17] These events provide the alternate fuel, the FFA (Free Fatty acids). A major determinant of the fuel adaptation to starvation is glucose requirement as the sole energy fuel for the brain. Because the other tissues can use the more abundant FFA, FFA becomes the dominant fuel for skeletal muscle, heart and other tissues, thus sparing glucose for the brain. Under further hypoglycemic tendencies, FFA is taken up to the liver and converted to acetoacetic acid and beta hydroxybutyric acid, and then released into the circulation. These are water-soluble and are readily oxidized by all tissues including the brain, thus providing approximately 50% of the energy fuel for the brain.

Hyperketonemia and hyperuroecemia are found during total caloric starvation,[18] but not in semi-starvation as in the prescribed fast. Semi-starved persons are hungry, unlike the totally starved. During starvation, the circulation and the CNS activities are maintained whatever the cost to less essential parts of the body.

In further starvation, when most of the gylcogen and fat reserves of the body are depleted, the amino acids, from the protein breakdown in the muscles, become a major precursor for the obligate glucose production necessary to support brain metabolism, until death ensues.

FASTING AND MAGNESIUM

During fasting, the serum magnesium is increased. The following points about magnesium are worthy of note.

(1) Several actions of magnesium ion can contribute towards its cardioprotective effects and hence magnesium is now more frequently used in the treatment of heart attacks.

Plasma magnesium levels are low for a day or two after myocardial infarction, and chances of patients recovering from a heart attack.[19] are increased if magnesium is given immediately after a heart attack Fasting halves the mortality rate in myocardial infarction, probably by reducing the risk of serious arrhythmias, especially ventricular fibrillation induced by raised local concentrations of catecholamines. Magnesium deficiency increases coronary artery tone.

Magnesium also has anti-platelet effects and hence, prevents extension of the thrombus. Magnesium deficiency favors thrombosis. Magnesium also acts as a vasodilator and prevents vascular stasis.

(2) Magnesium and calcium ions are inversely related. Ca and Mg ions compete with each other.[20] Magnesium inhibits calcium influx into myocardial cells. Magnesium deficiency can cause coronary spasm, correctable by giving calcium channel blockers.[21] When magnesium level is lowered, calcium is raised and may be deposited in tissues. Potassium acts as a cardio-protector in cardiac ischaemia in synergism with magnesium. Potassium in combination with magnesium produces more reduction in systolic and diastolic B.P. than magnesium alone.

(3) Magnesium acts on mitochondria and cell nuclei, and is essential for activity of many enzymes, especially for phosphorylation and energy transfer. Phosphates bind magnesium in the bowel and prevent its absorption. A 12 oz. can of carbonated soft drink might contain 30 mgms. of phosphate and could take up an equivalent amount of dietary magnesium. Average daily requirement of magnesium is 300-400 mgms. while an

average diet provides 250-500 mgms. daily. Signs and symptoms of hypomagnesemia occur usually at serum level below 1 mg.% but there may be other coexistent electrolyte disturbances e.g. hypocalcemia and hypokalemia. Hypocalcemia is partially explained by the fact that parathyroid hormone secretion is inhibited with hypomagnesemia.[22]

(4) Magnesium is a membrane stabilizer acting on the Na/K/Ca flux at the membrane level. When acting (a) on the specialized conducting system of the heart, it relieves cardiac dysrhythmia and therefore prevents sudden death in myocardial infarction; (b) on the vascular muscle cell of the coronary artery, it dilates the coronary arteries and relieves angina; (c) on the cell membrane of the neurons, it blocks transmission of nerve impulses, thus reducing neuro-muscular irritability. Magnesium therapy has a beneficial effect on most neuropathies; (d) on synapses, it relieves cerebral dysrhythmia and hence it is useful in various types of epilepsy; (e) on neuromuscular junctions, it prevents leg cramps; (f) on the bronchiolar muscle tissue, it relieves asthma; (g) on the uterus, it prevents hemorrhage and premature births. Magnesium deficiency during pregnancy can result in migraine, pregnancy-associated high B.P., low birth-weight babies, miscarriages and still births.

(5) Magnesium and Atheroma: (a) In atheroma, the arteries become hard and rusty due to deposits of cholesterol, beta-lipoproteins, aggregates of calcium, etc. all clumped together into a substance called phosphate-lipidcalcium complex. This deposit narrows the lumen of the arteries and may occlude them, aided by thrombosis. Fasting prevents the formation of atheroma as well as dissolves atheromatous plaques. During fasting, there is a lowering of serum cholesterol, phospholipid, triglyceride and insulin levels, all these factors depending on the quality and the quantity of food ingested at the pre-dawn meal. Fasting probably takes an active part in rejuvenating processes in the body through many channels, one being the reversal of atheroma and making the arteries more supple and pliable.

(6) Magnesium increases the fibrinlolytic activity of the

blood, which leads to prevention and also dissolution of any clot just formed.

(7) Both systemic and also pulmonary hypertension artificially produced in rats, could be normalized by addition of magnesium in the diet. There is a magnesium-lipid connection evidenced by high cholesterol-low magnesium diet in rabbits which produced much more atheroma than when they were on a high cholesterol-high magnesium diet.[23]

(8) Magnesium is also a powerful dilator of arteries, e.g. coronary and cerebral arteries, and hence, it is useful in ischaemic heart disease, angina pectoris, systemic and pulmonary hypertension, chronic skin ulcers, coronary and cerebral thrombosis. Other benefits attributed to magnesium are prevention of some complications of pregnancy, e.g. abortions and miscarriages.[24] However, recently, no association was found between a low dietary intake of magnesium and adverse outcome—pre-eclampsia, preterm labor, and infants small for gestational age. Magnesium is also beneficial in thyrotoxicosis, as well as to reduce the size of toxic and nontoxic goiter. Magnesium is also claimed to be useful in vertigo of undetermined etiology, and also in Miniere's syndrome. Magnesium can also prevent renal lithiasis, particularly calcium oxalate stones.

(9) Magnesium requirement is increased during stress, be it physical or psychological. Serum magnesium content is low in chronic alcoholics and in presence of delirium tremens.

(10) While acting as a membrane stabilizer on the intestinal mucosa, it may prevent, by some as yet unexplained mechanism, the absorption of any harmful atherogenic or other harmful component of the antigen-antibody reaction related to milk proteins, beef, egg proteins and others. It has not been conclusively demonstrated that magnesium can block absorption of any carcinogens, but the possibility cannot be ruled out.

(11) Magnesium therapy is also useful in decreasing gastrointestinal motility, when given parenterally.

FASTING WITH UNDERFEEDING

It has been observed that underfed animals live longer than their heavily fed counterparts. They also tend to suffer fewer illness including auto-immune diseases, which may help to explain their longevity. Inflammatory symptoms of rheumatoid arthritis in human beings, decrease during fasting.[25] Moreover, there are certain diseases which are benefited by loss of weight through fasting and caloric restriction e.g. hypertension, diabetes, obesity, osteoarthritis, radiculopathies, etc. We should not overeat at the post-sunset and pre-dawn meals if we wish to lose some weight. Weight reduction increases adipose tissue lipo-protein lipase responsiveness.[26]

If each of us eats one morsel of food less per meal and if we ensure that that morsel is transported to the needy, there would be 1000 million morsels of food for free distribution at each meal, considering that there are over one billion Muslims in this world. Prophet Muhammad (ص) is reported to have said that a plate of food for one is good for two. If, in fact, we really share our plate, then there should not be left a single hungry mouth whatsoever on the face of this earth. However, some countries, unfortunately, dump the excess food produce, to maintain their economy.

There is also an incident reported in the Traditions that once Prophet Muhammad (ص) was asked as to why such and such a tribe lived so long. He replied that they would not eat until and unless they were really hungry and that they would stop eating before their appetites were filled. He used to have a light post-sunset and a light pre-dawn meal. If after Ramadan is over, we find that we have put on weight instead of losing some, we better look critically at ourselves. It is obvious that we have not followed the practice of the Prophet.

FASTING AND GROWTH

During fasting there is increased secretion of growth hormone by the pituitary.[27] The following points about growth hormone are noteworthy: The Growth hormone, called somatotropin, is secreted by the pituitary gland. This growth hormone secretion is regulated by a G.H. inhibitory factor called somatostatin and a G.H. releasing factor (GRF).[28] Somatotropin is not only present in the hypothalamus but throughout the nervous system and the gut.[29] The G.H. acts through a second hormone (somatomedin C or insulin growth factor I), which is synthesized and released into the circulation by the growth hormone on hepatocytes. G.H. is necessary for normal growth of most of the soft tissues and of the skeleton, but it is not capable of promoting normal growth in the absence of thyroid hormone, glucocorticoids, gonadal steroids and insulin. The complex system that encompasses the release and action of G.H. includes many neuro-transmitters, hormones and organs.

More G.H. is released at night than during the day, especially during the first one and one-half hours of sleep. The plasma G.H. concentration rises steeply soon after onset of sleep and additional pulses of G.H. secretion occur primarily during the first half hour of the sleep period. The addition of daytime naps to the sleep activity cycle results in pulses of G.H. secretion during the nap periods. Sleep stages 3 and 4 (slow-wave sleep) occur more frequently in early sleep when G.H. secretion is maximal. More G.H. is released during afternoon naps than in morning naps. The G.H. rhythm, like that of cortisol, undergoes large amplitude oscillations, but is unlike the cortisol rhythm in its dependence on the sleep activity cycle.[30] The half-life of circulating G.H. in humans is 20-30 minutes.[31] Annual rhythms have been observed in the plasma concentration of G.H. which may be a beneficial factor in Muslims who fast regularly in each and every month of Ramadan. Not only the amount, but also the daily secretion pattern of frequency and amplitude of pulsatile G.H. secretion is vital for the maintenance of normal Insulin Growth Factor I and growth velocity.[32]

After G.H. is released into the circulation, it travels to the liver & other tissues, including chondrocytes in growing cartilage. In the liver and in cells of other tissues, G.H. stimulates production of pro-insulin Growth Factor (IGF 1 & IGF 11). Insulin Growth Factor 1 treatment can reverse weight loss induced by starvation.[33] It also reduces protein breakdown in the fasted state.[34]

G.H. is a protein anabolic hormone and produces a positive nitrogen and phosphorous balance. It stimulates erythropoiesis,[35] and increases gastro-intestinal absorption of calcium.

G.H. causes renal retention and body storage of Ca, P. Na, K as part of its generalized anabolic activity. G.H. is responsible for the elevated level of serum alkaline phosphates in growing children.[36] G.H. stimulates proportionate growth of the body by causing (1) skeletal growth, (2) growth of muscles, (3) growth of other organs.

The effects of G.H. secretion on protein metabolism, cartilage and growth are not due to a direct action of G.H. Instead, G.H. stimulates the liver to produce those sulfation factors responsible for stimulation of DNA and RNA synthesis, and collagen formation. There is a variety of growth factors called somatomedins, such as insulin growth factor I and II nerve growth factor, epidermal growth factor, fibrolast growth factor and others. Other actions of G.H. that appear to be direct rather than somatomedin-mediated include stimulation of erythropoiesis, increased insulin response to insulinogenic stimuli, and increased cellular uptake of aminoacids.

Levels of G.H. increase in the blood (a) during fasting and hypoglycemia, (b) after physical exercise, (c) after couple of hours of sleep, (d) with stress, including psychological stress. Stimuli that decrease secretion are REM sleep, glucose and cortisol.[37]

Physiological effects of G.H. are: (1) increased protein synthesis, (2) intracellular lipolysis, (3) stimulation of collagen synthesis. This latter may be responsible for the observation that the skin of Muslims who fast regularly during the month of Ramadan, does not wrinkle even when they are old, (4) stimulation of chondroitin-sulfate synthesis. G.H. accelerates chondrogensis, and as cartilaginous epiphysial plates widen they lay down more matrix at the end of long bones. In this way, stature is increased. In cartilage, G.H. stimulates proliferation of columnar cells and the incorporation of phosphates, and the synthesis of collagen.[38] Unlike anabolic steroids, G.H. causes no acceleration of the maturation of the bones.[39] Hence, children can safely fast during Ramadan from an early age.

G.H. increases gluconeogenesis from fat and proteins, causes loss of body fat and increased muscle mass with increased protein synthesis in muscle. Cardiac muscle glycogen is increased during fasting, unlike glycogen content of the liver and skeletal muscle. G.H. stimulates reticulocytes, suggesting stimulation of lymphopoiesiss. G.H. increases circulating FFA levels, which provides a ready source of energy for the tissues during hypoglycemia and other stressful stimuli. G.H. increases the ability of the pancreas to respond to insulinogenic stimuli such as glucose. This is an additional way G.H. promotes growth, since insulin has an anabolic action. However, the response of G.H. to hypoglycemia, fasting and exercise are reduced in obese patients.[40]

The background activity of the brain is called EEG and can be recorded with scalp electrodes. The dominant frequency and amplitude characteristic of the surface EEG vary with states of arousal.

Relaxed wakefulness in an adult with mind wandering and eyes closed, is accompanied by alpha waves, 8-12 Hz. (cycles/sec), 50 micro-volts, most marked in the parieto-occipital areas. These waves disappear when the subject opens his eyes. In addition to the dominant alpha rhythm, beta rhythm is seen symmetrically in the frontal regions characterized by waves of 13-30 Hz of low voltage (10-20 micro-volts), and are associated with intense mental activity. Theta activity with a pattern of large regular waves occurs in normal children and is briefly seen in stage I sleep and also in REM sleep (also called stage 5 sleep). Delta activity (very slow waves, 0.5 -4 Hz, high amplitude) is unusual in a normal record and accompanies deep sleep, i.e. stage 3 and 4 sleep.[41] It should be noted that excitement is characterized by a rapid frequency and small amplitude while varying degrees of sleep are marked by increasing irregularity and by the appearance of "slow-waves."

When the eyes are opened, the alpha rhythm is replaced by fast, irregular low voltage activity with no dominant frequency, called the alpha block. This break-up of the alpha rhythm could be produced by any form of sensory stimulation or mental concentration such as solving arithmetic problems. This replacement of the regular alpha rhythm with irregular low voltage activity is called de-synchronization. Because de-synchronization could be produced by sensory stimulation and is correctable by arousal, the alert state, it is also called the arousal or alert response. Adrenaline and noradrenaline produce EEG arousal by lowering the threshold of reticular neurons in the brain.

During tranquil states and meditation, slow brain-waves are induced as shown in the EEG. Stimulation of afferants from skin mechanical receptors at rates of 10 Hz produce sleep in animals; regularly repeated monotonous stimuli also put humans to sleep.

During the first few hours of the prescribed fast, the EEG is normal. However, the frequency of the alpha rhythm is decreased by a low blood glucose level.[42] This may happen at the end of the fasting day towards evening when the blood sugar is low.

Fasting improves the quality and intensifies the depth of sleep. The processes of repair of the body and of the brain takes place during sleep. Two hours of sleep during the month of Ramadan are more satisfying and refreshing than more hours of sleep otherwise.

Plasma adrenaline falls in deep sleep due to diminished sympathetic activity, as seen by constricted pupils, immovable eyelids and motionless eyes. Sleep soothes the nervous system and adjusts behavioral patterns. The body assumes a relaxed posture with low muscle tone. The pulse rate and cardiac output fall. Skin blood vessels dilate. Blood pressure is at its basal level, approx. 20-30 mm. Hg. less in systolic; B.M.R. falls by 10-20%. Body temperature is at its basal level. All bodily functions like digestive, cardiac, metabolic and adrenal are at basal level, though gastrointestinal motility is increased, due to increased parasympathetic activity. During sleep, a person periodically dreams, associated with involuntary jerks and rapid eye movements (REM). REM sleep occurs 3 or 4 times every night during normal sleep, the intervals lasting approximately 90 minutes. A person goes through 5 stages while going to sleep. Relaxed wakefulness is accompanied by alpha waves 8-12 Hz and low voltage fast activity of mixed frequency. This is called stage 1. As sleep deepens into stage 2, bursts of 12-14 Hz (sleep spindles) and high amplitude slow waves appear. The deep sleep of stages 3 and 4 is featured by an increasing proportion of high voltage, slow activity. Breathing is regular in slow-wave sleep or non-REM sleep. The presence of rhythmic slow-waves (in the alpha and slow wave pattern) indicates that neural discharges are being fired synchronously.

After about 70 minutes or so, mostly spent in stages 3 and 4, the first REM period occurs, usually heralded by an increase in body movements, and a shift in the EEG pattern from stage 4 to stage 2. These rapid low-voltage irregular waves resemble those seen in alert humans; however, sleep is not interrupted. This is called stage 5 or REM (rapid eye movements) sleep or paradoxical sleep, when the EEG activity gets desynchronized. There is marked muscle atonia, despite the rapid eye movements in REM sleep, and the breathing is irregular.[43]

Non-REM (NREM) sleep passes through stage 1 and 2, and spends 60-70 minutes in stages 3 and 4. Sleep then lightens and an REM period follows. This cycle is repeated 3 or 4 times per night, at intervals of about 90 minutes, throughout the night, depending on the length of sleep. REM sleep occupies 25% of total sleeping time. Children have more 3 and 4 stage sleep than young adults, and old people have much less. Sleep is most important for human efficiency and sense of well-being. There is a strong significant duration-dependent association between afternoon siestas and lowered coronary heart disease rates, to the extent that a 30 minute siesta seemed to offer a 30% reduction in coronary heart disease.[44]

Deprived of sleep, experimental animals will die in a few days, no matter how well they are fed, watered and housed.[45] Recovery after prolonged sleep deprivation shows that the amount of sleep required is never equal to the amount lost. If prevented night after night from REM sleep, subjects show a greater tendency to become anxious, irritable, hyperactive, emotionally labile and less able to control their impulses, a state corresponding to the heightened activity, excessive appetite and over-sexuality of REM deprived animals. Because old people have much less stage 3 and 4 sleep i.e. deep sleep. fasting is particularly important for them as it increases the depth of sleep. Sleep stages 3 and 4 or slow-wave sleep occur more frequently in early sleep, when growth hormone secretion is maximal. Growth hormone is responsible for protein synthesis and for repair of the body and of the brain, especially during the early hours of deep sleep.[46]

Significance of association between G.H. and sleep is an enigma. G.H. secretion is increased in subjects deprived of REM sleep and inhibited during normal sleep.

Humans aroused at a time when they show the EEG characteristic of REM sleep report that they were dreaming, whereas individuals wakened from slow-wave sleep do not. REM sleep and dreaming are closely associated. Teeth grinding (bruxism) is also associated with dreaming. Sleep-walking (somnambulism) and bed-wetting (nocturnal enuresis) occur during slow-wave sleep, especially during arousal from slow-wave sleep. They are not associated with REM sleep. Episodes of sleep-walking are more common in young boys than in girls, and may last several minutes; somnambulists walk with their eyes open and avoid obstacles, but when awakened, they cannot recall the episode. Dreaming may be necessary to maintain health, but prolonged REM deprivation has no adverse psychological effects. Dreaming sleep occupies 50% of sleep cycle in infants and decreases with age. Brain synthetic processes occur in deep sleep; brain protein molecules are synthesized in the brain during deep sleep or used in REM sleep in restoring cerebral function. Fasting significantly increases deep sleep and leads to a fall in REM sleeping time or dreaming time.

There is a large increase in REM sleep after one discontinues sleeping pills and this situation may be responsible for nightmares, restlessness and night awakenings.

The mechanism that triggers REM sleep is located in the posterior reticular formation; the rapid eye movements are motivated via the reticular nuclei. Drugs that inhibit monoamineoxidase increase brain noradrenaline and decrease REM sleep. Barbiturates also decrease the amount of REM sleep. Discharge of serotonin-secreting neurons is involved in production of slow-wave sleep. Serotoninergic neurons discharge rapidly in the awake state, slowly during drowsiness, more slowly with bursts during deep sleep and not at all during REM sleep. The psychomimetic responses to LSD is in effect dreaming in the awake state.

FASTING AND ENCEPHALINS

During fasting. certain endogenous. narcotic-like substances, known as opioids (or encephalins), are released into the body. They have a tranquilizing effect as well as an elating effect on the mind. Probably, these are also responsible for prevention of psychosomatic diseases. The opioids have several effects, including the slowing of the metabolism to conserve energy. Another effect of opioid may be that, although it produces elation as well as intense hunger, it does not drive the person to eat with sheer gluttony.

Brain and pituitary extracts revealed at least 3 separate opiatepeptidesystems: (a) Encephalins, (b)Endorphins, (c) Dynorphins.

Encephalins: Several times more potent than morphine.[47] Encephalins are not only present in the brain but also in the tissues of the gut and in the adrenal medulla.[48] The presence of encephalins in the spinal cord and thalamus is consistent with the well-known role of opiates in pain modulation. Encephalins co-exist in the adrenal medulla in the same granules containing catecholamines. Actions of encephalins are: (1) Analgesia: encephalins influence pain perception. (2) Inhibition of gut motility similar to morphine. (3) The adrenal medulla is a major source of encephalins in plasma, but it is rapidly de-activated. However, even the small amounts released during stress may be sufficient to influence opiate receptors throughout the body. The stress-induced analgesia in humans may be related to opiate peptides of adrenal origin. (4) are present in high concentrations in the posterior pituitary, which may influence the secretion of vasopressin and oxytocin.

Endorphins: Several times more potent than encephalins and a thousand times more potent than morphine.[49] The hormone (betaendorphin) increases in plasma dramatically in times of stress. Actions of endorphins are: (1) Analgesia. In contrast with encephalins, betaendorphins are not found in the spinal cord in high concentrations. (2) Sedation. Effect on eating, drinking, and reward and motivated behavior.

Dynorphins: More potent than beta-endorphin.[50] Does not

cause analgesia but can cause cataplexy and other behavioral effects.

SLEEP, MEMORY AND FASTING

There are 20-30 billion nerve cells in the human brain linked through various cross terminals. The neo-cortex, also called the association cortex, distinguishes the human brain from the animal brain. Memory is a series of molecular events due to biochemical changes in the nerve cells. Protein synthesis is involved in memory processes. Within the small volume of the human brain, experience of a life time could be recollected with the correct description of sights, sounds, smells, tastes and emotions. The external world is mirrored in the microscopic structure of the brain. Because of various connecting fibers of the limbic system to other parts of the cerebral cortex, a familiar voice on the telephone projects a visual memory of the person calling. Experience must be imprinted and encoded in the finer structures of the brain before they can be registered, retained and recalled. This encoding is done through a series of molecular events triggered by external stimuli. It is not known what molecular mechanisms translate visual experience into permanent neural architecture, as a result of chemical reactions influencing structural changes in the neurons.

Three mechanisms interact in memory production, one mediating immediate recall of events of the moment; another, of events that occurred minutes to hours before, and a third, of memories of the past. Memory for recent events is impaired in certain neurological diseases, but remote memories are remarkably unaffected, even in the presence of severe brain damage.

The cerebral cortex, especially the temporal lobes, is involved in memory. Stimulation of the temporal lobe evokes detailed memories of events that occurred in the remote past, often beyond the power of voluntary recall. The memories produced by temporal stimulation are "flashed back" complete, as if they were re-plays of a segment of experience.

There is frequently loss of memory for the events immediately preceding brain concussion or electro-shock therapy, but remote memory is not affected. Damage to the amygdala and the hippocampus, two major components of the brain known as the limbic system, can result in global amnesia.

It may take a few hours to "encode" or "consolidate" memory, this process probably involving the hippocampus. Seizures in the hippocampus cause loss of recent memory, and some alcoholics with brain damage develop impairment of recent memory, with pathological changes in the mammary bodies, a major site of hippocampal fibers for encoding memory molecules.[51]

Vasopressin secreted by the posterior pituitary is a typical neural hormone, i.e. a hormone secreted directly into the circulation by nerve cells. Vasopressin is also called Anti-Diuretic Hormone (ADH) because it causes retention of water by the kidneys. The urine becomes concentrated and its volume decreases. Vasopressin secretion is increased in hemorrhage, pain, stress, emotion, exercise, administration of morphine, nicotine and barbiturates, and decreased by alcohol. Vasopressin may also be involved in influencing memory processes.

Synthetic processes occur in deep sleep. Brain protein molecules are synthesized in the brain during sleep and they are also used in REM sleep in restoring cerebral function, Fasting significantly increases deep sleep and hence accelerates synthesis of memory molecules.

FASTING AND CIRCADIAN RHYTHM

"Circa" means "about" and "dies" means "day." Circa has also been applied to the other endogenous biological rhythms that have free-running periods, e.g. circatidal, circalunar and circannual. The period of circadian pacemaker is somewhat longer than 24 hours. Rhythm shorter than 24 hours is called ultradian such as secretion of Luteinising Hormone, while those longer than 24 hours, e.g. menstrual cycles are termed infradian. Hormonal secretion is frequently characterized by rhythmic fluctuations which may be regular or irregular in periodicity. The period of regular oscillation may be as short as a few minutes or as long as a year. Luteinising Hormone secretion in women acts as episodic bursts separated by 90 minutes to 8-12 hours depending on the menstrual cycle. Circulating levels of the cortisol and the GH exhibit pronounced 24 hour rhythm. The hormonal concomitants of ovarian cycles recur at 4-28 day intervals, depending on species. Integration of diverse endocrine rhythms with other biological functions requires a mechanism for biological time-keeping. The peak of the circadian rhythm in human plasma cortisol concentration occurs approximately at the time of arising in the mornings. Reversal of the lighting results in reversal of the cortico-steroid rhythm, but the coricosteroid rhythm is not controlled by the sleep-wakefulness cycle.[52] Laboratory measurements of physiological variables e.g. cortisol. ACTH, vasopressin, G.H., prolactin, drug effectiveness and gastric acid secretion also show circadian rhythm. Most ACTH and cortisol secretion occurs between midnight and morning. In the absence of any time cues, human circadian rhythm begins to free-run.

The body timing system that drives circadian rhythms is exposed to external factors from the imposed activity-rest cycle, the natural light-dark cycle, and the social activities outside the workplace. Night work is a major health hazard to millions of workers the world over, and may be responsible for an increased risk of cardiovascular illness, gastro-intestinal disorders, infertility and insomnia, and also results in diminished productivity and increased fatigue-related accident rates due to decreased vigilance. Despite the deprivation of night sleep, these workers experience day time insomnia. The circadian timing system fails to adjust to an inversion of the daily routine even after a week of night work, and this includes the endogenous circadian rhythms of body temperature, plasma cortisol concentration and urinary excretion rate. Misalignment of the circadian phase and sleep deprivation are the principal factors contributing to decreased performance and increased accident rates associated with night shift work. Exposure to bright light at night and darkness during the day can reduce the ill-effects of night work. Subjects slept an average of two hours longer during the period of imposed darkness than did the control subjects who were allowed to sleep under restricted conditions.[53]

There are biological pacemakers or oscillators within the

body with time keeping capacity which synchronize with the external environmental cycles such as light. Environmental cues (signals) that synchronize or entrain biological pacemakers have been given the name of "zeitgebers" (from the German meaning time-givers), and the process of re-setting the pacemaker is called the entrainment or re-synchronization. The light/dark cycle is a potent zeitgeber for circadian rhythm but daily cycles in temperature, food availability, social interaction (such as congregational prayers) and even electromagnetic field strength, entrain circadian rhythm in certain species. Because of recurring cycles of light, temperature and food availability, organisms evolved endogenous rhythms of metabolism and behavior providing response to specific environmental cycles. Many biological rhythms reflect the period of one of four environmental cycles viz., cycles of the tide, of day and night, of phases of the moon and of seasons. The first report of the daily biological rhythm persisting in the absence of environmental cues, was the leaf of a heliotrope plant opening and closing in constant darkness. Self-sustained rhythms with a period of 24 hours was first termed circadian rhythm.[54]

Time of day has an effect on most pituitary hormones, and in some animals, time of the year is also an important factor. Time of day is sensed through the use of a circadian oscillator(s) which has a periodicity of approx. 24 hours. This oscillator is synchronized to external cues, the primary cue for most animals being light. The suprachiasmatic nucleus is thought to contain the circadian oscillator. Daily variations in the secretion of pituitary hormones are probably due to inter-connections between the circardian oscillator and hypothalamic neurosecretory neurons.

Another important element in the coupling of the rhythmic activity with hormone release is in the pineal gland. The pineal gland plays an important part in directional sense. Its proximity to the surface of the skin in primitive animals has earned its title, "the third eye." It is associated with seasonal and diurnal rhythms. Pineal activity undergoes circadian variations that are also linked with the light cycle. Light information is transmitted via a circuitous route from the suprachiasmatic nucleus, down through the spinal cord, into the superior cervical ganglion and back up into the pineal via the sympathetic fibers. The most important of this is melatonin which is secreted into the circulation and acts primarily as an inhibitor of gonatotropic secretion, mediating the effects of day length.

Circadian rhythmically persists under constant environmental conditions. Annual rhythms have also been observed in plasma concentrations of cortisol and G.H. Population statistics for mortality, suicide and conception exhibit regular annual rhythms. Circadian rhythms persist under conditions of constant light or constant darkness. Serotonin plays some role in regulation of circadian rhythm.

Muslims who have been fasting regularly since childhood. have been exposed to different sleep/wake and light/darkness cycles on a daily basis in one annual lunar month. Hence, it may be easier for such persons to synchronize their circadian. circalunar and circannual biological rhythms under difficult conditions.

JET LAG

International travel across time zones produces symptoms of jet lag such as sleep disturbances, gastro-intestinal disorders, decreased alertness, fatigue and general malaise. Difficulty is experienced more while traveling eastward and accommodation to lengthened days (westward) is easier than to shortened days.

Factors contributing to symptoms of jet lag are (1) external de-synchronization due to the immediate difference between body time and local time at the end of the flight. (2) The second is internal de-synchronization due to the fact that different circadian rhythms in the body re-synchronize at different rates, and during the re-synchronization period, these rhythms will be out of phase with one another.[55]

Inability to sleep the night before due to circadian de-synchronization in pilots adds to the effect of jet lag, while traveling, especially eastwards. Age strongly affects sleepiness. Crew members who are over 50 experience increased number of awakenings, a high percentage of light drowsy (restless) sleep, and a lower percentage of deep slow-wave (restful) sleep, and a lower sleep efficiency. This may be responsible for cockpit human errors resulting from miscalculations, memory lapses and miscommunications and poor crew co-ordination, causing aircraft accidents.[56]

Jet lag also affects performance of athletes, when there is a rapid displacement across the earth's time zones, causing de-synchronization of their physiological and psychological cycles. General symptoms arising from de-synchronization include tiredness during the day and disturbed sleep and reaction time. The severity of these adverse effects and therefore the time required for re-synchronization depends on the ability to pre-set the bodily rhythms prior to flying, the number of time zones crossed, the direction of flight, age, social interaction and activity.[57]

Rapid adaptation to a new zone can be facilitated by maximizing exposure to zeitgebers for the new cycle, e.g. changing to meal times and sleep times appropriate to the new time zone. Maximizing social contact and exposure to natural lighting will result in faster re-synchronization than staying at home in a hotel and eating and sleeping without regard to local time.[58] There are widespread individual variations in the rapidity of re-synchronization. Muslims who fast regularly and who have experienced disturbed wakefulness/sleep cycles on a daily lunar annual basis, can adapt themselves much faster to different time zones during international travel and do not suffer from the ill effects of jet lag. Moreover, the social contact during the Special Night Prayer in congregation during Ramadan and other social cum spiritual activities should act as a zeitgeber which regulates any de-synchronized biological rhythm.

Shift workers also experience similar symptoms as jet lag, especially gastro-intestinal, cardiovascular, sleep disorders and also reproductive dysfunction in women. The inverted schedule of sleeping and waking also results in diminished alertness and performance during night-time work with attendant increase in the number of fatigue-related accidents during night time shift hours.[59] Normally, a period of 3 weeks is required for re-synchronization among shift workers, and as the fasting Muslim attunes himself to re-synchronization processes during the space of just over 4 weeks in Ramadan. his health problems as a shift worker would be negligible as his synchronization processes would be more rapid. whether during Ramadan or at any other time.

It is also a common observation that as soon as Ramadan is over, normal circadian rhythms are established in the fasted Muslims by the Festival day (the first day of the month of Shawwal) with such great rapidity as to be at par with pre-Ramadan levels.

FASTING, EXERCISE AND SPECIAL NIGHT PRAYER

Throughout the year, the average Muslim performs his five daily prescribed prayers, as well as some optional extras, which amount to gentle physical exercise, involving each and every muscle in the body. The various postures allow some muscles to contract isometrically and others isotonically. When contraction occurs without any significant decrease in the length of the whole muscle, it is called isometric (same length) contraction. When contraction occurs in the approximation of muscles, it is called isotonic (same tension) contraction. During exercise, the caloric needs of muscle are initially met by glycogenolysis in muscle.

During the fasting month of Ramadan, additional prayers are performed at night, called the Special Night Prayer, ranging from 8 to 20 cycles, accompanied by chanting Glory to God, at the end of every 4 cycles. Such additional exercise, besides expending any extra calories ingested at the post-sunset meal approximately one and one-half to two hours earlier (and at the same time when blood sugar level is rising from ingested nutrients), improve flexibility, coordination and relaxation response, reduce stress-related autonomic responses in normal persons, and relieve anxiety and depression.

Gentle exercise improves fitness and emotional well-being and increases longevity.[60] For there to be an improvement in the stamina and endurance, in flexibility and strength, the effort required needs to be only a little greater than the person is accustomed to. Not everyone could or should go jogging even walking at 3 MPH or the five times daily prescribed prayers would produce the same physiological changes without unpleasant effects. Apart from health-promoting qualities of exercise, mild exercise such as prayers, trains the person to be ever prepared for any unexpected physical exertion, such as running for a bus, which may be accomplished more safely and efficiently, an advantage for the elderly who will be able to maintain his independence much longer. Persons who fast and perform the Special Night Prayer report feeling much better and healthier.

In the elderly, the level of physiological activity drops. Bones become thinner and osteoporotic. The skin also becomes thinner and wrinkled. The repair processes of the body become slower and immune responses are reduced. Lower levels of Insulin Growth Factor 1 in aging men are related to diminished physical activity.[61] Reserve functions of all vital organs decline and the aged are more vulnerable to accidents and disease. But because prayers are prescribed, repeated and regular movements of the body during prayers will improve muscle power, tendon strength, joint flexibility and the cardiovascular reserve. This will enable them to improve the quality of life and to meet with unexpected challenges which could have resulted in their falls, with consequent damage to their bodies. This will improve their stamina, self-esteem and self-confidence in being independent.

Just before the post-sunset meal, both blood glucose and insulin are at their lowest level. Very little is metabolized by muscle and FFA is the predominant fuel. An hour or so after the post-sunset meal, the blood glucose begins to rise and also plasma insulin. Liver takes up much of the circulating glucose to replenish its glycogen content, and muscles may also do the same. Unless a lot of sweets are eaten very rapidly, the glucose level in the blood may not reach above the renal threshold and no sugar would spill in the urine. However. when the blood sugar begins to rise after the post-sunset meal to reach high levels in an hour or two, the benefits of the Special Night Prayer (the latter coinciding with the timing of the rising of the blood sugar) come into effect. The circulating glucose is oxidized to

CO_2 and H_2O during the Special Night Prayer.

Even trivial activity is accompanied by secretion of adrenaline. Once secretion starts, it may outlast the stimulus that gave rise to it e.g. the effects of adrenaline and noradrenaline are apparent even after the Special Night Prayer is over. Even the thought or the intention of performing the Special Night Prayer is sufficient to activate the sympathetic system. The adrenaline would re-distribute the blood in the body to the active muscles, would mobilize liver glycogen if necessary in order to provide glucose for the active tissues, would diminish fatigue in skeletal muscles and would facilitate alveolar ventilation by relaxing bronchiolar muscle, and would initiate cardiovascular changes. Exercise induces a more effective functioning of beta-adrenoreceptors located on cell membranes.

The Special Night Prayer is considered to be gentle exercise, and the beneficial effects of gentle exercise on the body are as follows:

SKELETAL MUSCLE

An unused muscle atrophies in spite of availability of ample proteins. During prescribed prayers, every muscle in the body contracts, some isotonically and others isometrically. Exercise also improves stamina and reduces fatigue. It helps the disabled to make the most of their residual capacities.

The blood flow of resting muscle is low. When a muscle contracts, it compresses the vessels in it if it develops more than 10% of its maximal tension. Between contractions, the blood flow is greatly increased. Blood flow sometimes increases even before the start of exercise, with just the thought of performing exercise or of performing the Special Night Prayer. Potassium ions cause vasodilation of arterioles. During the Special Night Prayer, systolic B.P. may rise a little and the diastolic B.P. may remain unchanged or even fall. However, after the Special Night Prayer is over, the B.P. may drop to just below normal levels, a very welcome sign.

Training increases the maximal oxygen consumption (VO_2 max) produced by exercise, such as the regular Special Night

Prayer. Just as persons who exercise regularly FEEL better, persons who perform the Special Night Prayer regularly have also observed that they FEEL better. Regular physical exertion also increases the probability that a person can remain active past the standard age of retirement. Similarly, all those who perform the extra Special Night Prayer, besides the prescribed daily prayers, are more alert and active than those who do not perform the optional Special Night Prayer even after age of retirement.

Tendons and Connective Tissues: Exercise improves physical strength and joint stability and reduces risk of injury

Skeleton: Bone mineral content falls with age, espy. after age 40. Decline in the bone density can be prevented or even reversed by mild exercise, in both menopausal and in elderly women. Exercise increases bone mineral density at sites of maximal stress.[62] Some areas of the skeleton have to bear some extra pressure during the bending forward and prostration in the prescribed prayers. The strain put on the forearm during prostration in lifting the body from the ground increases the bone mineral content of the forearm. Exercise also prevents osteoporosis and maintains normalcy in bone structures. The risk of osteoporosis and consequent hip fractures should be substantially less in those who take regular exercise or pray five times daily, in addition to praying the Special Night Prayer

Joints: Exercise improves lubrication and range of movement, and maintains flexibility. The varying load during the different postures of prayers causes a lubricating and therefore a protective flow of synovial fluid into the joint cavity. The reinforcement of the calf muscle pump by active ankle movements such as in the prescribed prayers, prevents deep vein thrombosis, the latter being the most common cause of ulceration of the legs in the elderly.

Erhythropoiette System: Repeated exercise activates the erythropoietic processes in the bone marrow.[63]

Metabolic Effects: Exercise improves body weight control and expends calories without proportionate increase in appetite. A combination of moderate dietary restriction, both at the post-sunset and pre-dawn meals, accompanied by the

Special Night Prayer, should achieve weight reduction. With exercise, both fat and body weight are reduced, but fat-free weight remains constant or may even increase slightly. When energy reduced diets are combined with exercise, the fat-free weight loss is considerably less, compared with programs using only diet. Hence, for persons who would like to lose some of the excess weight during Ramadan, it is important not to overeat at the post-sunset and pre-dawn meals and in addition, to perform the Special Night Prayer

Exercise prevents coronary heart disease, improves carbo-hydrate tolerance and ameliorates late-onset diabetes. Beneficial changes have been recorded in the lipid profile, B.P., clotting factors, weight reduction and insulin sensitivity of mus-cles and other tissues, in persons whom exercise regularly. Growth Hormone secretion elevated by fasting is further ele-vated by exercise such as the Special Night Prayer. As G. H. is necessary for collagen formation, this may be an important fac-tor as to why the skin of those Muslims who fast regularly and pray the Special Night Prayer do not get wrinkled even when they are very old.

Cardiovascular Effects: Exercise could exert benefits by its effects on the main coronary risk factors by (a) facilitating stop-ping smoking, (b) reducing obesity, (c) increasing High density lipo-proteins. Exercise increases maximum oxygen uptake, slows the heart, lowers the B.P. slightly, decreases ventricular ectopic activity, enlarges the lumen of the coronary arteries and increases cardiac output. Exercise also helps cases of chronic respiratory diseases.

Psychological Functions: Exercise improves mood, thought and behavior.[67] Exercise improves the quality of life, reduces anxiety and depression, influences mood favorably and con-tributes to self-esteem and self-confidence; improves memory in the elderly especially with constant repetition of the verses from the Holy Quran and other verses of His Glory would help to screen the mind from incoming thoughts. The repetition of a prayer, verse of glorification. remembrance of God or muscular activity coupled with passive disregard of intensive thoughts causes a relaxation response, leaded to lowering of B.P.

decrease in O2 consumption and a reduction in heart and respiratory rates. All these are combined in the Special Night Prayer which is an ideal situation for relaxation response. It combines repeated mummer activity with repetition of prayers, of words of glorification of God and of supplications. The Special Night Prayer puts the mind at ease. This relaxed state of the mind may be partly due to the release of encephalins, beta endorphins and others into the circulation.

Islam is the only religion where physical movements of prayers are combined with spiritual exercise. Prayers being prescribed throughout a person's life, recurring every few hours or so, trains a person to undertake the difficult task of meditating during physical movements of prayers, so that he benefits both from spiritual as well as physical exercise. Prescribed prayers are unique in that tension builds up in the muscles during physical movements while al the same time, tension is relieved in the mind due to the spiritual component.

17

RAMADAN RECIPES

Shabnam Zaman

It is recorded in the Traditions that the Messenger ended his daily prescribed fast in Ramadan with dates, water and often a barley broth called *talbina* or *tirbiyali*. Our Ramadan recipes begin with this broth.

TIRBIYALI (SYRIAN)

4 cups meat broth (whatever meat
    you are used to eating)
4 Tbls. barley flour
1 Tbl. lemon juice (fresh)
1 egg

Mix the barley flour, lemon and egg. Add to the lukewarm meat broth and add salt and pepper. Serves 4.

Other daily favorites for ending the prescribed fast include the following:

SWEET FRITTERS (PERSIAN)

Syrup
1 cup water   2 cups sugar

1 Tbl. lemon juice (fresh)

Dough

1 1/2 tsp. baking power

1 1/2 cups flour

3 cups vegetable oil for frying

3 Tbls. honey

1 cup lukewarm water

2 tsp. lemon juice (fresh)

Syrup

1. Place the water, sugar, lemon juice and honey in a saucepan. Bring to a boil over high heat. Reduce heat and simmer 10 minutes over low heat. Put aside.

Dough

1. Dissolve baking powder in 1 cup lukewarm water in a bowl. Add flour and lemon juice. Mix until creamy and set aside for 45 minutes.

2. Fill a plastic squeeze dispenser with the dough. Heat oil in a deep fryer to 375 degrees.

3. Hold bottle over fryer and squeeze dough in a pretzel shape directly into the oil. Fry until golden brown on all sides.

4. Gently remove the sweet fritter from the oil with a skimmer. Dip in syrup covering completely.

5. Using another skimmer, remove the pieces from the syrup and arrange on a serving platter.

FALUDA (MIDDLE EAST)

2 Tbls. ground almonds

2 cups milk

4 Tbls. condensed milk

1/4 cup seaweed

1 small tin cream

1/2 tsp. cardamom powder

2 Tbls. sugar

1 drop red food coloring

1. Boil milk and seaweed and simmer until the milk is slightly evaporated.

2. Add almonds to the milk liquid while it is simmering.

3. Remove from stove and add cardamom, sugar and condensed milk and tint a light pink color. Cool slightly then add cream.

4. Beat with a rotary beater until frothy and light.

5. Spoon gently into tall glasses or bowls and allow to set in the

refrigerator. Decorate the top with sliced almonds.

CARROT HALWA (PAKISTANI/INDIAN)

1 lb.peeled, finely grated carrots	3 Tbl. corn oil
1/2 cup nonfat dry milk	1 1/2 cups nonfat milk
1/8 tsp. saffron	1/2 tsp. grated nutmeg
1/2 tsp. crushed cardamom seed	1/4 cup sugar
1/4 cup golden or dark raisins	1 Tbl. slivered almonds

1. Melt oil in a saucepan and cook carrots for 5 to 6 minutes. Make sure to stir constantly
2. Add milk and milk powder and bring to boil. Reduce the heat and cook for 25 minutes, stirring constantly.
3. Add saffron, nutmeg, cardamom and raisins. Mix well.
4. Cook stirring occasionally until almost all of the liquid has evaporated.
5. Add sugar. Mix well and reduce heat. Stir occasionally until the mixture thickens. This will take 10 to 15 minutes.
6. Pour into serving dish, garnish with almonds and serve.

CHAPLI KABABS (PAKISTANI/INDIAN)

2 lbs. mince meat	1/2 cup chopped onions
1-2 tsp. crushed red chilies	2 Tbl. chopped fresh mint
2 Tbl. chopped coriander seeds	3 Tbl. finely chopped fresh coriander leaves
1 Tbl. cumin seeds	1 Tbl. yogurt
1 1/2 tsp. salt	2 tsp. freshly ground green chilies
1/2 cup mealie meal	1 egg

1. Roast chopped coriander and cumin seeds until slightly browned. Coarsely crush them and put aside.
2. Add all spices, onion and mealie meat to the mince meat.
3. Mix the mince meat well and knead mince mixture at half hour intervals.
4. After 2 hours, add chopped greens, egg and yogurt. Mix well.
5. Take mince mixture and make into hamburger like patties.

6. Place kababs on greased griddle or very thick pan and grill over slow heat, pouring a bit of oil when necessary. Press the kababs in the middle so that there is even contact with the griddle.

7. Serve warm with lemon wedges, chutneys or salad.

BREAD (PAKISTAN/INDIAN)

1/2 lb. whole wheat flour	1/2 tsp. salt
2 Tbl. oil	1/2 cup water

1. Arrange flour in a semi-flat try so that a small well is formed in the middle.
2. Add water and salt together, little by little.
3. Mix so that soft dough is formed.
4. Knead well for 5 minutes.
5. Set dough aside for at least an hour before making the bread.
6. Before making the bread, the dough should be kneaded well.
7. Break off a piece of dough and roll with hands into a small ball of about 1 1/2 " in diameter.
8. Roll flat with rolling pin to about 1/8" thickness.
9. Pour oil on the uncooked dough.
10. Fold in half and pour more oil.
11. Fold into cone shape and flatten slightly.
12. Roll it flat into 1/8" thickness.
13. Place in frying pan and cook for 1 minute.
14. Flip over and cook for another minute and add a little oil. Fry each side until golden brown.
15. You may add a little oil as necessary to do the frying.
16. Serve hot with any curry and chutney.

EGGS CURRY (MIDDLE EAST)

The pre-dawn meal is often something normally eaten for dinner but eggs curry is also a favorite.

4 hard boiled eggs	1 sm. onion chopped
1/2 tsp red chili powder	1 tsp. turmeric
1 Tbl. chopped fresh ginger	1/2 sm. ripe tomato chopped
2 Tbl. grated coconut	1 stick cinnamon

1 or 2 cardamom
pinch of curry leaves
4 Tbl. oil

1 or 2 cloves
1 cup coconut milk
salt to taste

1. Fry onions to a golden brown then add all the dry ingredients. Fry mixture well and keep slightly moist with water so that the mixture does not burn. Do not make the mixture too watery.
2. Now add garlic, ginger and tomatoes and cook on slow heat for about 4 to 5 minutes.
3. Add coconut milk and cook mixture for another 10 minutes.
4. Cut the eggs in half and add these to the mixture. Be sure not to stir too much as the eggs might break.
5. Once the curry has simmered for a few minutes so that the eggs absorb some of the mixture, turn off the heat.
6. Serve with rice or break with salad or pickle of your choice.

18

DREAMING OF PRESCRIBED FASTING

Ibn Sirin
Translated by Muhammad al-Akili

Fasting, Prescribed: (Armor; Protection) Fasting in a dream represents vows and offerings. Interrupting the fast in a dream means an illness, a journey or backbiting someone.

If one interrupts his prescribed fast through forgetfulness in a dream, it means that he will receive a pleasing gift or money.

Fasting in a dream also means honor, rising in station, or it could mean repentance from sin, repayment of a debt, penitence for a sinner or begetting a son.

Observing the prescribed fast of the month of Ramadan in a dream means understanding something about which one has doubt or recognizing the truth without falsification or distortion.

If one finds that he is the only person observing the prescribed fast in the dream, and if one is unlettered, it means that one will memorize the Holy Quran, attain spiritual maturity and receive glad tidings. This dream also indicates that one is a pious and a religious person.

If one is sick, it means that one will recover from one's illness.

If one is lost in heedlessness, it means that God Almighty will grant guidance.

If one is indebted, it means that one will be able to repay one's debts.

If in one's dream, one intentionally breaks one's fast during the prescribed fast of the month of Ramadan, it means that one could kill someone.

Similarly, if one sees oneself killing someone in a dream, it means that one has intentionally broken one's prescribed fast.

Observing the two months of atonement for the sin of breaking the prescribed fast during the holy month of Ramadan or for any such fast for the expiation of sins in a dream means that one may fall sick and repent to God Almighty for one's sins.

Intentionally breaking the prescribed fast of Ramadan in a dream also means neglecting one of the pillars of Islam. If one acknowledges that, then vows to offer the required duties in a dream, it means that one could receive an unexpected gift which will arrive shortly.

If one recognizes in one's dream the importance of the month of Ramadan, it means that one is on the right path.

If one is not fasting, it means that one may go on a journey.

Voluntary fasting in a dream means protection against one's enemies.

If a sick person sees self fasting in a dream, it could mean death, silence, celebrations or recovering from an illness. It could also represent one's faith in God Almighty and sincerity in one's words and actions.

If one sees masses of people performing prescribed fasting in a dream, it could mean a famine.

If one eats during the hours of observing the prescribed fast in a dream, it means that one will commit a sin, or it could mean indebtedness or falling sick.

Prescribed fasting in the month of Ramadan in a dream also means safety, protection from evil or repentance from sins.

Fasting an extra day in doubt about one's proper religious performance in a dream means committing a sin or lack of vigilance and certitude about one's devotion.

Fasting days of the month of Ramadan one has missed for a

permissible reason in a dream means release of a prisoner or repentance of a sinner.

Fasting a votive fast or a vowed fast for the purpose of an attainment in a dream means attaining one's goal, joy and happiness.

Observing a votive perpetual or an ongoing fast in a dream means undertaking a heavy responsibility or following innovation, or it could mean becoming a loner or abstaining from talking to others, or that one would only talk if the subject is beneficial to others, for fasting in a dream also means silence.

Observing a votive perpetual fast in a dream also represents a pious and a religious person. If the person is a sinner, such votive fast in a dream also may mean that he will get nothing out of what he wants. Paying the due charity *(sadaqat al-fitr)* after completing one's fast in a dream means recovering from an illness.

If one observes a fast for show in one's dream, it means that one will receive what one desires.

PART SIX:
HUMAN BONDING

19

RAMADAN AND INTERFAITH BONDING

Shahid Athar

In 1988, three wise men of our town, Rev. Jerry Zehr, Rabbi Jonathan Stein, and Imam Ihsan Bagby got together and thought of starting an interfaith group, then known as Northside Interfaith Project (NIP). In the first year, there were only social gatherings and interfaith dialogues like "our common Creator," 'life after death," and so forth. Subsequently, many individuals and organizations (twelve Christian churches, two Jewish synagogues, two Muslim organizations, one Bahai and one Unitarian Universalist church) joined in. The NIP changed its name in 1992 to Interfaith Alliance-Indianapolis.

At least six annual events are carried out to educate people of other faiths. Jewish people invite others to observe cedar marking the exodus, Bahais celebrate Unity Feast. Muslims invite others to the post-sunset ending of the prescribed fast during Ramadan. In addition, they all join together in non-religious functions like thanksgiving, art festivals, and "side-by-side," an annual event to repair the homes of the poor. All events have been well received by the public and the media.

Our Ramadan post-sunset ending of the prescribed fast program has been very successful. For the first four years, it was held at the Islamic Center in Plainfield. For the last two years, it has been held at the Al-Fajr Mosque, Indianapolis. The program is filled to capacity. Many had to be turned away because of lack of space. All those who purchase advance tickets for $6 per person. This year (1994), attendance was 170 people, 90% non-Muslims. Br. Mazen Ayoubi was in charge of planning and execution.

THE PROGRAM

After registration, everyone is seated. The program starts with recitation of Holy Quran, followed by translation. Then welcome is read on behalf of IAI. In the 1993 program, Dr. Athar said the following:

> It gives me great pleasure to welcome you all today on behalf of Interfaith Alliance, and I thank you for your participation in the 6th Interfaith Ramadan-Iftar.
>
> In spite of the fact that the world has become a global village, sometimes followers of religious traditions live in a small hut of their own, never to open their door, to venture out to see how other folks in other huts live. Thus our apprehension sometimes of each other is a result of not knowing each other. The Quran says, *"Oh humanity, We created you from a single pair of male and a female, and made you into nations and tribes that you know each other."* Thus, knowing each other is not only a social need but a Divine injunction. Just because another person, of skin color different from mine, born in a land different from where I was born, prays to the same God, but in a different manner or in a different language, he or she does not become less worthy of my love and respect for his life and views. We need to know and respect others religious beliefs and cultures.
>
> It is not easy these days to project a good image of Islam in a world which is hostile to Muslims. I want my non-Muslim friends to know that Islam and Muslims are somewhat two different things. Islam is a way of life, of peace and submission to the will of God. Muslim is a state of the degree to which one is practic-

ing Islam. Thus you may find those who have a Muslim name but are not practicing Islam, and you will find those who have opened the doors of their mosque, and extended their hands of friendship to invite their non-Muslim friends to end the fast and share a meal together. You should know the difference.

I also want my Muslim friends to know that there are also two types of non-Muslims. There are those who label all Muslims as terrorists while they themselves are doing all kinds of atrocities against Muslims such as what's happening in Bosnia by the Serbs and in India by Hindu fanatics. There is also the second kind like those who came here today to be with their Muslim friends to share a meal and learn more about Islam. We do realize the difference. While we pray to God for guidance for the former, we thank Him for giving us the company of the latter. Welcome to the beauty and majesty of the true Islamic hospitality in the blessed month of Ramadan.

After the welcome speech, a Muslim scholar speaks about the significance of Ramadan. When it is time to end the fast, the call to prescribed prayer is called, and all participants, Muslims and non-Muslims, end the fast with juice and dates. Muslims then go to the mosque area for the evening prescribed prayer, and non-Muslim watch from behind, sitting on chairs or on the floor.

Following the prescribed evening prayer, they all come back to their tables in the Community Hall, where dinner is already on their tables. Sometimes dinner is served buffet style, as well. Americans enjoy spicy Middle Eastern food and tasty desserts. There are separate areas for men and women. After dinner about one hour is spent on a question-answer session in an open forum. Usually, four knowledgeable Muslims, two men and two women, form the panel. The audience asks them all kinds of questions about Ramadan, dietary laws, the modest dress and other aspects of Islam. After the question-answer session, there is a thank-you note from the chairperson of the program, a future update note from the president of IAI, and a closing supplication by the Imam of the Mosque. Then the call to prayer for the night prescribed prayer is called. Muslims go for the pre-scribed prayer and the special night prayer of Ramadan and the guests go home.

THE SURVEY

For the last three years (1992, 1993 and 1994), I have given survey forms to all guests to complete before leaving. About 60% have returned the survey.

RESULTS OF THE SURVEY (91 RESPONDENTS)

1. When asked to identify their faith group:
36 classified themselves as Catholic, 25 as Protestant, 10 as Jews, 15 as Muslims, and 10 as others (Unitarian, Bahai).
2. When asked to describe the facility at the mosque:
78 said it was good and 13 said it was satisfactory.
3. When asked about the food served:
86 liked the food, 2 did not, and 3 had no comment.
4. When asked to judge the speakers:
31 said excellent, 57 said good, 3 said boring.
5. When asked to evaluate the question-answer session:
78 said it was informative, 13 said not.*
*Most of these 13 were Muslims.
6. When asked if they learned something new about Islam:
87 said yes, 4 said no.
7. When asked if the program decreased their misconception and stereotyping of Islam:
89 said yes, 2 said no.
8. When asked if they would like to come back next year:
78 said yes, 3 said no, and 10 were not sure.

COMMENTS

Some of the individual comments by our non-Muslim guests are interesting and mentioned below.
1994:

* I would appreciate your adding the teaching of Islam next year. -Mary J. Matheny

* Thank you for being so welcoming and generous. I have a much better feeling of Muslim religion and culture now. -Aliza Weidenbaum

* I feel very much at home in Islam. I would also like to con-

tinue studying Arabic and the fabric of Islam, the Koran. Peace be to you. - Karla Pate

* You have a very lovely facility. Everyone was warm and friendly. The question-answer segment was very good! Lots of good information. -Frances Geisaman

* Thank you for your hospitality and sincerity. It was a very interesting evening. Special appreciation for the food preparers. The food was a fun experience.

* I thought the evening was very helpful to an understanding of the importance of Ramadan and Islam as a whole. Plus, the interaction and fellowship among persons of various traditions is always valuable. My appreciation to the Muslim community for their gracious hospitality. -L. Lang Brownlee

• Thank you for sharing your faith with me. -Marta Spence

* I was truly blessed by the opportunity to come and learn your religious backgrounds in an environment of peace and love. Thank you for your gracious hospitality and willingness to promote education and understanding. -Marla Black

This was an outstanding event. The new mosque is beautiful and I feel honored to be invited to join the faithful in prayer. Each speaker spoke from his or her heart—it was very moving for me. The food was delicious, and conversation while eating was informative, warm and very enjoyable. I thank you for opening your doors to all who attended, and giving us so bountiful an experience. I look forward to the next-one. -Jeanne Sanchez-Laite

SUMMARY

In conclusion, while it is true that the image of Islam and Muslims has been distorted and defamed, being labeled as terrorists, hijackers, fanatics, backward, barbarians, oppressors of women, etc., thanks to the anti-Islam media and to some extent by non-practicing secular Muslims and extremists, there is room for improvement of our image, to clarify the misconceptions about Islam by going directly to the American people and sharing with them what Islam is and what Muslims have to offer.

We cannot change the ink of anti-Islamic writers, but with the help of God, maybe we will be able to soften the hearts of

Americans about Islam and Muslims, at least to the extent of earning their respect and diminishing their hostility. If such efforts are made constantly in every town in the US and non-Muslim countries, there is hope.

1994 IAI RAMADAN POST-SUNSET ENDING OF THE PRESCRIBED FAST PROGRAM

IAI thanks you for participating in our Ramadan-Iftar Program on February 22nd at Al-Fajr Mosque, Indianapolis. We consider your presence as a source of strength to IAI's objective of bringing people of different faith a little closer to each other through such interactions. In order to serve you better next year, we would like to have your valuable opinions about the program. Please circle the appropriate answers to each questions

1. Did you participate this year for the first time?

2. If no, how many times have you participated?

3 Are you a (circle one)?

Protestant Catholic Jewish Bahai Muslim Other

4. Was the facility at the Mosque? Good Satisfactory Unsatisfactory

5. Did you like the food? Yes No No Comment

6. Was the food service? Good Satisfactory Unsatisfactory

7. Were the speakers? Excellent Good Boring

8. Please rate on a scale of 1-4 (1 best 4 worst) these speakers:

(1) M. Saleem Kayani   (2) Adil Marzouk

(3) Shahid Athar   (4) Any other

9. Was the question-answer session informative? Yes No

10. Through this program did you learn something new about Islam? Yes No

11. Do you think this program helped decrease misconception and stereotyping about Muslims? Yes No

12. Would you like to participate in the same program next year? Yes No

13. Are you an IAI? Member Non-Member Male Female

14. Your comments and suggestions.

20

FASTING: AN HISTORIC PERSPECTIVE

Muhammad Zafarkhan

With the arising of human consciousness, we tend to question more—whether it be religion or science. We have a compelling need to ask, "Why?" This is true today of believers and non-believers alike. In some cases, the motive is a rational one, but in other cases, the motive is clearly adverse. What in the past had been normal religious practice is now the target of severe criticism. The human being seeks religion to serve him or her and not the reverse.

What is religion and what human needs do its practices fulfill? It clearly does not serve the passions (anger and lust), individual, ego-centric desires which compete with the common good, but rather serves that which is noble, fruitful and dignified within human creation. Many turn to a supermarket perspective of picking and choosing aspects of religious practices they "enjoy," cutting across traditional religions and failing to pick up or leaving aside those aspects which appear difficult because they require self-discipline. This eclectic view leads to religion for each individual which, in turn, reinforces a god or goddess who differs for each person. This god or goddess in traditional religious terminology is called "the ego" and its very presence proves the existence of the success of the satanic which traditional religions have predicted happens when a person turns away from the worship of the One God, Creator and Sustainer of the universe, and worships self-ego (the passions within) instead. The worship of the One God fosters unity, morality and the common good—human perfection and completion whereas self-worship simply fosters completion—living and dying at the horizontal level of life never having experienced the vertical ascent beyond individual ego to the All-encompassing Spirit which was, in addition, breathed into the human soul at the beginning of time, It Itself being primordial and eternal.

Among religious practices scrutinized by human egos is that of prescribed fasting. Perhaps putting the practice in an historic context will vouch for is universal validity as a means, and one of the best, to overcome the satanic ego.

Fasting as a practice of maintaining through abstaining from food, drink and/or sexual contact for a period of time arises out of an instinctive consciousness of subduing and controlling desires. Through experience or inspired by Divine Grace, the human being has throughout history realized the benefits of fasting.

While the emphasis here will be on the fast prescribed in Ramadan for those who submit to God's Will (*muslims*), sensing connectedness to other faiths serves to reinforce its validity.

Maulana Sayyid Abdul Razzaq writes,

> It is very true that every culture had had fasting as a permanent feature of its traditional conception of life and its progress. We find it in high esteem amongst the ancient Persians of Iran. It was most prominent in the ceremonies of Mithraism. The ancient Hindus with their primeval view of the transmigration of the soul and of the body as a temporary prison of a fallen spirit carried fasting to unnatural excess.[1]

Hinduism is an ancient religion in which fasting is observed. Professor Mahadevan of Madras says,

A different group of festivals are the prescribed fast. The followers of each cult have their own special days in the year which they spend exclusively in prayer and worship. Many people on these occasions fast and keep vigil during the night, read from the sacred texts and keep their minds engaged in thoughts on God. The day known as Vaikuvantha-Ekadasi is sacred to Vishnu. Not only Vaishanavas but even other Hindus observe this day as a day of fast and prayer. The whole night, which is thought to be auspicious for the worship of Shiva, is the Sivaratri. There are the days, again, on which the women fast and offer prayer to the Devi in her various manifestations like Gauri and Lakshmi. These fasts are significantly named Vratas or Vows. They are intended for the purification of the soul and providing it with spiritual food.[2]

Speaking of some other faiths, Syed Sulaiman Nadwi observes the following.

Among the ancient Egyptians fasting seems to have been associated with many religious festivals, notably with that of Isis, but it does not appear that so far as the common people were concerned, the observance of the fasts was compulsory. In Athens only the women attending the festival used to keep fasts on the third day of the Thosmophoria. Among the Zoroastrians, though fasting is not prescribed for the common people, it appears from a verse in the Sacred Book that the command of fasting was present in their midst. For the priests, in particular, the five-year fast was compulsory.[3]

In regard to fasting in Judaism, Maulana says,

Amongst the Semitic races, fasting was most popular. A day was set aside by the Mosaic Law for the sole purpose of fasting. Although it was only once in the

year it was still very important. The 10th day of the
seventh month of Tishri is called the 'Yom Kipper'
meaning the day of Atonement or the holiest of the
whole year. According to tradition it meant the
strictest and most rigorous abstinence from all food or
drink as also from washing, anointing, the putting on
of sandals, from the sunset of the 9th to the appearance of the three stars on the evening of the 10th day.
That amounts to 24 hours of complete abstinence
from food and liquid. The result of such a fast is obvious; in most cases it is conveniently shelved or over-
looked.[4]

Nadwi says,

Among the Jews fasting was instituted in Biblical
times as a sign of mourning, or when danger threatened, or when the seer was preparing himself for a
divine revelation. Occasional fasts were also instituted for the whole community, specially when the nation
believed itself to be under Divine displeasure, or a
great calamity befell the land, or pestilence raged, or
drought set in.

The Jewish calendar contains comparatively few
regular fast-days. Besides the day of Atonement,
which is the only fast-day prescribed by the Mosaic
Law, there were established after the captivity four
regular fast-days in commemoration of the various sad
days that had befallen the nation during that period.
There were fasts of the fourth month (May), of the
fifth month (June) of the sixth month (July) and the
tenth month (Tebet). According to some Rabbis of the
Talmud these fasts were obligatory only when the
nation was under oppression, but not when there was
peace for Israel.

In addition to these there are other fasts which are
observed in memory of certain disasters that befell
Israel. These are not regarded as obligatory and have
found little acceptance among the people. Their number, with a few changes, is twenty-five.

Besides the fixed fast-days, there are some other

fasts which may be described as local or regional. These fasts, too, are related to one unfortunate occurrence or another in the history of the Jews. Many fasts are divided among different classes, with each class observing the fast in memory of a certain calamity, or of a particular occasion of joy or sorrow. It is customary among many Jewish communities to fast on the eve of New Year's Day. The Synagogue is empowered to impose fasting in case of a misfortune befalling the people, such, as pestilence, famine, or an evil decree enforced by the ruler of the day.

Private fasts have also been frequent among the Jews during the earliest times. One may take upon oneself to fast on certain days, either in memory of certain events in his own life, or in expiation of his sins, or in time of trouble to arouse God's mercy. The Rabbis, however, did not encourage such abstinence. They positively forbade it in the case of a scholar who would be disturbed in his study, or of a teacher who would thereby be prevented from doing his work properly. Fasting was also done in consequence of seeing an evil dream. While in general no fast is permitted on Sabbaths or holidays the Talmud allows it to be undertaken on these days provided that it is complemented later by another fast.

The Jewish fasts begin at sunrise and end with the appearance of the first stars of the evening, except those of the Day of Atonement and the ninth of Ab which lasts from eve to eve. There is no special ritual for the ordinary fast-days. The giving of charity on a fast-day, specially the distribution of food necessary for the evening meal, is encouraged.

The first nine days of Ab, and with some Jewish communities, the period from the seventeenth of Tammuz to the tenth of Ab, are regarded as partial fasts in which the eating of meat and the drinking of wine alone are forbidden.[5]

In regard to fasting and Christianity, Maulana says,

Apart from the Mosaic dispensation we have with us

the wonderful religion of Jesus. It is however forgotten, but one can trace back the 40 days when Jesus continued fasting. The early Christians observed Lent, i.e. six weeks except Sundays. But the object of these fasts was definitely different from what the great master had taught. His fasting was for God and theirs was for penitence and the commemoration of Christ. Christians' were further obliged to see no benefit in it and gradually it fell into disuse. Christian theologians take great pains in explaining this point by emphasizing that the fasting of 40 days by Jesus was merely his own individual act. The *Chambers Encyclopedia* in fact elaborates much further and mentions the fact that Jesus was distinctly against such a command. He excused his disciples who neglected the fast. Thus Christendom soon lost every trace of fasting and eventually it was regarded as something of no validity. Later when it was thought to be revived it could only be done by proclamation. In the United Kingdom, the sovereign has from time to time appointed by proclamation a day for solemn national fast, humiliation and prayer as on the 21st March, 1855 (The Crimean War) and 7th October, 1857 (The Indian Mutiny).[6]

The *Encyclopedia of Religion and Ethics* states,

Although he (Christ) himself fasted for 40 days before the beginning of his ministry, and probably as a devout Jew, kept the one fast-day that was obligatory at the time—the Day of Atonement—he left no regulations for fasting. He gave the principles and left his Church to make rules for carrying them out. No rules on the subject could claim to come directly from the Master himself.... The Jewish Christians, doubtlessly, continued to keep the Day of Atonement, and St. Luke mentions it as an epoch but the Gentiles were almost certainly not pressed to observe: When we review the century and a half that followed the death of St Paul we are at once struck by the want of regulations as to fasting. There was a general sense of the duty of fasting and frequent warnings against making it an external act. Irenaes say that there was great variety in its observance, some fasting for one day, others for two or for several days, and that this variety was of long-standing. It was a common custom in the Second Century, at least in some countries, to fast on Wednesdays and Fridays. Pre-baptismal fast was observed by the candidate, the baptizer and others.

From the 3rd Century onwards manuals of instruction and worship, now conveniently called 'Church Orders' became common, basing their injunctions in most cases on supposed Apostolic authority. Fasting, accordingly, was more regulated and the Orthodox became stricter than the Montanists. In the 4th Century we find only two days before Easter named as fast in some authorities The fast ends at midnight. Sick people who can not fast on both days were allowed to fast on Saturday. There was also a diversity as to the time of ending the fast. In Rome they ended it at cockcrow, elsewhere at nightfall.

A forty days' fast is not found until the 4th Century and made its way gradually. At Rome three successive weeks before Easter were kept except Saturdays and Sundays. In Illyria and Greece and Alexandria they fasted six weeks. The mode of fasting also varied; some abstained from things that had life; some ate fish only, others both fish and fowl; some did not eat eggs and fruit, some ate dry bread only, some not even this.

Since the Reformation the Church of England while fixing the fasting days, has made no rule how they are to be observed, leaving it to the individual conscience, but Acts of Parliament of Edward VI and James I and proclamations of Elizabeth vigorously enforced fasting, ordered abstinence from fresh-meat on fast days and gave the curious reason for the injunction that fish and shipping trade might be benefited.[7]

DISADVANTAGES OF FREEDOM OF CHOICE IN THE DAYS AND METHOD OF FASTING

Nadwi continues,

There were, thus, no fixed days of fasting nor detailed regulations concerning it in some of the earlier faiths. It was left to their followers to decide whether to abstain totally from food and drink or only partly. With most of the religions originating in India it is the same, so that while some of their adherents simply refrain from eating meat on fast-days others avoid only such articles of food as are cooked on fire. There is also a section which takes only water with a little salt or lime juice added to it or something of the sort.

These practices have, to a great extent, destroyed the spirit of fasting and impaired its efficacy. Since the choice was left to the individual who kept the fast and the determination of the days of fasting and the degree and duration of abstinence was made a matter of his preferment it paved the way for slackness and evasion. People began to take all kinds of liberties with the fasting and it became very difficult to keep an eye on them for if anyone who was fasting, was asked how it was that he was eating at day time he could very well say that his fast had ended. Similarly if it was inquired why was he keeping fast at the time of breaking it he could reply that his fast had just begun. The ancient religious communities were deprived of the moral and spiritual advantages of fasting due to this drawback. After their experience the wisdom of fixing the days and time schedule of fasting and framing elaborate rules for it becomes apparent.

As Shah Waliullah writes, 'If the right to exercise one's own judgment in fasting is conceded, it will open the door of evasion, the path of sanctioning what is allowed and forbidden, what is prohibited will be obstructed and this foremost event of obeisance in Islam will fall into negligence.'"8

With regard to the prescribing of the period of fasting he remarks,

It was also necessary to determine its period and duration so that no room is left for excess or slackness.

But for it, some people would have observed so little of fasting that it would have been fruitless while others would have carried it so far as to inflict upon themselves excessive hardship. In truth, fasting is a remedy to counteract the effects of the poison of sensuality and, therefore, it is essential that it should be administered in the right quantity.[9]

If one adopts the view that the human being is a casual concourse of atoms one favors materialism and if one considers self to be a spiritual being, one tends to favor monasticism. Islam encourages neither but adopts the middle way for the human being which, in this view, is body, soul and spirit. It is only when the functions of all three aspects of self are regulated through moderation that there will be well-being. This moderation only arises when the innate passions (anger to preserve the individual and lust to preserve the species), the animal aspects of self are controlled by reason/intuition. This is conditional upon the response being initiated by reason/intuition and not imagination. Reason/intuition innately preserve the eternal possibility of self. It is through the sublimation of the energies of the passions to that of reason/intuition, uninfluenced by imagination, that the human being can perfect self. As seen through the glance at the historic origins of fasting, it is one of the best methods to aid reason/intuition to control the passions.

The Quran says, "*Fasting is prescribed for you as it was prescribed for those before you so that you may guard against wrongdoing..*" Here is a major distinction. Whereas fasting in other faiths was done as a mark of sorrow, to propitiate an angry god or goddess or for the expiation of wrongdoing, the motive for doing it has completely changed. The believer is commanded to fast no matter what individual or communal calamity has been suffered. The significance has changed. The believer told to perform the prescribed fast not in order to appease God or for the atonement of wrongdoing, but because it helps in developing and enhancing self-esteem, self-development, human perfection by teaching the believer to guard against wrongdoing (*taqwa*) and this is the only characteristic which makes one believer more superior to another in the view of those who submit to God's Will (*muslim*s). There is no superiority based on gender, race or class, but solely on who is best able to guard against wrongdoing. Being on one's guard against going beyond God's limits or bounds requires constant vigilance. Moral lapses are avoided by intensifying consciousness and this is enhanced by the prescribed fast whereby one learns to perceive the approach of a possible wrongdoing. "To be forewarned is to be forearmed," as the expression goes.

The prescribed fast, then, is not based on starvation or abstinence from food, drink and sexual intercourse from dawn to dusk, but from everything that is beyond God's bounds. The Quran says, *"Perform the prescribed fast a number of days."* If the intention had been starvation as a virtue, it would have been everyday and not for a number of days. It is not a question of asceticism because believers are encouraged to enjoy the lawful things in life, but when the believer becomes absorbed in worldly pleasures, the guard is dropped, causing the person to easily exceed God's bounds.

Someone may argue that it is not necessary to have a prescribed fast for a whole month to maintain well-being. This argument, however, assumes that the human being is solely a physical form. This is only a part of the total person and should be kept in a sound state, but this happens when the controlling agent is sound. In the traditional perspective, it is the spirit manifested as reason/intuition only which can act as a positive control agent in controlling the passions which are constantly on the verge of rebellion. The prescribed fast strengthens the spirit to withstand the pressures of the passions and thereby the body. In other words, it works from inside out and not outside in. The controlling forces are inward and are other than just physical.

The prescribed fast strengthens will-power by denying that which is available, for a period of time and which, other than for the prescribed fast, would be lawful. This then reinforces the ability to deny wrongdoing at other times when one is not fasting. It is one of the only forms of worship which is completely based on one's conscience and God. No one else need ever know.

It is because of this that performing the prescribed fast during Ramadan enhances the feeling of nearness to God for the believer. It is not a question of killing desires of the passions, but of disciplining and controlling them leading to mastery over them rather than the reverse, being at their mercy.

TOTAL ABSTINENCE OR PARTIAL?

Nadwi says,

> Drawing a comparison between the two categories of fasting (one in which complete abstinence is observed from all the things that are inimical to fasting and the other in which only partial abstinence in practiced) Shah Waliullah shows his preference for the former and explains its superiority in the following words: 'There are two ways of reduction in diet. One is to eat sparingly and the other is to observe such a long interval between meals that the object of curtailment is gained. In the Divine Law the latter course has been prescribed, it is because it induces an adequate appreciation of the torments of hunger and thirst and strikes first the root of the carnal appetites (anger and lust), a definite reduction in whose force and intensity is noticed. On the contrary, in the former case, these results are not obtained owing to the continuity of meals. Besides, it is not possible to lay down a general rule for reduction as the circumstances differ from one individual to another. A person takes half a *sir* of food while for the other only a quarter of a *sir* suffices. Thus, if a general limit is laid down for everyone, one will profit by it and the other will suffer.'
>
> Shah Waliullah goes on to observe that moderation should be the rule in the determination of the hours of fasting. It, again, was desirable, he says, that the hours of fasting were not so long as to entail unbearable hardship as for instance, three days and three nights. Apart from being opposed to the spirit of the Divine Law, it would also have generally been impracticable.[10]

CONTINUOUS FASTING: DAYS OR PERIODIC?

Nadwi continues,

> A common practice among the ancient religions was that fasting was observed at intervals. Different days of the year were set aside for it and the gap between them was so long that the effectiveness of the act was lost. The period of fasting would end before one was morally, mentally and spiritually brought into accord with it. In the words of Hazrat Shah Waliullah It was necessary that the opportunity to abjure food and drink occurred repeatedly and in succession in order that it could serve the purpose of an exercise in submission. To go without food only once (however hard it is) would avail nothing. Viewed against it, Islamic fasting will seem to satisfy all the essential requisites of fasting and be capable of yielding the desired moral, social and spiritual benefits.[11]

TIME, MANNER, MOTIVE

Maulana says,

> In fasting, then, three important issue are involved; time manner and motive. When does one fast and what is the duration of the fast? How does one fast? And why does one have to subscribe to fasting? A cursory glance over all the religions that keep fast makes it clear that it was a privilege of the few, especially the very healthy. The layman in the street could hardly benefit by it. To stay away from food and water for 24 hours is medically unhealthy. Delicate tissues of the body burn out and the human being loses a great amount of stamina. Apart from these considerations it is highly impossible for the ordinary person to keep such a long fast. Thus it involves extremity in time which renders the fast an impossibility. Besides

the above fact such fasts amounts to self-mortification which in every sense is injustice to the body and unwarranted cruelty to the flesh.

We also have the Hermits, Sadhoos, and monks on the hill tops who fast for long periods. Some fast for months and some drag on for years fasting on very scanty tit-bits seeking salvation and spiritual progress. They are divorced from all social activities and have severed all relations with families and friends. This, in reality, is not fasting.In fact it is renunciation of the world and just how many can do it? Obviously such a gesture in the principles of fasting cannot receive universal appraisal nor can it bring any positive fruit.

On the other hand, we have fasting prescribed for brief periods. This is usually instructed by the medical specialist. Fasting for a few hours is most popular amongst the doctors and it hardly involves any spiritual aspect. From the medical point of view it is true that the physiology of a condition where solid and liquid foods are withheld from a person results in chemical changes in the tissues of the body. The doctors recommendation for fasting is in every way limited. The most significant change in this aspect came with Islam. *"And eat and drink until the white thread of dawn appear to you distinct from the black thread*; (about 1 1/2 hours before sunrise) *till the night appears"* (exactly after sunset).

The time prescribed for daily fasting in Islam involves the normal hours of routine life wherein all the human senses are functioning and the human faculties are active. A person has to start at the early dawn and end up after sunset. This is norm and yet has a character building restraint on the human mind and body. It is even within the reach of the youths of tender age as well as people of advanced age. Neither find it impossible. This moderation renders fasting an act for everybody and that is precisely why so many millions of people fast during Ramadan. Muslims in the deserts, on the hills, and ploughing fields do not have to take days off to fast nor do they have to abandon their activities.

The manner of fasting is significant too. Amongst many religious groups fasting implies abandoning their homes and seeking seclusion. The son leaves for the hills and others, while at home, do not enjoy the company of their families. The idea of becoming 'holy' through fasting has seriously affected social life. Many regard social activities during fasting a kind of wrongdoing. This has been completely revised in Islam. The whole conception of fast in this respect is to render both the spiritual aspect and physic one. Fasting has something to do with daily life. The believer must therefore see its fruit not on the hill tops or away from family and friends, but in the center of society. The Holy Quran is quite clear on this point.

In Islam the manner of fasting is simple. Early in the morning, just before dawn, before sunrise, the believer takes his or her only meal for the day called pre-dawn breakfast and thereafter he or she devotes the time to prayer. The person may even return to bed after performing the early morning prescribed prayers. One does this with the expressed intensity of fasting for God and keeping away from any type of food, including energy restoring injections, liquids and cohabitation with one's spouse. This empowers a person to control the passions, but does not restrict one from social activities, domestic duties and intermingling with society. Apart from the physical side, the human being has to guard his or her spiritual side at all times and every action issuing from that person must have bearing on his or her character and discipline.

Fasting means discipline and character building too. As the day proceeds the mind is focused on higher spiritual ideals. It all goes with the normal day to day life. At the end of the day after sunset the breaking of the fast and once again the body prepares for the next day. The meal after sunset is called *iftar*. During the night the person is free to resume the above three things which were abstained from during the day.

The most important aspect of a fast is its motive. Why does one really have to fast? Why should one fast according to Islamic teachings. It must be remembered that fasting is not a new institution. What are the changes as far as motives of fasting are concerned? Before us are all the religions and cultures that have prescribed fasting in some way or the other but the motives certainly vary. In every instance there is profound difference. Amongst the ancient people, the prescribed fast was instituted to appease the hunger of mythical gods and mysterious spirits. In some cases it was an act of penitence and repentance for sins. To some it played the role of commemoration. They commemorated the occasions of the birth and deaths of their heroes and human gods and to some it was the best means to arrive at spiritual purity. Islam on the other hand emerged with a comprehensive over-all change in this respect.[12]

CONCLUSION

Historically the concept of fasting has existed in some form or other in all religious traditions. It reaches its fruition in the school of thought and action of submission to the Will of God (*islam*) as the most natural way to strengthen will power. It is the strengthened will power which will be able to dominate, discipline and control the passions, the ego. This development of the concept of fasting avoids self-torture and self-mortification by limiting the time period for each day's fast based on the length of time the sun is with us during that season. It also avoids the spiritually useless momentary abstention from food, drink and sexual intercourse. It enhances the experience through encouraging social gatherings to end the daily prescribed fast. It is not so stringent to require isolation from work, family or friends. All of this social and individual spiritual development is reinforced by times of meditation and contemplation, voluntary congregational Special Night Prayer, retreating to a mosque in the last ten days of Ramadan, celebrating the Night of Power, helping the poor by paying the prescribed poor-due at the end of the month, and joining in the congregational festival prayer. The motive of strengthening one's ability to guard against wrongdoing is thereby attained at least one month during the year through practices that are ideally suited to every age and every people.

PART SEVEN: MASTER COMMUNICATORS

21

UTILIZING RAMADAN
TO COMMUNICATE

Tariq Butt

Communications is seen at three levels by believers: communication between self and God, self and others and self with self. Ramadan serves to further all three levels of communication.

Seen as an individual, the believer takes advantage of the two months preceding Ramadan, the months of Rajab and Shaban, where voluntary and supererogatory fasts are recommended, pre-training, in a sense, for what the Quran refers to as becoming *"pious and virtuous"* (2:183). This is seen as a means of drawing closer to God.

Ramadan is considered to be a blessed month because it is the month in which the Quran was revealed. In terms of strengthening the believers mastery of communication with God, certain strategies have been traditionally provided. These consist of special and recommended prayers, performing the prescribed fasting during the whole month of Ramadan, retreating to a mosque during the last ten days of Ramadan, anticipating the Night of Power and remembering God, spending in the Way of God by paying the poor-due before the end of the month of Ramadan and participating in the congregational prescribed Festival prayer. Each one of these strategies reinforce the goal and belief of the believers allowing them to move away from self-centeredness and egotism towards humility and spiritual poverty in furthering moral character development. This, in turn, fosters brotherhoods and sisterhoods and closer ties of communication between people.

Ramadan brings special and recommended prayers in addition to the five daily prescribed prayers. A Tradition is recorded in which Muhammad (ص) used to counsel his Companions to observe the special prayer (*tarawhih*) every night during the month of Ramadan. In addition, the late night prayer (*tahajjud*) was also recommended. Believers, however, are cautioned to perform these prayers with the intention of drawing nearer to God and not in order to show off to others. Offering prayers in order to show righteousness to others leads to hypocrisy and self-conceit, both negative and undesirable traits for a believer.

Performing the prescribed fast in obedience to God's command strengthens the believers faith, furthering the believers ability to see God's Presence everywhere. "*Wheresoever you turn, there is the Presence of God.*" A Tradition confirms this for the believer where it is recorded Muhammad (ص) said, "There are two pleasures for the person performing the prescribed fast, one at the post-sunset ending of the prescribed fast and the other at the time when the believer sees his/her Lord. Then the believer will be pleased with having performed the prescribed fast."

It is recorded in a Tradition by Ayisha, the wife of the Messenger, "When the last ten days of Ramadan began, the Messenger used to prepare himself for prayer. He stayed awake throughout the night and also awakened members of his family." She reports that he also secluded or retreated to the mosque for the last ten days of the month of fasting, advising people to look for the Night of Power in the five odd numbered nights of the last days of Ramadan (that is, the 21st, 23rd, 25th, 27th, and 29th).

During this retreat to the mosque, in addition to recitation of the Quran, believers engage in a practice known as remembrance (*dhikr*) of God. This is often done by learning the 99 Most Beautiful Names of God through which He self-disclosed in the universe. There is a Tradition which says whoever recites the 99 Most Beautiful Names will go to heaven.

It is recorded by his Companions that Muhammad (ص) was the most generous of people. This was particularly so in Ramadan. Therefore, acts of charity, prescribed as well as supererogatory, are continuously practiced by believers. A Tradition says, "This is a month in which attention must be paid to the sufferings of the poor and their hunger." Believers pay the poor-due at the end of the month of fasting which is itself a purifying act. Finally, in a direct attempt to grow closer to God, believers participate in the prescribed, congregational Festival prayer.

Through these spiritual practices, the believer will have fulfilled the Sign (*ayah*) in the Quran which says, *"And when My servants ask you concerning Me, then verily I am near. I answer the prayer of the supplicant when he calls on Me, so they should answer My call and believe in Me so that they may walk in the right way"* (2:186).

Strengthening communications with self are also important and occur as the indirect result of the above practices. Through special and supererogatory prayer as well as the prescribed fast, the believer develops humility and a sense of spiritual poverty. Self-control is strengthened through the disciplinary practices. Believers are empowered to overcome their inappropriate lust and anger at least during this time span, increasing their self of self-esteem as believers and creatures of God. There is a well-known Tradition which says that the Messenger's character was the Quran. A contemporary philosopher-poet, Muhammad Iqbal, said in one of his writings that he had considered himself to be the best Muslim among Muslims until he looked into the Quran as a mirror but could not see his face.

As proof of having internalized these spiritual practices, resulting in furthering humility and spiritual poverty, behavior patterns should change towards others reflecting moral and spiritual growth. This proof may appear in the gatherings held in homes and mosques for the post-sunset ending of the pre-scribed fast and the performance of the voluntary Special Night Prayer in congregation. For believers living in the West as a minority community, it is a time for familiarizing others with their practices and organizing study programs to renew beliefs thereby strengthening their power as master communicators.

22

SPECIAL NIGHT PRAYER OF RAMADAN

Muhammad Aslam

The Special Night Prayer of Ramadan is called *tarawih* (pl., *tarwihah*) which means "to rest" because the devotee take a brief rest after every four cycles of prescribed prayer. This prayer is also called qiyamu Ramadan, "the standing in prayer during the nights of Ramadan."

There is a Tradition in which the Messenger says that he used to recommend people to perform the Special Night Prayer of Ramadan without making it a religious obligation. He said, "Whoever prays at night in the month of the prescribed fast out of faith and hope for spiritual reward, his (or her) former sins are forgiven." The importance of the Special Night Prayer for both men and women is clear in the practice of both the second rightly guided caliph and the fourth rightly guided caliph. Each of them appointed a leader (*imam*) for the men and a separate one for the women.

The Special Night Prayer may be performed individually or in congregation, but the majority of jurisprudents say that it is better to perform it in congregation. The difference of opinion arose because the Messenger did not make it consistent for fear that it would be made obligatory by God. A Tradition confirms this view. Zayd ibn Thabit reported that the Messenger reserved a room in the mosque made of reed mats. He prayed therein on some nights so the people began to gather expecting to pray behind him. He said to them, "Pray, O people, within your houses because the best prayer of a person is in his (or her) house except the prescribed prayers."

After the death of the Messenger, the practice of performing the Special Night Prayer of Ramadan continued individually as well as in congregation. It was during the caliphate of Umar ibn al-Khattab that he established the practice of one congregation in the mosque behind one leader.

The Special Night Prayer may be either eight cycles, twenty cycles or thirty-six cycles as it is a recommended prayer and not obligatory. It may be offered anytime after the night prescribed prayer.

Each night during the month of Ramadan, the Special Night Prayer is performed and one-thirtieth of the Quran is recited so that by the end of the month, the entire Quran has been recited. The devotees stand behind the leader (*imam*). They recite a two cycle prayer, just like the dawn prescribed prayer, but the recitation part is extended so that once they have performed ten such prayers, one-thirtieth of the Quran has been recited. The congregation usually rests after five two-cycle prayers.

It is a beautiful experience to be part of the congregation at this time. While the Quran is divided into thirty parts and a person tries to read one part each night throughout the month, it is spiritually enhancing to hear it recited by the imam while in congregational prayer.

23

RETREAT TO A MOSQUE

Muhammad Zakariyya Kandhlawi

Retreat, religious retirement or seclusion for the purpose of devotion, meditation or peace of mind is fostered not only by the major religions of the world but also by various cults, sects, fads and by even the worshippers of idols and graves.

The form and extent of the retreat differ primarily as a result of the varying outlooks and perceptions of God, the human being and the universe. There are some who live their entire lives in retreat i.e.. secluding themselves from the world. Then there are others whose retreat would extend to months and years while others 'religious retirement' would be an abstention from certain biological or social roles and functions.

At the time Muhammad (ﷺ) it was Arabia's custom for the pious and thoughtful to devote a period of each year to a retreat of worship, asceticism, and prayer. They would seek an empty place far away from their people where they could concentrate on their prayers and genuinely seek a new level of seriousness, wisdom, and ethical goodness through meditation. This practice was called *tahannuth* or *tahannuf*.

At the peak of Mount Hira', two miles north of Makkah, Muhammad (ﷺ) discovered a cave whose perfect silence and total separation from Makkah made it a perfect place for retreat. In that cave he used to spend the whole month of Ramadan. He would satisfy himself with the least provisions, carried to him from time to time by a servant, while devoting himself uninterruptedly to his spiritual pursuits in peace, solitude and tranquillity. During his retreat he would busily engage himself in meditation prayer and fasting.

It was during his retreat in the cave in the month of Ramadan at the age of forty that he, Muhammad (ص), was called to prophethood. It is very noteworthy indeed that the first revelation occurred during a period of retreat and as a result of such it may be very easily misconstrued that the practice of retreat can lead to prophethood. Also, the importance, form and extent of retreat in Islam may not only be overemphasized and exaggerated but may be developed into a way of life for many who profess to be Muslims.

Islam's approach to man's earthly existence is not one of renunciation, repression nor suppression of his nature. It seeks, however, to mold the human being's character by providing guidance, developing control and encouraging indulgence in acceptable opportunities for his natural growth and development. It calls on the human being to actively participate in the reconstruction of society. It was not surprising then, that the Messenger discontinued his retreats to Hira' after having received guidance from God.

Immediately after his initiation to prophethood, the Messenger was taught by the Angel Gabriel the performance of the prescribed prayer. On accepting Islam the Companions were all taught how to pray and the prayer was institutionalized and made a pillar of Islam just before the migration to Madinah (*hijrah*). Prescribed fasting, although practiced by the Messenger during the Makkan period was made obligatory during Ramadan in the second year of the migration. However, it was only during the latter part of his life after the injunction of fasting in Ramadan that the Messenger reverted to the practice of retreat. The retreat, however, was observed in the mosque. This form of retreat is called *i'tikaf*.

The practice of retreat as a form of worship in Islam is sanctioned in the following verses of the Quran, *"And We covenant-ed with Abraham and Ishmael that they should sanctify My House for those who compass it round, or use it as a retreat, or bow, or prostrate themselves (therein in prayer)"* (2:125). *".... but do not associate with your wives while you are in retreat in the mosque"* (2: 187).

It should be noted however, that both verses mentioned the place of retreat to be a mosque. This obviously denounces and has closed the door to the association of anyone or thing with God in the observance of retreat. The Muslim, therefore, is pro-hibited to perform the retreat in a tomb, at a gravesite or in the presence of any idols, statues and pictures.

LAWS PERTAINING TO THE RETREAT IN A MOSQUE DURING RAMADAN

The fundamentals of the retreat include the following: Intention to perform the retreat and staying in the mosque dur-ing the retreat.

There are three types of retreat: Obligatory, recommended and supererogatory. Obligatory retreat becomes obligatory on an individual when he or she makes a vow to observe such. Recommended retreat is the retreat performed during the last ten days and nights of Ramadan; supererogatory retreat is a retreat which is not the fulfillment of a vow nor during the last ten days of Ramadan.

There are varying opinions on the minimum period for the recommended and supererogatory retreat. The following are some opinions: there is no limit or minimum; it must be long enough so as to say 'Praise be to God' (Shafi'i); it should be at least the time it takes to perform one prescribed prayer; and it should be at least a day and night (Malik). Imam Hanifah and Imam Malik did not approve of less than a day. Imam Shafi'i preferred at least a day.

It should be noted that the retreat to a mosque which is based on a vow is governed in accordance with the nature of the vow. That is, if someone vowed to spend a week in retreat to a mosque then he or she is committed to spending that length of time in retreat.

The conditions of the retreat: The person must be sane, not mad. The person must be mature, not a child. The person must be in a mosque. The person must be free from major impurities. In the case of a wife, she must have her husband's consent.

That which breaks the retreat includes: intentional sexual intercourse even though there is no seminal emission; seminal emission as a result of sexual activity even without sexual intercourse; leaving the mosque intentionally without necessity, even though it may be for a very short time; insanity; and menstruation and post-natal bleeding.

The disapproved actions during retreat are: Cupping and bloodletting; too much involvement in business: sewing, weaving, etc; the presence of commodities for sale in the mosque; too much involvement in studies and writing; visiting the sick; and attending the prayer for the dead.

Manners during the retreat include: Preoccupation with the obedience to and worship of God in the form of prescribed prayers, reading the Quran and Traditions, remembrance of God, supplication, seeking forgiveness for sins and repentance, etc; fasting is recommended during the retreat; speaking well of others and avoiding foolish talk; refraining from arguing and getting angry or speaking badly about anyone; keeping oneself, clean,with well-groomed hair and use of perfumes.

THE TIME OF ENTERING THE RETREAT AND LEAVING IT

With respect to the last ten of Ramadan the time of entering into retreat is before sunset on the 20th or 21st night. The leaving of the retreat during the last ten of Ramadan is after sunset of the last day of the month, in the opinion of Abu Hanifah and Shafi'i. Malik and Hanbal, however, consider it to be recommended to stay in the mosque until the time for going to the prescribed Festival prayer. Malik and Hanbal, also do consider it lawful for the person in retreat to come out of retreat after the sunset of the last day of Ramadan.

BENEFITS OF THE RETREAT

The basic purpose of the retreat is that the heart becomes attached to God. With it, one attains inner composure and equanimity. One puts aside pre-occupation with the mundane things of life.Absorption in the Eternal Reality takes its place. A state is reached in which all fears, hopes and apprehensions are superseded by the love and remembrance of God. Every anxiety in transformed into the anxiety for Him. Every thought and feeling is blended with the eagerness to gain His nearness and earn His good favor. Devotion to the Almighty is generated instead of devotion to the world. It becomes the provision for the grave where there will be neither a friend nor a helper. This is the high aim and purpose of retreat which is the specialty of the most sublime part of Ramadan i.e.; the last ten days.[1]

Similarly, Shah Waliullah remarks that retreat in the mosque is a means to the attainment of peace of mind and purification of the heart. It affords an excellent opportunity for forging an identity with the angels, sharing in the blissfulness on the Night of Power and for devoting oneself to prayer and meditation. It is because of these blessings that God set apart the last ten days of the month of Ramadan for it and made it a *sunnah* for His pious and virtuous slaves.[2]

TRADITION

It has been reported that the Messenger once performed retreat to the mosque in a tent (inside the mosque) for the first ten days of Ramadan. Thereafter, he extended it to the middle ten days. Thereafter, he put his head out of the tent and said, "Verily in search of "the Night of Power did I perform retreat to the mosque for the first ten days and extended it to the next ten days for the same purpose. Then I was told that this night is in the last ten days. Those with me should also continue the retreat to the mosque I had indeed been shown that night and then made to forget which one it shall be. And verily did I see myself prostrating to God with my forehead in mud on the morning after that night. Therefore, seek the Night of Power among the last ten nights of Ramadan. Seek it among the odd ones." Abu Saeed says, "That same night it rained. The roof of the mosque leaked, and I saw the Messenger performing prostration in muddy clay; and that was the morning of the 21st night."

COMMENTARY

It used to be the general practice of the Messenger to perform retreat to the mosque in Ramadan. At times he used to remain in the mosque for the whole month and, during the last year of his life, he was in retreat to the mosque for twenty days. Because he usually secluded himself in the mosque for the last ten days of Ramadan, the religious scholars consider it strongly recommended to perform the retreat to the mosque for that period.

From the above Tradition it can be deduced that the object behind retreat to the mosque was to anticipate the Night of Power. What better manner can there be for this search than to remain in worship all the time, as in retreat to the mosque, whether one is awake or asleep. Furthermore, in retreat to the mosque, one is free from all daily tasks and thus has all the time to be devote to the remembrance of God and meditation.

Throughout Ramadan, the Messenger remained in worship and particularly, when the last ten days came along, he set no limit in exerting himself. He himself remained awake throughout the night and set the example of waking up his family for the same purpose. Ayisha reports, "During the last ten days of Ramadan, the Messenger tied his *"lungi"* (trouser-cloth) tightly about him, staying awake all night, and waking his family for the purpose of worship. "Tied his *lungi* tightly about him" could mean either that he set no limits in exerting himself in worship or that he completely avoided all forms of sexual contact with his wives.

TRADITION

Ibn Abbas relates that the Messenger said, "The person performing retreat to the mosque remains free from sins, and he is indeed given the same reward as for those who do righteous deeds (in spite of not having done these deeds) as a result of having been secluded in the mosque."

COMMENTARY

Now this Tradition points to two great benefits of retreat to the mosque. First, one avoids sin. The world all around us is full of temptations and very often one falls into sin without even intending to do so. To commit sin in the blessed month of Ramadan is indeed a great injury to ourselves. Through remaining secluded in the mosque, one completely avoids the temptation to sin.

Secondly, it would appear outwardly that, when one is secluded in the mosque, one is apparently at a disadvantage by not being able to perform certain good deeds like joining in funeral prayers, attending burials, visiting the sick, and so forth. Therefore, according to this Tradition, one is rewarded for these deeds even though not performing them. What a great favor from God! How great is God's bounty! If only we can understand and properly appreciate these favors, which can attract the Mercy of God, but we are very neglectful of this and place little value on our faith.

TRADITION

Hazrat Ibn Abbas reports that, while he was once in retreat to the mosque in the *Masjid al-Nabi* (the Messenger's mosque) a certain man came to him, greeted him and sat down. Ibn Abbas said to him, "l see that you seem sad and troubled." The man replied, "Yes. O son of the uncle of the Messenger, I am indeed troubled in that I have an obligation to fulfill towards someone. I swear by the holiness of the inmate of the grave of this honored resting place that I am not able to fulfill this obligation." Ibn Abbas inquired, "Shall I intercede with that person on your behalf?" The man replied, "By all means, if you so wish." Ibn Abbas put on his shoes and proceeded out from the mosque. The man, seeing this, said, "Have you then forgotten that you are in retreat to the mosque?" Tears filling his eyes, Ibn Abbas replied, "No, but the occasion is still fresh in my mind when I heard the esteemed inmate of this tomb say, 'Whoever sets forth in the way of settling a necessary affair on behalf of his brother, that service shall be better for him than to perform retreat to the mosque for ten years; and whosoever performs retreat to the mosque for a day (thereby seeking the pleasure of God), God will spread three trenches between him and hellfire, the width of each trench being greater than the distance between heaven and the earth.'"

COMMENTARY

Two things are clear from this Tradition. In the first place, we are told that by way of reward for one day's retreat to the mosque, God spreads three trenches between him and the hellfire, the width of which equals the distance between the heavens and the earth.

In the second place, we are told that performing a service for one's brother brings a reward greater than ten years of retreat to a mosque. For this reason. Ibn Abbas broke off his retreat to the mosque. It was of course possible for him to continue it afterwards. The Sufis say that God has such sympathy for very few things as He has for a broken heart. It is for this reason that we have been so much warned of the appeals to God of that person whose heart has been hurt through any unjust treatment or persecution. Whenever the Messenger appointed anyone as a governor, in addition to advising him, he would also warn him to beware of the invocation (to God) of the persecuted. Note that the retreat to the mosque terminates when one leaves the mosque, even for a task on behalf of a fellow Muslim. When that retreat to the mosque is obligatory, it will mean that it has to be performed all over again. The Messenger never left the mosque during retreat to the mosque, except for the calls of nature and ablution. As for Ibn Abbas leaving the mosque to do some favor to a friend, it was in the spirit that is reminiscent of the soldier lying near death on the battle field of Yarmouk, refusing to drink water until his wounded comrade had been given the drink. On the other hand, it is quite possible that Ibn Abbas was performing a supererogatory retreat to a mosque, in which case it was permissible for him to break it off.

TRADITION

Ibn Abbas says that he heard the Messenger say, "Paradise is made fragrant with the sweetest perfumes in Ramadan. From the very beginning of the year until the end, it is brightly decorated for the coming of this blessed month. And when the first night of Ramadan appears, a wind blows from beneath the Throne. It is called perfumed and causes the leaves of the trees of paradise to rustle and door handles to vibrate, thus giving forth such a melodious sound as had never been heard before. The dark-eyed damsels of paradise then step forth until they appear in the center of the balconies of paradise, exclaiming, 'Is there anyone praying to God for us that God may join us in marriage with him?' Then these damsels call out, "Oh Ridwan, Keeper of Paradise! what night is this?" He replies, *"Labbayk,"* it is indeed the first night of Ramadan, when the doors of paradise are opened to those who observe the fast from among the community of Muhammad.

COMMENTARY

We see here that there are a few people who are deprived of the general forgiveness in Ramadan. Among them are those who fight and quarrel among themselves and those disobedient to their parents. The Messenger said, "The bankrupt one from among my community is that person, who shall appear on the day of judgment bringing with him/her righteous deeds like prescribed prayer, prescribed fasting and giving of charity; but he/she had also sworn at someone, falsely accused someone else, and hurt someone, with the result that all these people shall come forward with complaints against him/her bearing witness against him/her.

TRADITION

In Bukhari we read a Tradition,"On the Day of Judgment, Noah shall be called and asked, 'Did you deliver the message in the proper manner?' He shall reply, 'Yes I did.' Then his community shall be asked, 'Did he deliver My commandments?' They shall reply, 'No, neither did a bringer of glad tidings came to us, nor a warner.' Thereupon Noah shall be asked to bring a witness. He shall call upon the community of Muhammad. This community shall be called forward and they shall testify (as to the truth of Noah's evidence.)"

In some versions of this Tradition, this community shall be cross-questioned. "How do you know that Noah did deliver commands of God, when you were not present at the time?" They shall reply, "Our Messenger informed us of that; the True Book revealed to him informed us of that." In this same manner, all the communities of prophets shall be questioned. For this reason the Quran says, *"Thus we made you a community, justly balanced, that you might stand witnesses over the nations."*

COMMENTARY

The contents of this Tradition are found in many other collections of Traditions also that faults of those who obey God and seek His pleasure are forgiven. One should therefore be careful of not humiliating and attacking the righteous ones for their faults, lest we may be the real losers through backbiting and jeering at those who in their own manner seek to please God, Who may cover up their faults and forgive them through the blessings of their other good deeds, while we, who continue to backbite, scoff and jeer at them, may be causing our own destruction. May God in His Mercy Pardon us all. This Tradition also states that the night before the day of the Festival is called the night of prize giving, the night when God gives a reward to his servants who should also properly value this night. It is usual that, once an announcement is made that next day is the Festival, the majority of us (including the good Muslims) feel fatigued because of Ramadan and prefer on this night to enjoy rest and sleep, whereas this too is a valuable night that should be spent in worship. The Messenger said, "Whoever stays awake for worship on the night preceding either Festival with the aim of gaining reward, his/her heart shall not die on that day when hearts shall wither." The meaning here is that at the time when evil will have over-powered everybody, his/her heart shall stay alive (guarding against wrongdoing).

24

THE NIGHT OF POWER

Seyyed Qutb

"Lo! We revealed it on the Night of Power And what will convey to you what the Night of Power is? The Night of Power is better than a thousand months. The Angels and the Spirit descend therein, by the permission of their Lord, with all decree. Peace it is until the rising of the dawn."

This chapter (*surah*) of the Quran speaks about that great night promised in advance which the whole universe marks with joy, happiness and prayers. It is the night of the absolute and perfect contact between this world and the highest abode. It is the night which marked the beginning of the revelation of the Quran sent to Muhammad (ص), the night of that great event, unparalleled in the history of mankind for its splendor and the significance it brought to bear on the life of mankind as a whole. Its greatness is far beyond human realization.

"Lo! We revealed it on the Night of Power. And what will convey to you what the Night of Power is? The Night of Power is better than a thousand months."

The Quranic statements which relate this great event glitter and shine. They flow with a light which is serene and friendly. It is God's light shining in His Quran, *"Lo! We revealed it on the Night of Power."*

It is also the light of the Angels and of the Spirit moving to and fro between the earth and highest abode. *'The Angels and the Spirit descend therein with the permission of their Lord, with all decrees.'* In addition, there is also the light at dawn which the chapter portrays harmoniously along with the light of revelation and the angels as well as the Spirit of peace. *"Peace it is until the rising of the dawn."*

The night which is the subject of this chapter is the same night of which mention is made in another chapter (44), Dukhan (The Smoke), *"Lo! We revealed it on a blessed night. Lo! We are ever warning . whereupon every wise matter is made distinct. This is a command from Our Presence. Lo! We are ever sending a mercy from your Lord. Lo! He is the Hearer, the All-Knowing."*

It is established that it is a night in the month of Ramadan as stated in chapter 2, *"The month of Ramadan in which was revealed the Quran, a guidance for humanity and clear proofs of the guidance, and the Criterion."* It is the night when the revelation of the Quran to the Messenger, peace be upon him, started in order that he should convey it to humanity. Ibn Ishaq, one of the earliest biographers of the Messenger, related that the first revelation consisting of the opening of the chapter, The Clot, took place in the month of Ramadan. The Messenger of God, peace be on him, was then at his devotions in the cave of Hira'.

A number of statements placing this night have come down to us. Some stress that it is the 27th of Ramadan, others, the 21st. A few others say it is one of the last ten days and some others do not go beyond saying that it is in Ramadan.

Its title "The Night of Power" may be meant to denote assignment designation and organization or its value, position and rank. Both meanings are relevant to that great universal event of the Quran, the revelation and the message assigned to the Messenger. It is the greatest and most valuable of all events in this universe. It is also the event which explains more clearly than any other, the place of assignment, designation and organization in the life of humanity. *"This night is better than a thousand months."* The figure here and in similar places in the

Quran does not signify its precise number. It is meant to denote a large number. This night is better than thousands of months in the lives of people. Many thousand months and many thousand years have passed without leaving behind a fraction of the changes and results brought about in that blessed and happy night.

This night is of an essence too great to be understood by the human intellect. *"And what will convey to you what the Night of Power is?"* There is no reason to attach any value to the legends circulated amongst the masses concerning this night. It is great because God has chosen it for the announcement of the revelation of the Quran, the spreading of its light throughout the universe, the overflowing of peace originating from the Divine Spirit on the conscience and lives of people It is great because of what the Quran includes: an ideology, a perception of values and standards, a way of life and a code of moral behavior, all of which promote peace in the world and in the mind. It is great because of the descent of the angels and Gabriel, in particular, with the permission of their Lord, carrying this Quran, which was sent down on that night, and their filling all the space between heaven and earth in such a splendid universal manifestation, strikingly portrayed in this chapter.

If today we look in retrospect, after the lapse of a long chain of generations, to that glorious and happy night, and perceive that fascinating manifestation the world witnessed on that night, and ponder over the essence and dimensions of life on the earth, and on the concepts of hearts and minds, we behold a great reality. We then realize a part of the significance of this Quranic reference to that night, *"And what will convey to you what the Night of Power is?"*

On that night every essential matter was made distinct, new values and standards were established, and positions were decided which are greater than those of individuals, because they belong to nations and countries. Positions still greater were also designated and these belong to situations and hearts.

Humanity, out of ignorance and to its misfortune, may overlook the value of the Night of Power, the essence of that great event and the greatness of the whole issue. When humanity ignored all that, it lost the happiest and most beautiful Sign of grace which God bestowed on it, lost the real happiness and peace gifted to it by Islam, namely the peace of conscience, family and society. The ways of material civilization which were opened to it cannot be a compensation for its loss. Humanity is miserable in spite of higher production levels and better means of existence. The splendid light which once illuminated its soul was put out. The brilliant touch of happiness which carried it high up to the highest society was smothered. The peace which overflowed on the hearts and minds disappeared and nothing can compensate for the happiness of the soul, the heavenly light and the elevation to the loftiest ranks.

We, the believers of Islam, are commanded not to forget or neglect this episode. The Messenger, peace be on him, has provided us with an easy and enjoyable way for the commemoration of this night, so that our souls may always be in close communion with it and with the universal episode which took place in it. He has urged us to spend this night of each year in devotions. We are asked to seek it in the last ten nights of the month of Ramadan. He said, "Seek the Night of Power in the last ten nights of Ramadan." And, "One who spends the Night of Power in worship, one's motive being faith and devotion, will have all one's previous sins forgiven."

Islam is not mere formalities. Hence the Messenger, peace be upon him, specified that the consecration of that night must be motivated by faith and devotion. This would make its consecration an awareness of the far-reaching implication of what took place on that night and would ensure it being practiced in complete devotion and dedication to God, praised be He. The consecration of that night causes the heart actually to feel a certain truth related to the concept stressed in the Quran. Regarding this night, in a Tradition reported by Anas (Durr Manthur), the Messenger is reported to have said, "The Night of Power was granted to this community and not to any other before this." As regards the reason for the granting of the Night of Power, various views are held. According to some Traditions, one reason is given that the Messenger used to ponder over the longer lives of people of the past ages and when comparing them with the much shorter lives of his community, he became greatly saddened because if his community wished to compete with the people before them, then because of their shorter lives, it would be impossible for them to either emulate or surpass the previous communities in the doing of righteous deeds. Therefore, God in His Infinite Mercy granted them this night of great blessings. This means that if any fortunate person of this community during his lifetime spends ten such nights in the worship of his/her Maker, he/she would have gained the reward of worship for 833 years and even more.

Another Tradition states that the Messenger once related to the Companions the story of a very righteous man from among the Israel tribe who spent 1000 months in struggle. On hearing this, the Companions enviously felt that they could not attain the same reward, whereupon God granted them the Night of Power.

Still another Tradition states that it so happened that the Messenger once mentioned the names of the four most pious people from among the Israel tribe, each of whom spent eighty years in God's sincere service, worshipping Him and not transgressing in the least. They were Jonah, Zachariah, Ezekiel and Joshua. The Companions heard this, wondering how to emulate their achievements. Then Gabriel appeared and recited the chapter called The Night of Power wherein the blessings of this particular night were revealed.

There are other Traditions, too, explaining the origin of the Night of Power but no matter which of these we accept, the important fact remains that God has granted believers this night as a great favor. How fortunate are those believers who have never missed worship on this night. As to which particular night it is, here again approximately fifty different views are recorded. It is not easy for me to enumerate them all, but the most generally accepted versions shall follow. As the Quran itself mentions the Night of Power, we shall commence with a short commentary on this chapter.

"We have indeed revealed this message on the Night of Power." Reference here is made to the fact that on this special night, the Quran was sent down from the Guarded Tablet to the

heavens. The mere fact that the Quran was revealed on this Night would have been sufficient to ensure its greatness. But apart from this fact, it is also noted for many other things. In the very next verse, by way of increasing our interest in the matter under discussion, a question is asked, "And what will explain to you what the Night of Power is?" In other words, the question asked here is, "Have you any knowledge as to the greatness and importance of this night? Have you any knowledge as to the great favors and bounties that go with it?" The next verse proceeds to explain its greatness.

"The Night of Power is better than a thousand months." The true meaning here is that the reward for spending this night in worship is better and more than that for having spent one thousand months in worship; but as to how much more regarding it is, we are not told here.

"Therein come down the angels and the spirit by God's permission on every errand."

A fine explanation is given for this verse by Imam Razi. Commenting on this verse, he explains that when the human being first appeared on earth, the angels looked upon Adam with concern. They even ventured to ask God, *"Will you place on this earth one who shall shed blood?"*

In regard to the spirit that descends during this Night, commentators of the Quran have given various meanings of this word.

(a) The vast majority of commentators are agreed that it refers to Gabriel and, according to Imam Razi, this is the most correct meaning. God first makes mention of the angels and then because of Gabriel's special status among them, a separate mention is made.

(b) Some commentators hold the view that the spirit here means one specific angel of such extraordinary and gigantic proportions that before this angel the heavens and the earth appear as small as a morsel.

(c) Another group of commentators hold the opinion that spirit here means one group of angels who never ordinarily appear and only on this night are they seen by other angels.

(e) There is also a view that spirit here refers to the Messenger Jesus who on this night comes down to look at the righteous deeds of this community.

(f) The last interpretation we wish to mention here is that the spirit means God's special Mercy which comes in the wake of the angels descent. There are other interpretations also but as already stated, the first opinion given above is the best known. In this connection, Imam Bayhaqi relates a Tradition from Anas where the Messenger is reported to have said, "On the Night of Power, Gabriel comes down with a group of angels and prays for mercy for everyone whom they find busy in worship."

"By God's permission descend on the earth for blessed errands." The author of *Mazahir Haq* writes that on this night, ages ago, the angels were created long before the creation of Adam was begun in the shape of a nucleus on this same night that the Messenger Jesus was lifted up bodily into the heavens and also it was on this night that the repentance of the Israel tribes was accepted.

"Peace reigns until the break of dawn."

Indeed this night is the very embodiment of peace. Throughout its span, the angels offer salutations to the faithful believers adoring their Lord. As one group ascends, another group descends (with the same greetings), as indicated in some narrations. Another interpretation is that it is a night of complete safety from wrongdoing and mischief. These blessings last all night until the break of dawn, and are not limited to anyone part of the night.

25

THE POOR-DUE
AT THE END OF RAMADAN

Navid Hanif

DEFINITION

Poor-due at the end of Ramadan (*zikat al-fitr*) is the prescribed poor-due which every Muslim is required to make at the conclusion of the month of Ramadan.

ITS INJUNCTION

It is binding upon every Muslim, freeman or slave, male or female, child, young or old. The Messenger made incumbent on every male or female, freeman or slave, young or old, the payment of one *sa'* of dates or barley as charity or poor-due or charity for Ramadan. The people then equalized one sa' of dates or barley with half a *sa'* of wheat. Others used to give dates. Once there was scarcity of dates in Madinah and they gave barley. Even if a baby is born to the family before the Festival prayer, the poor-due at the end of Ramadan (*zakat al-fitr*) becomes obligatory on the guardians to be paid on behalf of the newly born child. The head of the family is responsible to pay on behalf of each member of the family, especially if they are young, but if they are adults then they must pay it by themselves. Husband must pay on behalf of the wife. Any person who possesses the day's provision for self and family has to pay the poor-due at the end of Ramadan.

The poor-due purifies the soul of the fasting person. Ibn Abbas narrated, "The Messenger, upon whom be peace, made charity of poor-due compulsory as purification of a fasting person from vile discourse and vain talks and also as food to the poor and the needy." In another narration, Ibn Abbas said, "The Messenger enjoined charity of the poor-due so that those who observe fasting are purified of their indecent and shameful errors, and the poor and the needy ones are enabled to arrange for their necessities of food and clothing." Therefore a person who gives his poor-due before the prescribed Festival prayer will be accepted by God as poor-due marking the end of Ramadan, but whosoever gives it after the prescribed Festival prayer will be treated as an ordinary charity. Poor-due also serves as a token of thankfulness to God for having enabled him or her to observe the fast.

THE AMOUNT OF POOR-DUE AND WHEN IT IS TO BE GIVEN

The measurement or amount of poor-due is *sa* (equivalent to four handfuls of both hands). It is normally given in the staple food crops of the country such as rice, barley, corn, dates, raisin, etc. except wheat which is two handfuls of both hands (i. e. half of *sa*) per head.

HOW TO MEASURE IT

Since one *sa* is equivalent to 4 *mudd*s (that is, four handfuls of both hands according to the Tradition in Bukhari), just take rice or any item and measure it by simply taking from it four handfuls of both hands (preferably middle size hands, not too big nor too small) and that four handfuls of rice or any item becomes your poor-due marking the end of Ramadan.

It can be weighted and the cash value paid according to Imam Abu Hanifah. But the majority of religious scholars are of the opinion that it cannot be given in cash as it was not the practice of the Messenger and his Companions. In the case of Imam Abu Hanifah's opinion that it can be given in cash, there will not be one price for charity of the poor-due marking the end of Ramadan. Even with rice, one may have different prices, for example the price of American rice is higher than the price of Pakistani rice if one takes four handfuls of each and values it in cash. One should give of the same quality one eats in one's home.

Therefore, for those Imams who tell their people to have their poor-due in cash, they must make sure that they go to the market and find out the different prices of different rice in their country as well as different articles and their prices like peas, corn, split peas, wheat, dates, raisins, barley and so forth and take four handfuls of each, except wheat which is two handfuls and then value it and give the choice to the people to choose any article they want instead of telling that this years charity for poor-due marking the end of Ramadan is $3 or $4.

The best way to do this is that every Imam should bring the articles of different kinds with a scale to the mosque. He should show it to the people to see how the poor-due should be given so that the people may not depend upon the Imam to tell them how much poor-due should be given every year.

THE TIME TO GIVE

Abu Hanifah and Shafi'i said the poor-due marking the end of Ramadan can be given at the beginning of Ramadan while Malik and Hanbal say it can be given a day to two before the Festival day. However, it must be given before going to the prescribed Festival prayer.

ITS RECIPIENTS

The recipients of the poor-due at the end of Ramadan are the same eight types of people mentioned in the Quran: *The alms are only for the poor, and the needy, and those who collect them, and those whose hearts are to be reconciled, and to free the captives, and the debtors, and for the cause of God, and the way-*

farers; a duty imposed by God, God is Knower, Wise (9:60).

However, the preference must be given to the poor and the needy as the Messenger said, "It is food to the poor and the needy."

Abu Hanifah and others said, that it is permissible to give the poor-due to non-Muslims based upon this Quranic verse: *"God forbids you not those who warred not against you on account of religion and drove you not out from homes, that you should show them kindness and deal justly with them. Lo! God loves the just dealers."*

NOTEWORTHY POINTS

1. It is permissible for a wealthy woman to give her poor-due to her poor husband, but not the reverse because a wife's maintenance is the responsibility of her husband.

2. A person who does not possess his or her daily provision is exempted from paying the poor-due, as God does not burden a soul except according to its capacity.

3. When the poor-due at the end of Ramadan is collected is collected it must not be used for any other purpose than to give it to the poor and needy. Thus, everything must be given to the poor or the needy before the Festival or on the day of the Festival.

4. The poor-due marking the end of Ramadan must not be kept for more than three days after the Festival, unless in an extreme case where a poor or needy person may be absent and who may be living in a far place. In such case, his or her portion can be kept and given within three days after the Festival.

5. It is not permissible to take poor-due from one country to the other except in emergency case.

6. A Muslim must pay his or her poor-due for the end of Ramadan anywhere he or she resides.

7. It is advisable, as the practice of the Companions of the Messenger, to have officially appointed people for the collection of the poor-due a week before the Festival and have it distributed to the poor and the needy three or two days before the Festival.

In other words, the officially appointed people must go house to house to collect the poor-due for the end of Ramadan. Naafi narrated that Ibn Umar used to give it to those who had been officially appointed for its collection, and they used to give it a day or two before the Festival.

Collectors have been warned and strictly prohibited from taking presents from people, not to speak of illegal gratification. Abu Humaid as-Sa'idi reported, "The Messenger appointed a man of Azd tribe called Ibn al-Latbiyyah as collector of poor-due. When he returned to Madinah, he said, 'This is for you (Messenger) and these are presents to me." The Messenger then delivered a sermon, praised God and glorified Him and said, 'The next thing is that I have appointed some men among you to manage some affairs of which God gave me authority. One of them comes and says, "This is for you and this is a present given to me." Why then does he not sit down in the house of his mother or in the house of his father and then see whether he will be given presents or not? By Him in whose hands there stands my life, nobody will take anything out of it but he will be brought on the Resurrection Day carrying it on his shoulder. If he had a mule, it will be braying, if he had a cow, it will bellow, or if he had a goat, it will make its particular sound.' Then he raised up his hands, till we saw the whiteness of his two armpits and said, 'O God, have I proclaimed! O God! have I proclaimed it (the message?' All agreed that he had."

8. It is not lawful for any Imam to take any portion of the poor-due for the end of Ramadan for himself, unless he does not possess daily provision for himself and his family. In such a case, he must be treated like any other poor or needy person. It was narrated by Ziyad bin Al-Harith: "I came to the Messenger and took the oath of allegiance to him. He narrated a long tradition. Then a man came to him (the Messenger) and said, 'Give me something of the poor-due.' The Messenger said, 'God was not pleased with the direction of a prophet or of those besides him about the poor-due until He passed order about it. He divided it into eight divisions. If you then come within those divisions, I shall give you from it.'"

26

THE FESTIVAL DAY: SUGGESTIONS FOR SCHOOL CELEBRATIONS

Ismat Bano Siddiqi

The word *'id* means festival, holiday, a happy time when Muslim families and friends get together to celebrate a special occasion. Muslims have two festivals or holidays. One is celebrated on the first of the month of Shawwal marking the and of the fasting period of the month of Ramadan and the other is in remembrance of the Prophet Abraham's sacrifice of a lamb.

'Id is a time for the Muslims to praise and thank God for His blessings by offering special prescribed prayers. It is also a time to remember those loved ones who are far from their homes, the poor and the needy and the orphans who do not have the means of celebrating the occasion, the friends and relatives who are dear and near to those celebrating the festival. It is also a time to forgive one's enemies, settle quarrels between Muslims and to see people one has not seen for some time. It is a time of reducing tensions and renewing friendships. It is a time for having an air of good will, of rejoicing, and of praising God.

The Muslim calendar is based on the lunar (moon) cycle and not on the solar (sun). Since the lunar year is ten days shorter than the solar year and eleven days shorter in a leap year, the festivals are approximately ten days earlier every year and eleven days in a leap year. It is because of this that festivals do not occur at the same time every year and are celebrated at various seasons of the year. The lunar year dates from the migration of the Messenger (‎ﺹ) from Makkah to Madinah which happened in the year 622 CE.

The festival that marks the end of the prescribed fasting is called *'id al-fitr*. The lunar months are either twenty-nine days or thirty-days long so one has to depend on the appearance of the new moon to find out whether it was twenty-nine days of fasting or thirty. Muslims go out and try to see the new moon on the night ending the twenty-ninth day of fasting. Sighting the new moon means that the period of prescribed fasting has ended and the festival of *'id al-fitr* has begun.

Muslims in the West stay in contact with their local mosque to find out if the new moon has been sighted. If the new moon is not sighted at the end of the twenty-ninth, then Muslims fast the next day as well. Once it is established that the new moon has been seen, greetings of "Happy *'id*" to each other fill the air and there is a festive spirit everywhere. Muslim families had been preparing throughout the month for the festival day by planning and preparing food, buying new clothes and shoes, sending cards to relatives and friends, and preparing the poor-due which must be put aside the night before the festival to be distributed to the deserving to help them celebrate as well.

The next morning Muslims put on new clothes, eat a quick breakfast and gather in their local mosque. Sometimes the local mosque is not large enough to handle the crowd so the people go to a park area to join in the festival prayer of thanksgiving for the successful completion of the obligation. This prayer is other than that of the five daily prescribed prayers. After the *'id* prayer, people embrace and greet each other and go home and then eating and visiting and more greetings start. It is a holiday in Muslim homes.

PROJECTS

There are many projects which children can undertake in their schools to help their friends learn about Ramadan and what it means to be a Muslim. The class may form into various groups who do something different or they may prepare something individually. The presentation should have an introduction and a conclusion and may last for ten to fifteen minutes. Each group should present at least five facts to their fellow classmates. All this needs to be coordinated by the teacher.

RESEARCH PROJECTS

1. Explain the Arabic alphabet and how it differs from English.

2. Present information on one or more major Muslim contributions to mathematics, medicine, other sciences or literature.

3. Prepare a presentation of the different clothes worn by Muslims in various parts of the world.

4. Explain how Muslims follow the command of God, "You shall have no other gods before Me."

5. Show how Muslims call Friday the "Sabbath" and go to congregational prescribed prayer. Show also how the Sabbath of the Muslims differs from the Sabbath of the Jews and the Christians.

PLAY/STORY/MELODY PROJECTS

1. Write a story or a poem on some aspect of the life of the Messenger Muhammad (ﷺ).

2. Using tapes or CD-ROMS, present a demonstration of the recitation of the Quran with an English translation.

3. Write a short play on the life of a Muslim who lived at the time of the Messenger Muhammad (ﷺ) and of a Muslim today.

4. Write a short play about the importance of not misusing the name of God.

5. Write a story on how Muslims learn the importance of honoring their mother and father.

ART-GRAPHICS PROJECTS

1. Study Islamic geometric patterns and explain how they are used to decorate mosques and crafts.

2. Explain why there are no graven images in places where Muslim pray following the command of God, "You shall not make for yourself no idol."

3. Draw a timeline on Muslim culture or history. Use pictures from magazines, your own drawings and so forth.

4. Draw a map of the Muslim world and show how it affects our lives today.

5. Collect pictures of Islamic art and architecture. Mount them and explain to your class.

6. Draw a chart of the various languages spoken by Muslim people. Briefly explain each one.

7. Make 'id greeting cards. Beautify them and add some words that may depict your feelings for the occasion.

NOTES

Part One: Goal-Setters
1 The Goal of Prescribed Fasting
1. *Sahih Bukhari*, Book 30, 43.
2. *Sahih Bukhari*, Book 65, 11, 25.
3. See the Quran 2:184.
4. *Sunan Abi Daud*, Book 36, 13.
5. *Sahih Bukhar*i, Book 30, 2.
6. See *Sahih Bukhari.*
7. See *Sahih Bukhari.*
8. See Ibn Majah, Nisai, and Bukhari.
9. See Ibn Majah, Nisai, and Bukhari.
10. See *Miskhat al-Masabih.*
11. See *Bayan ul-Quran.*

2 The Mysteries of Fasting
1. Unidentified Tradition.
2. Unidentified Tradition.
3. *Sahih Bukhari, sawm*, 2; *Ibn Muslim, siyam*, 160, 162-164.
4. *Ibid.*
5. *Ibid.*
6. *Ibid.*
7. *Ibn Muslim, siyam*, 162, 164, 165; *Sahih Bukhari, sawm*, 9.
8. Unidentified Tradition.
9. Unidentified Tradition.
10. *Ibn Majah, siyam*, 1.

11. Ibn al-Jarrah (AH 197/812 CE; *Ibn Sa'd*, vol. 6, p. 275.

12. al-Tabari, *Jami' al-Bayan*, vol. 29, p. 39.

13. Ibn Majah, *Masajid*, 19.

14. Unidentified Tradition.

15. The Kabah.

16. *Ibn Majah*, 65; *Abu Daud, sawm*, 78.

17. Unidentified Tradition.

18. Unidentified Tradition.

19. *Ibn Majah, siyam*, 1; *Sahih Bukhari, sawm*, 2.

20. *Sahih Bukhari, laylat al-qadr*, 5.

21. *Abu Daud, i'tikaf*, 4.

22. *Sahih Bukhari, i'tikaf*, 19.

23. Unidentified Tradition.

24. Unidentified Tradition.

25. Ibn Sulayman (d. AH 136/754 or 760 CE); *Ibn Sa'd*, vol. 6. pp. 243-44; *Ibn Qutaybah*, p. 241; *Sadharat al-dhahab*, vol. 1, pp. 207, 212.

26. *Sahih Bukhari, sawm*, 2.

27. Unidentified Tradition.

28. Unidentified Tradition.

29. *Ibn Majah, siyam*, 21.

30. *Ibid*.

31. Unidentified Tradition.

32. *Sahih Bukhari, sawm*, 2.

3 Sufis on Prescribed Fasting and Spiritual Poverty

1. Seyyed Hossein Nasr, *Muhammad Man of God*, p. 50.

2. *Ibid*.

3. *Khulasa yi sharh-i ta'arruf*.

4. Shibli, *Kashf al-asrar* (Maybudi).

5. Abu Said, *Kashf al-mahjub*.

6. Muzaffar Kermanshahi, *Majma yi-rasa'il-i Ansari*.

7. Shah Nimatullah, *Rasalaha-yi Shah Ni'matu'llah-i Wali*.

8. Weinsinck, vol. 8, p. 460.

9. Sayf al-Din, *Faith and Practice of Islam*, translated by William Chittick.

10. *Safinat al-bihar*, II, p. 378.

11. *Ibid*.

12. *Jami' saqir*, vol. 2, p. 88.

13. *Kashf al-mahjub*, p. 23.

14. *Tafsir-i irfani wa adabi-yi Quran-i majid*, II, p. 516.

15. Ansari, *Nafahat al-uns*, p. 97.

16. Ruwaim, *Tabaqat as-sufyyah* (Sulami), p. 182.

17. Attar, *Tadhkirat al-awliya*, p. 403.

18. *Ibid.*, p. 237.

19. *Ibid.*, p. 461.

20. Abu Hafs Haddad, *Risala-yi Qushayriya*, p. 458.

21. Attar, *Tadhkirat al-awliya*, p. 817.

Part Three: Strategists
8 Prescribed Fasting According to the Five Schools of Law

1. Seyyed Hossein Nasr, *Ideals and Realities of Islam*, pp. 94-95.

2. *Ibid*, p. 95.

3. *Ibid*. See chapter on the Shari'ah in *Ideals and Realities of Islam*.

Part Four: Moral Healers
12 Moral Healing Through Fasting

1. Sayf al-Din, p. 142-146

2. *Ibid*.

3. *Ibid*.

4. *Ibid*.

Part Five: Energizers
16 Medical Benefits of Fasting

1. L. Douglas. et al. Thyroid Function Studies in Fasting Obese Subjects. *Metabolism*, 16:12, 1075-1085, December. 1967.

2. H. G. Van Riet et al. Metabolic observations during the treatment of obese patients by periods of total starvation. *Metabolism*, 13:291, 1964.

3. V. R. Folsch et al. Effects of long term fasting of obese patients on pancreatic plasma. *Gastroenterol*, 22(7), 357-64, July, 1984.

4. F. A. Evans et al. The treatment of obesity with low caloric diets. *JAMA* 97:1063-1069, 1931.

5. L Douglas et al. Thyroid function studies in fasting obese subjects. *Metabolism*. 16:12, 1075-1085, December, 1967.

6. Z. Einstein et al. Effects of starvation on the proudction and peripheral metabolism of T3 in euthyroid subjects. J. Clin Endocrinol. *Metabolism*, 47:889-893, 1987.

7. N. E. Butkus. et al. Anqiotensin-converting enzyme (ACE) activity decreases during fasting. *Horm-Metabres*, 19 (2), 76-9, February, 1987.

8. A. Rapoport. *Metabolism*. 14, 7:31-46, 1965.

9. Hanrahan et al. *American Journal of Clinical Pathology*, 40-43, 1963.

10. D. H. Wasserman and Vranic M. Interaction between insulin and counter-regulatory hormones in substrate utilization in health and diabetes during exercise. *Diabetes /Metabolism Review*, 1:359-384, 1986.

11. S. H. Schachner et al. Alterations in adrenal cortical functions in fasting obese subjects. Metabolism, 14:1051-1058, 1965.

12. Samson Wright. The Bile. *Samson Wright's Applied Physiology*. 11th edition. Oxford University Press: 1965, 362-364.

13. J. L. Gamble. Extracellular Fluid. In *Samson Wright's Applied Physiology*. 11th edition, Cambridge MA: Oxford University Press, 38-40, 1965.

14. J. F. Cahill. Physiology of insulin in man. *Diabetes*, 20:785-799, 1971.

15. R. H. Unger. Studies on the physiological role of glucagon. *Diabetes*. 13:563, 1964.

16. R. H. Unger, Insulin-glucagon relationships in the defence against hypoglycemia (Berson Memorial Lecture). *Diabetes*. 32:575-583, 1986.

17. D. J. Koerker et al. Regulation of lipolysis early and late in fasting. *American Journal of Physiology*. 29:350-354, 1975.

18. T. B. Van Hallie. Starvation: protein calorie malnutrition. In *Harrison's Principles of Internal Medicine*. 8th ed. McGraw-Hill, Kogakusha Ltd, 449-452, 1977.

19. H. S. Rasmussen et all. I V magnesium in acute myocardial infarction. *Lancet*. 234-6, 1986.

20. F. A. Dodge Jr. and R. Rahamimoff. Co-operative action of

calcium ions in transmitter release at the neuromuscular junction. *Journal of Physiology* (London), 193:419-423, 1976.

21. K. Goto et al. Magnesium deficiency detected by intravenous loading test in variant angina pectoris. *American Journal of Cardiology*. 65:709-12, 1990.

22. K. Lau. Magnesium metabolism: normal and abnormal. In Ariegg, AI, De Fronzo RA, eds. *Fluid, Electrolyte and Acid-base Disorders*. 1:575-623. New York: Churchill Livingstone, 1985.

23. B. M. Altura, B. T. Altura. Magnesium, sodium and potassium interacton and cornorary heart disease. *Magnesium*, 1:241-65, 1982.

24. G. Spatling. Magnesium supplementation in pregnancy. A double blind study. *Obstetrics Cynecology*. 95:120-5, 1988.

25. I. Hafstorm et al. Effects of fasting on disease activity, neutrophil function fatty acid composition and leucotrine biosynthesis in patients with rheumatoid arthritis. *Arthritis-Rheumatism*. 31:5, 585-92, May, 1988.

26. R. H. Eckel and T. J. Yost. Weight reduction increases adipose tissue lipoprotein responsiveness in obese women. *Journal of Clinical Investment*. 80 (4), 992-7, October, 1980.

27. J. Roth et al. Hypoglycemia: a potent stimulus to secretion of GH. *Science*. 140:987, 1963.

28. J. B. Martin, Neutral regulation of GH secretion. *New England Journal of Medicine*, 288:1384, 1973.

29. L. E. Eiden and M. J. Brownstein. Extrahypothalamic distributions and functions of hypothalamic peptide hormones. *Fed Pro*. 40:2553-2559, 1981.

30. D. C. Parker et al. Rhythmicities in human growth hormone concentrations in plasma. In D. T. Krieger, ed. *Endocrine Rhythms*. New York: Raven Press, 1979, 142-173.

31. Glick, et al. Recent program. *Hormone Res*. 21:241, 1965.

32. B. E. Spilotos. GH neurosecretory dysfunction. A treatable cau;se of short stature. *JAMA* 251:2223-2230, 1984.

33. Y. O'Sullivan et al. IGF 1 in mice reduces weight loss during starvation. *Endocrinology*. 125:2793-4, 1989.

34. R. Jacob et al. Acute effects of insulin-like growth factor on glucose and amino acid metabolism in the awake fasted rat. *Journal of Clinical Investment*, 83:1717-23, 1989.

35. J. M. Fisher. Control of erythropoeitin production. *Proc. Soc. Exp. Biol. Med.* 173:289, 1983.

36. D. H. Nelson. Diseases of Hypophysis. In *Harrison's Principles of Interna Medicine.* McGraw-Hill: Kogakusha Ltd. 8th ed. 478-489, 1977.

37. Hunter and Greenwood. *Brit. Med. J.* 1:804, 1964.

38. Daughaday and Parker. *Amer. Rev. Med.* 16:47, 1965.

39. Geigy Scientific Tables. *Growth Hormone.* 7th ed. Ciba-Geigy Ltd. Basle, Switzerland. 719-721, 1975.

40. W. F. Ganong. *Review of Med. Physiology.* 12th ed. Lange Med. Publicatons: Los Altos, CA. 332-339, 1985.

41. T. C. Ruch and H. D. Patton. *Physiology and Biophysics.* The brain and neural function. W. B. Saunders: Philadelphia, PA, 1979.

42. W. F. Ganong. *Review of Med. Physiology.* 12th ed. Lange Med Publicatons: Los Altos CA, 152-159, 1985.

43. J. Orem. Breathing during sleep. In D. G. Davies and C. D. Barnes, *Regulation of Ventilation and Gas Exchange.* New York: Academic Press, 1978, 131-166.

44. D. Trichopolous et al. *Lancet,* 2:269-70, 1987.

45. R. D. Adams, M. Victor. *Principles of Neurology.* New York: McGraw-Hill, 1977.

46. W. Fa. Ganong. The pituitary gland. *Review of Med. Physiology.* 12th ed. Lange Med Publicatons: Los Altos, CA, 329-341.

47. J. Hughes, et al. Identification of two related pentapeptides from brain with potent opiate against activity. *Nature.* 255:577-579, 1975.

48. H. Khachaturian et al. Anatomy of CNS opioid systems. *Trends Neurosc.* 8 (3) 111-119, 1985.

49. R. Guillemin. Endorphins, brain peptides that act like opiates. *New England Journal of Medicine.* 296:266-278, 1977.

50. A. Goldstein. Dynophin: an extraordinary potent opioid peptide. *Proc. Nat. Acad. Sci.* 76:6666-6670, 1979.

51. W. F. Ganong. Memory. *Review of Medical Physiology.* 12th ed. Los Altos, CA: Lange Med. Publications, 218-223, 1985.

52. C. W. Wilkinson. Endocrine rhythms and the pineal gland. In *Textbook of Physiology.* 21st ed. WB Saunders Co, vol. 2

Patton et al. 1239-1259, 1989.

53. C. A. Czeisler et al. Exposure to bright light and darkness to treat physiological maladaptation to night work. *New England Journal of Medicine*, 322:1253-9, 1990.

54. F. Halberg. Physiologic 24-hour periodicity in human biengs and mice, the lighting regime and daily routine. In R. B. Withrow, ed. *Photoperiodism and Related Phenomena in Plants and Animals*. Washington, D. C.:American Association for the Advancement of Science, 803-878, 1959.

55. M. C. Moore-ede et al. *The Clocks That Time Us*. Cambridge, MA: Harward University Press, 1982.

56. C. Graeber. The tired pilot. *The Log: Journal of the British Airline Pilots Association*, 51:4, 7-10, August, 1990.

57. C. E. Loat and E. C. Rhodes. Jet lag and human performance. *Sports Medicine*. 8(4), 226-38, October, 1989.

58. M. C. More-ede et al. *The Clocks That Time Us*. Cambridge, MA: Harvard University Press, 1982.

59. T. Akerstedt. Sleepiness as a consequence of shift work. *Sleep*. 11:17-34, 1988.

60. K. E. Powell and R. S. Paffenbarger. Worship on epidemiologic and public health aspects of physical activity and exercise: a summary. *Public Health Rep*. 100:118-26, 1985.

61. E. T. Poehlman and K. C. Copeland. Influence of physical acticvity on insulin-like growth factor 1 in healthy younger and older men. *Journal of Clincial Endocrinol Metabolism*. 71(6), 1468-73, December 1990.

62. M. C. Veberly. Local bone mineral response to brief exercise that stresses the skeleton. BMJ. 299:233-235, July 1989.

63. Z. Szugula. Erythropoietic system under the influence of physical exercise and training. *Sports-Medicine*. 10(3) 181-97, September 1990.

64. B. H. Marcus et al. Usefulness of physical exercise for maintaining smoking cessation in women. *Amercian Journal of Cardiology*, 68:406-7, 1991.

65. G. A. Bray. Exercise and obesity. In C. Bouchard et al, eds. *Exercise, Fitness and Health: Concensus of Current Knowledge*. Champaign, IL: Human Kinetics Books.

66. L. Goldberg and D. L. Elliot. The effect of exercise on lipid

metabolism in men and women. *Sports Medicine.* 4:307-21, 1987.

67. P. O. Astrand and K. Rodhal. *Textbook of Work Physiology.* New York: McGraw-Hill, 1970.

Part Six: Human Bonding
20 Fasting: An Historic Perspective

1. Maulana Sayyid Abdul Razzaq. *ASJA Eid ul-Fitr Annual,* 1981.

2. *Ibid.*

3. Syed Sulaiman Nadwi. *Ramadan Manual.* 2. Muslim Credit Union Cooperative: Republic of Trinidad and Tobago.

4. Maulana, *op. cit.*

5. Nadwi, *op. cit.*

6. Maulana, *op. cit.*

7. *Encylopedia of Ethics,* Ramadan.

8. Nadwi, *op. cit.*

9. Nadwi, *op. cit.*

10. Nadwi, *op. cit.*

11. Nadwi, *op. cit.*

12. Maulana, *op. cit.*

CONTRIBUTORS

Abu Salman, Munir: Presently involved in Islamic activities in the United States, he has traveled extensively and been an active member of his Muslim community in the greater Chicago area.

Akili, Muhammad al-: Imam and well known translator of classical Islamic works, he lives in Philadelphia where he runs his own publishing house called Pearl Publishers. His most recent work, *Natural Healing Through the Medicine of the Prophet,* has become a Muslim best seller.

Ali, Syed Anwar. Presently residing in Pakistan, he is the author of *The Quran: The Fundamental Law of Human Life*, and a well known jurisprudent and author on Islamic subjects.

Aslam, Muhammad: Educated in the UK with an MS in Industrial Engineering, this industrialist is an advisor to the government of Pakistan as well as being a scholar of Islam. He has numerous writings to his credit and has attended many international conferences.

Athar, Shahid: Resident of Indianapolis, Indiana, the author is a practicing physician who is also involved in missionary and interfaith work. He is a prolific lecturer and writer whose most recent work is *Reflections of an American Muslim*, published by KAZI Publications.

Bakhtiar, Laleh: Presently, President of the Institute for Traditional Psychoethics and Guidance in Chicago, she has her Ph.D. in educational psychology and is a well known author of books on Islam and Sufism. Her most recent work is a trilogy on monotheistic psychology (*God's Will Be Done* series) which explains Islamic psychology in depth for the first time in any language.

Butt, Tariq: The author lives in Chicago and has a busy medical practice.

Ghazzali, Muhammad (d. 1111 CE): Theologian and Sufi, he was the great synthesizer of Islamic thought to his time. His best known work is *Ihya Ulum al-Din*, the English title of which is *Revival of the Religious Sciences*.

Gilani, Muhyiddin Abul Qadir: (d. 1166). Founder of the Qadiriyyah Sufi movement, his works have been translated into many languages and serves as the basis for the work of various Sufi orders in the United States.

Hanif, Navid: Presently at the Pakistan mission to the UN, he is a career diplomat who graduated from Columbia University and who has many articles to his credit.

Hanif, Pervez: With a MA in history, member of the Pakistani Chamber of Commerce, this industrialist brings new insights into understanding Islam. Advisor to the Pakistani government, he has traveled extensively and written many books. His latest two titles are *How to Succeed as a Muslim Husband* and *How to Succeed as a Muslim Wife*.

Kandhlawi, Muhammad Zakariyya: Author of *Hikayat assahabah* or its English title of *Stories of the Companions*, one of the most popular books among Muslims. Its present title is *Teachings of Islam*.

Kazim, Ebrahim: A practicing physician, he lives in Trinidad where he is actively involved in missionary work donating thousands of books each year to this cause.

Mawdudi, Abul Ala (d. 1979): Founder of the Jamat Islami in Pakistan, this well known and well loved jurisprudent has many followers throughout the world. A prolific writer and lecturer, he has written several excellent commentaries upon the Quran.

Mughaniyyah, Muhammad: Author of the *Five Schools of Islamic Law*, he is a well known traditional Muslim scholar.

Nasr, Seyyed Hossein: Presently, University Professor of Islamic Studies, George Washington University, Washington, DC. Born in Tehran in a family of traditional scholars and physicians, he came to America where he studied physics and history of science and philosophy at M.I.T. and Harvard, from which he received his doctorate. He was professor at Tehran University and founder and first president of the Iranian Academy of Philosophy. His most recent work is *A Young Muslim Guide to the Modern World*, published by KAZI Publications, which was reviewed on NPR and awarded the best radio interview of 1993. His *Muhammad: Man of God* is also now available from KAZI Publications. His essay, "Why do Muslims fast?" reprinted from *Islamic Life and Thought*, pp. 214-5 with the permission of SUNY Press.

Nurbakhsh, Javad: Pir or Master of the Ni'matullahi Sufi order, he resides in London. Trained as a psychiatrist, his works include *Sufi Women, Jesus in the Eyes of the Sufis, In the Tavern of Ruins, Sufi Symbolism* (5 vols.), *Masters of the Path* and many more.

Qutb, Seyyed (d. 1966): Author of *In the Shade of the Quran*, he is a well respected member of the twentieth century Islamic movement. Born in 1906 in Egypt, he began his career as a writer and progressed to become one of the most original thinkers of the contemporary Islamic Movement. He wrote with a profound sense of conviction which led him to give his life for his beliefs when he was executed in 1966 by the Nasser regime of Egypt.

Siddiqui, Ismat Bano: The author, who has her Ed.D. in Counseling and Guidance from Indiana University is active in her Muslim community in Indianapolis, Indiana where she is chair of the curriculum committee and educational advisor, training educators. She has also taught in Pakistan where she began the PACC program for the teaching of English as a Second Language.

Tabataba'i, Muhammad Husayn: Philosopher, theologian, author, teacher, he is best known for this twenty volume commentary on the Quran in Arabic called *al-Mizan*.

Zafarkhan, Muhammad: A practicing dentist, the author is active in his Islamic community in Libertyville, concentrating on interfaith dialog.

Zaman, Shabnam: A Chicago resident, her hobby is cooking. She is a specialist in applying henna to the hands of brides and is learning traditional healing from a spiritual master. She has written many articles for various journals.